MW01275700

Fully Rely On God

366 Dynamic devotions for cool kids

CHRISTIAN ART
PUBLISHERS

Originally published by Christian Publishing Company
under the title *Ek, my Tekkies en Christus*

© 1999

English edition © 1999
CHRISTIAN ART PUBLISHERS
P O Box 1599, Vereeniging, 1930

First edition 1999
Second edition 2003

Translated by San-Mari Mills
Cover designed by Christian Art Publishers

Scripture taken from Scripture taken from the HOLY BIBLE, NEW
INTERNATIONAL VERSION®. Copyright © 1973, 1978, 1984, by International
Bible Society. Used by permission of Zondervan
Publishing House. All rights reserved.

Set in 13 on 15 pt GoudySans Lt BT by Christian Art Publishers

Printed in China

ISBN 1-86920-279-1

© All rights reserved. No part of this book may be reproduced in
any form without permission in writing from the publisher, except
in the case of brief quotations in critical articles or reviews.

03 04 05 06 07 08 09 10 11 12 – 10 9 8 7 6 5 4 3 2 1

A Word from the Publisher

*F*ully rely on God is a daily devotional compiled especially for young children of primary school age.

It consists of 366 devotions in which spiritual truths are presented in a way that is easy to understand. Every day's devotion is particularly suitable to be incorporated in the young reader's daily quiet time. Topical themes contribute towards making this devotional something special.

Each devotion offers the following to make your daily quiet time a wonderful experience:

- A daily verse from Scripture.

- A discussion based on the verse from Scripture.

- A key thought which summarizes the message for the day.

– The Publisher –

NINA SMIT is the wife of a minister of the Dutch Reformed Church, Helderberg, Somerset West. She is very fond of reading and writing, classical music, paintings, nature, and enjoys travelling with her husband, Johan.

Devotions by
Nina Smit

ANNE McFARLANE has four sons and has been involved in youth work at her church for many years. She is also a versatile writer.

Devotions by
Anne McFarlane

JAN DE WET is a well-known South African gospel singer. He was a minister in the Cape for a number of years before he went into full-time music ministry. He has already released 35 CDs and albums.

He has been responsible for several successful children's productions with the Afrikaans title – Loflaaities. Jan has taken part in approximately 100 television and radio programmes and also presented a weekly radio program me for a few years. He has also published a song-book. Jan is married, has three children and lives at Hartebeestpoort Dam.

Devotions by
Jan de Wet

4 January; 9 January; 16 January; 21 January; 28 January; 2 February; 9 February; 14 February; 21 February; 26 February; 4 March; 9 March; 16 March; 21 March; 28 March; 2 April; 9 April; 14 April; 21 April; 26 April; 3 May; 8 May; 15 May; 20 May; 27 May; 1 June; 8 June; 13 June; 20 June; 25 June; 2 July; 7 July; 14 July; 19 July; 26 July; 31 July; 7 August; 12 August; 19 August; 24 August; 31 August; 5 September; 12 September; 17 September; 24 September; 29 September; 6 October; 11 October; 18 October; 23 October; 30 October; 4 November; 11 November; 16 November; 23 November; 28 November; 2 December; 7 December; 12 December; 17 December; 22 December; 27 December

JOHAN VAN SCHALKWYK thinks of himself as an "ordinary parish minister". He was born in Paarl and studied at the University of Stellenbosch and the Hebrew University of Jerusalem. He has been a minister in the Dutch Reformed church, Lynnwood Ridge, since 1988. He is married to Marinda, and they have four children: GJ, Marhette, MC and Johan.

Devotions by
Johan van Schalkwyk

5 January; 10 January; 11 January; 17 January; 22 January; 23 January; 29 January; 3 February; 4 February; 10 February; 15 February; 16 February; 22 February; 27 February; 28 February; 5 March; 10 March; 11 March; 17 March; 22 March; 23 March; 29 March; 3 April; 4 April; 10 April; 15 April; 16 April; 22 April; 27 April; 28 April; 4 May; 9 May; 10 May; 16 May; 21 May; 22 May; 28 May; 2 June; 3 June; 9 June; 14 June; 15 June; 21 June; 26 June; 27 June; 3 July; 8 July; 9 July; 15 July; 20 July; 21 July; 27 July; 1 August; 2 August; 8 August; 13 August; 14 August; 20 August; 25 August; 26 August; 1 September; 6 September; 7 September; 13 September; 18 September; 19 September; 25 September; 30 September; 1 October; 7 October; 12 October; 13 October; 19 October; 24 October; 25 October; 31 October; 5 November; 6 November; 12 November; 17 November; 18 November; 24 November 29 November; 30 November; 6 December; 10 December; 11 December; 16 December; 20 December; 21 December; 25 December; 26 December; 30 December; 31 December

HENNIE SYMINGTON was born in Johannesburg and grew up in Zimbabwe and the United States of America. She studied BA (Drama) at the University of Pretoria and later obtained an HED and an honours degree in English. She teaches at a school in Johannesburg and is the mother of three teenagers.

Devotions by
Hennie Symington

6 January; 12 January; 18 January; 24 January; 30 January; 5 February; 11 February; 17 February; 23 February; 29 February; 6 March; 12 March; 18 March; 24 March; 30 March; 5 April; 11 April; 17 April; 23 April; 29 April; 5 May; 11 May; 17 May; 23 May; 29 May; 4 June; 10 June; 16 June; 22 June; 28 June; 4 July; 10 July; 16 July; 22 July; 28 July; 3 August; 9 August; 15 August; 21 August; 27 August; 2 September; 8 September; 14 September; 20 September; 26 September; 2 October; 8 October; 14 October; 20 October; 26 October; 1 November; 7 November; 13 November; 19 November; 25 November; 1 December

Obey!

"To obey is better than sacrifice, and to heed is better than the fat of rams" (1 Samuel 15:22).

It is very important to the Lord that His children listen to Him and do what He tells them to do in His Word. Obedience is more important to God than offerings.

King Saul, the very first king of Israel, did not obey the Lord. He did exactly as he pleased. The Lord was not happy with this, and He sent the prophet Samuel to Saul with a message: Saul would not be king anymore; the Lord was going to make someone else king in his place.

Saul paid a price for his disobedience to the Lord, and the same goes for you. If you do not obey the things the Word of God shows you, this could mean big trouble. The Lord gives us His commandments because He loves us and so we can learn how He wants us to live.

God asks you to be obedient not only to His laws but also obedient to those He has put over you to guide you, such as your parents and teachers. Will you try to obey this year?

What miracle took place when Moses obeyed the Lord (see Exodus 14:16-17, 21-22) and what happened when Moses did not listen to the Lord (see Numbers 20:7-12)?

1 January

We Can't Understand God

"Can you fathom the mysteries of God? Can you probe the limits of the Almighty?" (Job 11:7)

"There's something I don't understand!" Jack said to his mom. "How can God hear everybody's prayers and be in different places at the same time?"

His mom answered, "Well, if you could understand Him, then He wouldn't be God."

Mom put a lettuce leaf through the bars of Polly's cage. Polly pecked at it greedily. "Just as impossible as it is for Polly to understand you, so it is impossible for you to grasp the greatness of God. But we do know enough about God to love and serve Him. And that's what He expects us to do," Jack's mom said. She added, *"I Am what I Am,"*

"What?" said Jack.

"That is what the Lord said to Moses when He spoke to him from the burning bush. I think He wanted to explain something about Himself."

"What could that be?" Jack wondered, a puzzled frown on his forehead.

"I think it means He is always the same, and nothing that people say and think about Him will make any difference to His nature."

God's greatness is bigger than our understanding.

2 January

God Is Holy

"Who will not fear you, O Lord, and bring glory to your name? For you alone are holy" (Revelation 15:4).

One need not be afraid of God, because He is a God of love. But one must have a holy respect for Him. The Bible tells us to "fear" Him. This means we are not to treat the Lord like we would just any person and become too familiar with Him. We must also not use His name just any old way. The old scribes who recopied the Bible scrolls did not even write God's name without first washing their hands.

Moses had to take his shoes off when he saw the burning bush that God spoke from, and we read in Revelation that the angels in heaven cover their faces with their wings when they come before the throne of God.

Sometimes people joke about the Lord. Maybe they don't realize what a terrible thing they are doing, because people should not laugh at the works of almighty God. The Lord Jesus became angry when people didn't show respect for His Father's house. He overturned the tables in the temple, and with a whip He drove out the people who were buying and selling things there.

Only when we think of God with great respect and awe can we call Him "Father," and then we can even imagine sitting on His lap and feeling His warmth and love.

We must be God-fearing.

3 January

Someone After God's Own Heart

"The LORD has sought out a man after his own heart" (1 Samuel 13:14).

The Lord is always looking for someone He can use. He wants to reach out to others and bless them through people like you and me. He is looking for someone who will do what He wants. A person like this is said to be after the Lord's own heart. David was such a person. David was an ordinary man, and he had his faults, the same as we do. (Just think of his sexual sin with Bathsheba in 2 Samuel 11.) But one thing is clear: He loved the Lord very much.

David lived very close to the Lord as a young boy. He was a shepherd, and out there in the fields looking after his sheep, he must have often talked to the Lord. He also sang songs to God. When a lion or a bear wanted to attack his sheep, he asked for the Lord's help, and God helped him. That is why he was also not afraid of the giant Goliath. David knew the Lord was with him and would help him.

David loved the Lord and believed in Him. He was someone after God's own heart. Let's try to love the Lord just as much as David did. Let's be people He can use today.

The Bible says, "David had served God's purpose in his own generation ... " (Acts 13:36)

4 January

See Nature Around You!

"From the lips of children and infants you have ordained praise" (Psalm 8:2).

There are probably tall buildings in the town or city where you live. Cars, bicycles, and buses race by like mad! Saturday mornings are especially hectic – grown-ups rush around as if it is their last chance to shop. As time goes by, this becomes habit. What a pity that because of all their rushing, they don't see the trees and mountains, the sky, and the clouds anymore.

Luckily children are not quite as busy. In the verse above, David says that it is you who are still able to see things that are really important. You can still notice trees, a blue sky, the lovely stream that you can splash through, and animals that play with you if you let them. In Matthew 21:16, Jesus quotes this very same text when the children recognized Him as the Lord Jesus. He spoke this in the temple when the educated grown-ups there did not want to admit that He was the Savior who had come to save the world. But the children knew and were happy to have Him there, and that is why the Lord quoted today's verse.

Enjoy the candor of childhood and the spontaneity which is part of it, before it becomes necessary to start worrying about all kinds of adult matters.

5 January

Can Your Parents Count on You?

"Where you go I will go, and where you stay I will stay. Your people will be my people and your God my God. Where you die I will die" (Ruth 1:16-17).

Children don't always realize that parents can also hurt. They think of their parents as "adults" who never get sick and tired of the responsibilities of every day.

The fact is that parents don't always manage that well.

They often feel threatened in a world that is moving too fast for them. Marriages go through difficult patches, and parents try to hide this from children. Sometimes they have financial problems. Sometimes they become depressed or have problems with their health. Sometimes they are just swallowed up by life with its many demands.

Can you, a child, make things easier for them? Of course you can. After all, you give meaning and joy to their existence. Your happy laughter can iron out all the wrinkles. A friendly greeting from an obedient child is worth all the trouble and heartache. You would be surprised what "love letters" under their pillows can mean to your parents.

Go and read the lovely story of Ruth, who would not let her mother-in-law go back to her own country all by herself.

Realize that your parents are just ordinary people.

6 January

Adam and Eve Are Disobedient

"When the woman saw that the fruit of the tree was good for food and pleasing to the eye, ... she took some and ate it. She also gave some to her husband, who was with her, and he ate it" (Genesis 3:6).

God loved the first two people He made very much. He let them live in a beautiful garden. There were many fruit trees in this garden, and Adam and Eve could eat as much fruit as they wanted. But there was one tree from which the Lord did not allow them to eat: the tree of all knowledge. (See Genesis 2:17.)

Unfortunately, it did not take the devil long to get Eve to disobey the Lord. He persuaded her to eat the forbidden fruit. Then she went and gave Adam some, and he started eating as well! The consequence of this act of disobedience was that sin entered into the world. Ever since that day, all people – including you – are sinners. Fortunately, God promised Adam and Eve that although they would be punished for their disobedience, He would send Someone one day who would free the world from sin again.

The devil is just as clever today as in Adam and Eve's time. Don't listen to him when he wants to trick you into being disobedient.

What was Adam and Eve's punishment for their disobedience? (See Genesis 3:16-19.)

7 January

God Knows Everything

"This is what the LORD says: ... I know what is going through your mind" (Ezekiel 11:5).

There is nothing God does not know. He knows, to the smallest detail, all there is to know about everything and everybody in heaven and on earth. Nothing can happen without His knowing about it, and we can hide nothing from Him. It should be a great comfort to us to have a Father like this. God knows everything and He can protect us from harm.

We see only one tiny part of the world at a time. But He sees everything from above, and He has the full picture of what happens to us. That is why He can send his angels to protect us when He sees danger approaching, or His Holy Spirit can lead us in the right way if we are headed in the wrong direction.

He also knows when we are sad and need some cheering up. Even if we hide it from others, the Lord sees deep into our hearts and knows how we feel. Then He can comfort us. The Bible tells us that God is on His throne in heaven. He doesn't run around all over the place and panic when bad things happen on earth. Nothing surprises Him. He knows about everything, and He is busy working out His plan for the world. One day every knee will bow before Him, and everybody will know that He is God.

God is an all-knowing God.

8 January

What Do You Live In?

Don't you know that you yourselves are God's temple?
(1 Corinthians 3:16)

Every one of us is unique. We look different. We walk differently. There is a difference in the way we sing and in the color of our hair. Some of us are short; others are tall. Everybody looks different – except, of course, identical twins! And not even they are exactly the same, because their personalities are different.

Look at yourself in the mirror. You have a body. Inside that body is someone with a personality. That is you. You take care of your body. You feed it, dress it, keep it healthy, rest it, exercise it, and wash it. That's the way it should be, because our bodies are very precious.

The Lord loves us so much that He wants to live inside our bodies. If we receive Him (See John 1:12.) or invite Him in (See Revelation 3:20.), then He comes to live in us. He lives in us through His Holy Spirit, and in this way our bodies become almost like a beautiful church building or a temple. In the old days, people made the temple very beautiful – only the best was good enough.

When the Lord comes to live in you, you must know that it is necessary to look after your body and take good care of it. Does the greatest King in the whole world live in you?

The Bible tells us: "So whether you eat or drink or whatever you do, do it all for the glory of God" *(1 Corinthians 10:31).*

9 January

Make the Lord
Smile on His Throne

"The LORD ... has established his throne"(Psalm 9:7).

One easily forgets that the Lord is always on His throne. From there He sees good and evil, His friends and enemies, His children and those who are against Him. Remember this during your free time too when you're having fun or playing a sport! Children sometimes forget that the Lord knows about everything they do. Luckily many of those who believe in Him try not to be naughty because they know God can see everything they do. Don't forget that God smiles when He notices that you praise Him in the way you spend your free time – like being honest when you're playing a game.

But if you shout, "The ball was in!" when you're playing a tennis match, while you actually hit it out, then of course, He is not pleased with your dishonesty. Remember this wherever you may be or whatever you do. One day, I was watching kids play tennis at school, and a few times I noticed the same kid shouting that the ball was out when it really wasn't. Some adults watching the game were not impressed at all. Can you think how the Lord must feel when He sees such dishonesty from His throne?

Make sure that your conduct always makes the Lord smile.

10 January

Trouble, Trouble, Trouble

*In the L*ORD *I take refuge. How then can you say to me: "Flee like a bird to your mountain" (Psalm 11:1).*

Any community in today's world experiences danger and accidents. Often children are the victims. The other day I joined a few children who were standing around at the scene of an accident in which a friend of theirs had been hit by a car while he was riding his bicycle. One of the youngsters suddenly looked up at a bird that was flying past and said, "I wish I could be like a bird, and fly away when trouble comes!" Too bad this isn't possible, right?

Psalm 11 tells us how the Lord takes care of the righteous as well as the wicked and those who shoot their arrows to hurt others. It is in circumstances like these that the believer can find shelter with the Lord. It is not necessary to fly away to the mountains like a bird. Of course, this doesn't mean that the children of the Lord will never be in danger or be involved in an accident. The devil is always around to set traps for us and to bring misfortune our way. But because we find refuge in the Lord, we do not have to live in fear. This is what is so wonderful – the Lord is with us when trouble comes. Jesus Himself said in John 10:28, *"No one can snatch them [my children] out of my hand."*

I imagine it would be wonderful to fly high like a bird. But it is much better when the Lord holds you in His hand, and you know that He will protect you, today and always.

It is hard when troubles come, but in those times, the Lord will hold you tight.

11 January

Faith Is a Firm Belief

But Daniel resolved not to defile himself with the royal food and wine (Daniel 1:8).

If someone asks you, "What do you believe?" you will probably say, "I am a Christian because I believe in Jesus Christ." But when it comes to proving your faith with your lifestyle, how will you fare then? If you want to be part of the "in" group, how far will your faith carry you when the group does things that go against your principles?

Principles are not of much use to you if they are just in your head. You must be sure of what you believe, and you must stand up for it.

Are your rules of conduct only a loose framework in which you try more or less to stay, or are they firm beliefs of right and wrong? Make a list of all the things you feel very strongly about and which you are not prepared to give up, no matter what the circumstances.

If you have few firm beliefs or maybe none, read the story of Daniel, who was a young man living in a foreign country and who never gave up even one of his principles. See how much he was respected in the country of the enemy.

Principles are not formed in a void. They must be founded on the Bible. Daniel's faith survived in a foreign country because he kept strictly to the principles of his faith.

12 January

Noah Is Obedient

So God said to Noah, " ... Make yourself an ark of cypress wood, ... You are to bring into the ark two of all living creatures ... " Noah did everything just as God commanded him (Genesis 6:13-14, 19, 22).

Noah's story boggles the mind! What would you do if the Lord should ask you to build a giant-sized ship on dry ground and, on top of that, to get two of every kind of animal and bird into that ship? One can honestly not imagine anything more impossible.

Noah probably also thought the Lord was asking a bit much. His wife and children and neighbors would probably make fun of him and think he was behaving very strangely. But what did Noah do? He wasn't ready with a lot of excuses for why it was absolutely impossible for him to do what the Lord told him. No, he "did everything just as God commanded him."

And when the ark was finished, God Himself made the animals go inside. (See Genesis 7:8-9.) With God everything is possible!

Because Noah was obedient, God spared his life and the lives of his family and all the animals. Don't you want to make the effort to be just as obedient as Noah from now on?

What happened to the disobedient people in Noah's time? (See Genesis 7:21-23.)

13 January

God Sees Everything!

His eyes are on the ways of men; he sees their every step (Job 34:21).

"Linda, where are you?" Mom calls. Linda doesn't answer. She is hiding under her bed and keeps very still. She has done something terrible! She took the goldfish bowl from the shelf, dropped it, and broke it! That's exactly what her mother said would happen. "Never try to pick up the goldfish bowl, Linda. You'll drop it!" her mother warned.

Linda keeps perfectly still, but she doesn't know her feet are showing. When her mother comes into the room, she sees immediately where her little girl is hiding. "You can come out now!" her mother says. Linda feels very bad. She can't look her mother in the eyes. Linda's mom speaks to her sternly, "You were disobedient. You will have to give me some of your pocket-money to help buy a new goldfish bowl. And you will have to clean up the study. Luckily I was able to save the goldfish!"

While Linda carefully picks up the broken pieces of glass, Mom pulls up a chair and sits down. "Linda," she says softly, "Remember, it's no good hiding when you have done something wrong. Even if I didn't see you, the Lord would have. It's always better to be honest if you've been naughty."

"I'm sorry, Mommy!" Linda says. Mom gets up and gives her a hug. Now Linda can look her mother in the eyes again.

You can't hide from God.

14 January

God Always Keeps His Promises

The one who calls you is faithful and he will do it (1 Thessalonians 5:24).

Do you get fed up when someone has promised to do something and then doesn't? Perhaps a friend promised to take you on a vacation with him or her and in the end never invited you. Perhaps your grandfather promised you a bicycle and forgot all about it. Perhaps your father promised to take you hiking, but now there's never time for it.

Yes, it does happen that people promise things and then don't keep their promises. But God never breaks a promise. If He makes a promise, He always keeps it. There is even a sign in nature to remind us of this. Do you know what it is? Yes, it is the rainbow. Remember that God promised Noah that He would never again send a flood as bad as the one that destroyed the earth? And God said that the rainbow, which usually appears in the sky after a shower of rain, will remind us that all His promises come true.

If you should decide to highlight all God's promises in the Bible with a yellow highlighter, your Bible will look like a field of sunflowers in places! And just think, He is going to keep all those promises!

You can count on God's promises.

15 January

Not Like This

F.R.O.G

F.R.O.G

F.R.O.G

Some time later, he fell in love with a woman ... whose name was Delilah (Judges 16:4).

Samson is a well known character in the Bible. He was called to be the Lord's instrument from childhood. When he grew his hair, he had great strength. He was able to help the Israelites win battles against the Philistines, their enemies.

Then he made a wrong choice. He fell in love with a Philistine girl who did not love the Lord. Soon after he got involved with her, his life ended very sadly. She started nagging him to tell her the secret of his great strength. She didn't really love him, and when the Philistines bribed her, she chose money above her feelings for Samson. When he told her his strength was in his hair, she cut it all off and called the Philistines to come and capture him. They captured him, poked his eyes out, and put him in a cage, taunting him and making fun of him, and also saying bad things about the Lord.

It is so important that we choose the right people as our friends. That is why your friends, both girls and boys, must know the Lord and love Him. And it's not too soon to ask the Lord even now to help us choose the right husband or wife one day.

The Bible says, "Let her be the one you have chosen for ... Isaac" (Genesis 24:14). Read Genesis 24.

16 January

If You've Messed Up ...

You bestow glory on me and lift up my head (Psalm 3:3).

There was a time when King David and his son Absalom were enemies. Poor old David even had to flee from his son's attacks! In Old Testament days it happened quite often that there was this kind of enmity between children and parents – especially in ruling families vying for power. Though there are instances of family problems today, luckily we do not see much of the same kind of enmity that King David experienced. This is good, because it does not please the Lord.

But even if you have a great relationship with your parents, don't think this means you can never do wrong. What about the time you pelted the neighbor's newly painted wall with eggs or mud balls because you were mad at his son? You just wanted to get back at him for something and went and did something crazy like that. What were you thinking?

First of all you need to tell your parents what you have been up to, and then you should go to the neighbor and offer to wash the wall and clean up the mess. The Lord tells us in today's verse that a good name is better than many riches. Someone who admits that he has behaved foolishly and tries to make up for it will always be respected afterwards, and that's a fact. It could be you, and the Lord will give you back your good name.

Why is making up so much more difficult than messing up?

17 January

Communicating with Parents

"Son, why have you treated us like this? Your father and I have been anxiously searching for you." ... [Jesus] asked, "Didn't you know I had to be in my Father's house?" (Luke 2:48-49)

Choose the right answer: Communicating with your parents is: a) easier than you think; b) more difficult than you think; c) both are true.

Of course there's the generation gap. But your parents want to communicate with you just as badly as you do with them. There are effective ways and means of doing it.

How to wreck any chance of communication:
- Sulk: Refuse to say what's bothering you.
- Try the pout: Grumble to yourself about everything.
- Scheme: Pretend to do what your parents want.
- Start shouting at the top of your voice, if you think the one who shouts the loudest wins.
- Manipulate: Play one parent off against the other.

Hey, presto! No possibility of open and sincere communication.

In Luke 2 we read about what seems to be a misunderstanding between Jesus and His parents. They were not aware of His calling and saw Him only as a young boy who was missing. Jesus is a little disappointed because they don't understand and tells them so.

Don't play games. Say what you mean.

18 January

Abraham Does What God Wants

Some time later God tested Abraham. He said to him, …
"Take your son, your only son, Isaac, whom you love, and
go to the region of Moriah. Sacrifice him there as a burnt
offering on one of the mountains I will tell you about"
(Genesis 22:1-2).

The Lord asked Abraham to do a terribly difficult thing: "Go and kill the son you love so much, Abraham," God said. "Go and sacrifice him on a mountain in Moriah."

Abraham loved Isaac very much. He and his wife Sarah waited many years for this son the Lord had promised them. When they were actually already too old to have children, Isaac was born. It was Isaac's offspring that would become the great nation that God promised Abraham. And now God expected him to kill this son!

But Abraham trusted God – without hesitation he started preparing to sacrifice his son. Fortunately the Lord stopped him in time and provided a ram for the burnt offering instead.

Sometimes the Lord also wants us to do something very difficult. Do you love the Lord as much as Abraham did? Would you be willing to give up your most precious possession if He asked you to?

How did the Lord reward Abraham's obedience when he was
on the point of sacrificing Isaac? (See Genesis 22:12-13.)

19 January

God Cares for His Creation

F.R.O.G. F.R.O.G. F.R.O.G.

He makes grass grow for the cattle, and plants for man to cultivate – bringing forth food from the earth ... and bread that sustains his heart. ... When you hide your face, they are terrified (Psalm 104:14-15, 29).

In a lovely song, the words: "He's got the whole world in his hands!" are sung. It's good to know this, isn't it? It would be terrible to think the Lord made the world and then just left it like that. There are people who believe God created nature, made its rules, and then wound it up like an alarm clock to run on its own. They think the universal clock must now tick on until it winds down one day, and stops. They don't believe God is still involved in His creation.

But today's text makes it clear: If God left us to ourselves, that would be bad. Think about a furniture maker who makes beautiful furniture. When he eventually dies, all the tables and chairs he made are still there to see. His death didn't change his creations in any way. But God and His creation are a different story. If our Creator withdrew His caring hand, there would be chaos!

Fortunately the Bible teaches us that He will keep up everything by His powerful word (See Hebrews 1:3). God's hand made us, and that is where we'll stay – in His hand.

God takes care of us.

20 January

Athletes on Their Knees

"Call upon me in the day of trouble; I will deliver you, and you will honor me" (Psalm 50:15).

When the South African Springbok rugby team won the World Cup for the first time in history, something wonderful happened.

When the final whistle blew, the captain of the Springboks called all his teammates together, and then millions of people all over the world watched as they went down on their knees and prayed. They thanked the Lord that He supported them and helped them. By doing this, they were admitting that their strength and ability came from God. Before the game they had asked the Lord to be with them, so they thanked and honored Him afterwards.

What a wonderful moment! We must follow this example. Every day we must acknowledge that we need the Lord and tell Him this. And then we must also remember to thank and praise Him for being with us and helping us. We must also not be embarrassed to do it in front of our friends or other people.

The Bible tells us: "My help comes from the LORD, the Maker of heaven and earth" *(Psalm 121:2).*

21 January

Better Than
the Olympic Games

Do you not know that in a race all the runners run, but only one gets the prize? Run in such a way as to get the prize (1 Corinthians 9:24).

I'm sure all of you have heard about the Olympic Games! The first modern Games took place in Athens on April 6, 1896. The Frenchman, Pierre de Coubert, was the driving force behind it all, and 80,000 spectators attended. The occasion was officially opened by the King of Greece.

Paul uses the image of an athlete to tell Christians how to run the race of life. He encourages us to run in such a way that we can win first prize. "But I'm not even an athlete, let alone a good one!" you might want to say. That doesn't matter. The question is, whether you take part in athletics or only watch sports on television, do you think about the fact that you are running on the track of life every day?

How are you running? Are you simply jogging along, or do you put all your effort into the race? How good to know beforehand that there are no losers among Christians. Every one of us is a winner in Christ. This means that He has already won the winner's crown for us. He keeps it ready and will award it to each of His children when they reach Him at the finish.

Put your all into the race, because you know the victory is certain.

22 January

You Take
Part at a Price

Everyone who competes in the games goes into strict training. They do it to get a crown that will not last; but we do it to get a crown that will last forever (1 Corinthians 9:25).

"**C**ome on, faster, faster!" I'm sure you've heard a coach at school encourage athletes like this during practice. And, "Don't eat so many sweets. You'll get fat and lazy!"

This is exactly what Paul is saying when he uses the image of athletes. If they want to do well, they have to be disciplined and miss out on many things while they are in strict training. Just like athletes need to go to bed early, cut down on soda pop or sweets, and not eat the wrong foods if they want to do well, it is necessary that you must discipline yourself for the spiritual race.

This means that you do not associate with friends who can make you stumble and that you will stay away from things like smoking, drugs, or alcohol. In the spiritual race of life you must not only keep away from certain things, but you must also concentrate on serving the Lord with devotion. Otherwise you will never become a balanced, mature Christian.

Keep yourself from doing the wrong things if you want to develop strong spiritual muscles.

23 January

When Parents Are Unbelievers

[Amon] did evil in the eyes of the LORD, as his father Manasseh had done. ... [Josiah] did what was right in the eyes of the LORD (2 Kings 21:20; 22:2).

Just paging through a newspaper makes you realize that the world is full of bad parents who set a bad example for their children. There are parents who do not teach their children to pray because they do not pray themselves. For many children the Bible is just another book they haven't read, and the church is there only for christening ceremonies, weddings, and funerals.

But there are children who are believers in spite of their parents and who try to live a life of faith. This is not always easy. If your parents are not believers, you can do the following:

- Pray that the unbelievers in your family will become believers.
- Follow the example of other adult believers.
- Become actively involved in a Christian youth group.
- Have a quiet time every day to strengthen your faith.

Don't give up. Think of Josiah who became king when he was eight years old and did not stray one step to the left or right, but stayed on the right way, in spite of his evil father, Amon. Read his story in 2 Kings 21 and 22.

You have been placed in your family for a purpose. Stand firm in your faith and God will, in His own time and in His own way, speak to your parents.

24 January

Joseph Obeys God

"How then could I do such a wicked thing and sin against God?" (Genesis 39:9)

Joseph's master, an Egyptian named Potiphar, had a very pretty wife. She noticed immediately that Joseph was an attractive young man, and she wanted him to go to bed with her. But Joseph refused. He explained to her that her husband had put him in charge of all his possessions, and that he could never do anything to betray that trust.

The real reason why Joseph didn't want to listen to his boss's wife was that he did not want to disobey God. He knew very well it would be sinful to sleep with a married woman.

"How can I do something I know is wrong?" Joseph asked Potiphar's wife. "It will be a sin against God!" Potiphar's wife was so angry with Joseph that she accused him of something he didn't do and saw to it that he was sent to jail. This almost looks as if Joseph landed in jail because of his obedience. But in Genesis 39:20-21 we read that the Lord was with him there in the prison.

Because Joseph was obedient, the Lord used him later on, not only to save the Egyptians from famine, but also to save the lives of his own family.

How did the Lord use Joseph in prison? (See Genesis 39: 20-23.) And afterwards? (See Genesis 41:56-57.)

25 January

God Also Gets Angry Sometimes

Serve the LORD with fear and rejoice with trembling ... lest he be angry (Psalm 2:11-12).

Many stories in the Bible show us that God can get very angry. When people are stubborn and don't do what He tells them to do, God punishes them. Think about what happened to the people in Noah's time when they wouldn't listen and kept on living sinful lives: God sent a flood in which everybody drowned except Noah and his children. And He was so angry with the people of Sodom and Gomorrah that He burned their cities to the ground. Only Lot and his family escaped. He also let the Egyptians drown in the sea because they wanted to take the Israelites back to Egypt.

Take note, though, that the Lord always protects His children. Noah and his family were spared in a wonderful way. Lot and his two daughters were not harmed by the fire. And the Israelites arrived safely on the other side of the sea.

The Bible asks the question, "If God is for us, who can be against us?" We must make sure we are on God's side and not be disobedient and make Him angry. Then we have nothing to fear.

We know that God is a God of love, but if a person keeps on sinning and is not even sorry about it, he will be up against a God that can make even the devil tremble.

God cannot treat good and bad the same.

26 January

God Is Love

God is love. Whoever lives in love lives in God, and God in him (1 John 4:16).

The verse from Scripture, "God is love," is very well known. You probably learned it as a tiny tot in Sunday school, and you must have seen it often on bookmarks, cards, and posters. But when John wrote it down, it was the first time in history that these three words were used in this way. By then people already believed in God's goodness, and they had often experienced His love, but no one had ever spelled it out like this.

A preacher once said he could see a picture in his mind of heaven on the day John wrote down these words. He said he believed the angels were looking over John's shoulder as he wrote down the three words and then suddenly they burst into joyful applause. "Now they know! At last people know it: God is love!" the angels rejoiced. A sigh of contentment and great happiness filled heaven, he said, because the greatest truth about God had now been made crystal clear.

These words mean that God does not really need a reason to love. He loves even the greatest sinner. And what is more, His love never stops. What a comforting thought this is! Our hearts should be on fire with love for our God, who is so full of love.

We love Him because He first loved us.

27 January

The Light

"I am the light of the world" (John 8:12).

We need light. We can hurt ourselves in the dark because we bump into things we can't see. We can trip over things or fall down stairs if we don't know about them. Darkness on a path can make us lose our way. These are just a few reasons why we need light.

But there is also another type of darkness. This is the darkness caused by sin. Let's call it a spiritual darkness. Sin can make it "dark" in a person's heart, and then he or she can't find the right way in life.

Jesus said very clearly that He is the light of the world. By this He meant the world is dark because of sin. But He came to bring light. You and I can drive away the dark by switching on a light. In the same way, Jesus shines like a bright light in the darkness of sin!

He Himself is the light. And if we invite Him into our lives, it becomes light wherever He is.

The Bible says: "In him was life, and that life was the light of men. The light shines in the darkness, but the darkness has not understood it" *(John 1:4-5).*

28 January

Call Out to God
When You Are in Trouble

The LORD will hear when I call to him (Psalm 4:3).

Once a fifth-grade boy told me how anxious he was when he got lost at the Easter show in the big city of Johannesburg, South Africa. He said he literally broke out in a sweat and eventually was so tired from all the walking that he felt he was going to collapse and fall down dead right there. He could see nothing he liked anymore, so he went and sat on a bench somewhere and started praying out loud to God to help him.

The next moment a thought flashed through his mind: "I must go to the information counter for help!" Right then he put his thoughts into action. When his plight was broadcast over the loudspeaker system, his parents were there to fetch him in no time. "That was a smart thing to do. What made you do it?" his mother asked.

"Well, I called to the Lord like the Bible says, and He helped me!"

An unbeliever might find this a bit hard to believe, don't you think? But definitely not the believer. After all, God does promise in His Word to help us if we call to Him. And it doesn't have to be only in difficult times either! Can you think of a situation like this one when you were afraid and called to the Lord, and He helped you?

Remember – call to the Lord in anxious moments!

29 January

Rebel Without a Cause

Then the LORD opened the donkey's mouth, and she said ...
(Numbers 22:28).

Through the ages, young people have found it hard to obey authority: Parents set all kinds of rules and regulations; teachers always give homework; the principal enforces all the school rules, and the minister nags kids to take part in youth activities. It's enough to drive any young person up the wall.

Some young people don't find it difficult to be obedient. Perhaps they see the need for rules and regulations, or they don't really mind the older generation with all their instructions.

Others see red when they hear "you must," "you must not," "you ought to." Rules are made to break, they believe. If their mothers say do this, then they do that. They go out of their way to annoy teachers with their rebellious attitudes, and if they go to church, they wear the most outrageous clothes just to show they are doing their own thing.

Sometimes something unusual happens to teach them obedience. Something or someone is sent to stop them in their tracks, like in the story of Balaam and his talking donkey. Why don't you read about it in Numbers 22?

Swimming against the stream is not necessarily wrong. Just make sure it's for the right reasons. Why did God want to stop Balaam? (See Numbers 22:21-35.)

30 January

Moses Makes Excuses

Moses answered, "What if they [the Israelites] do not believe me or listen to me? ... I am slow of speech and tongue" (Exodus 4:1, 10).

When the Lord told Moses He had chosen him to bring His people, the Israelites, out of Egypt, Moses did not feel like obeying at all. Surely this task the Lord had given him was too difficult! He started thinking of one excuse after another.

First he told the Lord he was not important enough. Then he said he couldn't speak well enough.

Finally – after the Lord had convinced him that He would help him with this difficult task – Moses gave in and agreed to do what the Lord wanted. And the Lord used him to lead the people of Israel out of slavery in Egypt.

Often we know very well that the Lord wants us to do things for Him. And then we make excuses like Moses did! Perhaps you tell yourself you have far too much homework, you are shy, or your friends will laugh at you if you speak to them about the Lord. How about forgetting all those excuses for once and obeying God? He will help you just like He helped Moses.

Count how many excuses Moses made for not wanting to obey God. (See Exodus 3:11, 13; 4:1, 10, 13.)

31 January

God Hates Sin

But your iniquities have separated you from your God (Isaiah 59:2).

"I don't think Cecilia's mother really loves her," Cindy told her friend Liezl on their way to school one morning.

"Why do you say that?" Liezl asked.

"She can do as she likes! She goes wherever she wants, stays out till all hours, and is never punished for anything. Just the other day she even skipped school and her mother said nothing. If I should dare do something like that, my mother would skin me alive!"

"That will be the day!" Liezl teased. "Your mother loves her little girl far too much!"

"I'll be punished. You can be sure of it!" Cindy said. "Because my mother loves me, she won't just leave me to go my own way."

"Yes," answered Liezl. "My mother also tells me she needs to discipline me because she loves me."

In today's verse, Isaiah says that our sins can stand between God and us like a solid brick wall. Can you understand now why God hates sin and why He is strict with us? He doesn't want anything to come between Him and us. He loves us and always wants us close to Him. Then He can protect us and help us and give us advice.

God hates sin like a mother hates a deadly snake that wants to attack her child.

Sin separates us from God.

1 February

Ouch!

Even my close friend, whom I trusted ... has lifted up his heel against me (Psalm 41:9).

Friendship is great, but you can also be hurt by it. You trust your friend. If you tell him or her something very special, you don't expect your friend to tell others about it. Trust is very important in a friendship. That is why it hurts when a friend does something that shows you can't trust him. Something else that hurts is if your friend is nice to you one day and turns against you the next day.

What should we do when this happens? The Bible says we all make mistakes. And no matter how difficult it might be, we must forgive. Even if your friend does not apologize, you must forgive anyway and still be nice to him or her. But it makes sense that you are going to find it difficult to trust that person again.

The worst thing you can do is to pay him back. The Lord says one must not return evil for evil. Don't say, "I'll get her for this!" Ask the Lord to heal your hurt, and to help you so that you feel no bitterness. Jesus said on the cross, "Father, forgive them, for they do not know what they are doing." Let's try to do the same.

The Bible says: "If you hold anything against anyone, forgive him, so that your Father in heaven may forgive you your sins" *(Mark 11:25).*

2 February

Reach for Your Goal with Determination

I do not run like a man running aimlessly; I do not fight like a man beating the air (1 Corinthians 9:26).

One sport I don't like at all is boxing. Maybe you don't feel the same way. It just seems like unnecessary torture to me. Nevertheless, one thing I do know about boxing is that a boxer who does not have the will to win and punches the air aimlessly all the time will not win a single fight! The point the apostle Paul wants to make in today's verse is that, spiritually, we should not be like a boxer beating the air. "No," the apostle says, "we must be purposeful in the boxing ring of life!" One cannot help agreeing with that.

Let me give you an example. If you don't know that your life is headed towards the Lord Jesus Christ and that you may look forward to the joyful day when you will stand before Him in person, then you will easily make the wrong turns in life. You will not grow and make progress in your spiritual life. You will bear no clear witness and never stand up for the Lord in anything. You will always be stuck at the side of life's road, afraid and miserable, and no one will ever know you belong to God. Surely this is not the way it's meant to be.

Be very sure of your aim in life (to be like Christ), otherwise you will never be a convincing witness for Him.

3 February

Practice to Control Yourself

No, I beat [discipline] my body and make it my slave [control it] so that after I have preached to others, I myself will not be disqualified for the prize (1 Corinthians 9:27).

At the school our children attend, the teachers often ask parents to help coach and tutor children. I have sympathy with the poor teachers because the work just gets to be too much, with teaching in the mornings and running around all afternoon in the hot sun coaching sports teams.

But I must say, it's quite something to watch some of the fathers who help with the coaching. Quite a few of them are already a little potbellied, and all this running around really makes them sweat! This is a good example of what Paul means when he talks about people who preach to others and do not qualify themselves! Of course the apostle's real message is, "Don't preach to your friends about living Christian lives while you don't do it yourself." What's the use of telling others not to swear if you do it? Or telling people to be a witness for Christ, but you're not one?

Examine your own life for a change. Is it possible that you are busy telling others what to do while you yourself don't do it? Practice what you preach!

Do what the Bible expects from a Christian.

4 February

The Most Important Person in the Kingdom

My spirit rejoices in God my Savior, for he has been mindful of the humble state of his servant (Luke 1:47-48).

Parents like bragging about their children. They think that their children must be winners at all costs. Otherwise, the world might think they have failed as parents.

In the eyes of the world there is no room for the dreamer, and you simply don't make mistakes. You must prove yourself before anyone notices you. The result is that only the so-called talented and clever children are noticed. Those who struggle to keep up don't count.

Fortunately God does not think so. He says, "To Me you are important, not because you are one of the in-group or you are smart and cute, but because you have been created in My image and likeness." It doesn't matter what the sports coach or the math teacher says about you; you are important in God's eyes. To Him even the most humble person is important. That is why He chose a poor, simple girl to be the mother of His Son.

If you ever have doubts about your importance in God's eyes, read Psalm 139:13, *"For you created my inmost being; you knit me together in my mother's womb."*

Mary was a plain, ordinary girl from a poor, small town. Yet God chose her to be the mother of Jesus.

5 February

God Wants You to Be Obedient

Children, obey your parents in the Lord, for this is right (Ephesians 6:1).

Being obedient is "doing what one is told to do" – this is how the dictionary explains obedience. Today's verse tells God's children to obey their parents.

When I look around me at the children I know, I'm not so sure they're quite as obedient as the Bible wants them to be. It isn't always easy to listen to your parents! Sometimes you feel what they expect from you is really not fair. Perhaps you don't get as much spending money as the rest of your friends. Perhaps your parents don't allow you to go parties your friends go to, or perhaps you have to do odd jobs around the house that you are not paid for.

If you read your Bible, you will discover that the Lord expects all children who love Him to obey their parents. This is so important to Him that it is written down in His law as one of the Ten Commandments. Children who are not prepared to obey their parents are not prepared to listen to the Lord.

What about you? Are you going to make an effort to try to be obedient, starting today?

In which way does the fifth commandment differ from all the others? (See Ephesians 6:2-3.)

6 February

God Can Forgive

Who is a God like you, who pardons sin and forgives the transgression? (Micah 7:18)

There was a major upset at the Anderson home. Stephanie and Michael had to be picked up from the police station that afternoon. They were caught behind the municipal buildings with a group of youngsters smoking marijuana. "What a disgrace!" Mrs. Anderson cried when she picked up the children. "I never ever thought this would happen to any of my children."

"But we didn't do anything wrong, Mom!" explained Michael. "We actually told them it was wrong!" Stephanie sobbed.

At home their father waited for them, his face grim: "You should not be with children who do things like this! Now see what has happened. Everybody is going to think you were also smoking marijuana."

"Sorry, Dad!" both children said.

That night during family devotions Dad read the story of Jonah. He read how God forgave the people of Nineveh because they were truly sorry about their sins. "What you did was wrong," Dad said. "But if you are truly sorry about it, God will forgive you."

"Does this mean you're not going to punish us?" Michael wanted to know. "That's right!" Dad answered. "I also forgive you. Come, let's thank the Lord for His mercy."

God does not like punishing us. He would rather have us pay attention to His warnings.

7 February

Jesus' Name

"You are to give him the name Jesus" (Luke 1:31).

Do you know what your name means? Why don't you try to find out? Maybe the meaning does not suit you at all, but you might just like it so much that it inspires you to reach new heights!

I'm sure you know that the name Peter means "rock." Theo and John both mean "gift from God." Anne means "grace," and Sonia means "wisdom." Those of you who are called by these names should find the meanings quite an inspiration!

Jesus' name means "Savior" or "Redeemer." This name really suits Him. He spent His whole life on earth saving or freeing people – some from illness, others from evil spirits, and many from lives without purpose. For example, think about the poor man from Bethesda who was sick for thirty-eight years before Jesus healed him. And what about the demon-possessed man from Gadara, who had to be chained hand and foot because he was so violent? Jesus freed him from the evil spirits. There's also Zacchaeus, who lived only for money and possessions. When Jesus spoke to him, he stopped sinning and started giving his money to the poor. Jesus freed him from his greed for money.

Is there something you would like to be saved or freed from? Perhaps a quick temper? Or laziness or lovelessness? Then remember, Jesus' name means "Savior." Ask Him to set you free from the things that are standing in your way and preventing you from living the way you should.

Jesus came to save us.

8 February

Life or Death?

"I am ... the life" (John 14:6).

Every day people die around us – in cars, in airplanes, in hospitals, and in every country in the world. Death puts an end to life here on earth. Death began with humankind's disobedience towards the Lord in the Garden of Eden, when the devil, who is also called the "lord of death," made humans believe his lies.

But Jesus Christ came to the rescue. He is the King of life. He came to live on earth as a human being, and He came to tell people that if they believe in Him they will live with Him forever. He knew, though, that all the people on earth must first die. And He was also prepared to die – on a cross on Golgotha.

When He died, He paid with His life for the sins of us all. But the greatest miracle is that He rose from the dead! We don't know exactly how it happened, but it was the most amazing thing that could have happened. Jesus triumphed over death! He is stronger than the devil and death.

If you and I believe in Him, ask Him to forgive our sins, and are prepared to follow Him, then we receive everlasting life. Then our bodies will still die on earth, but our spirits will live forever!

The Bible tells us: "I am the resurrection and the life. He who believes in me will live, even though he dies. ... Do you believe this?" *(John 11:25-26)*

9 February

Make the Lord Proud of You

In order that I may boast on the day of Christ that I did not run or labor for nothing (Philippians 2:16).

Parents love attending the awards ceremony at the end of the year to watch their children get prizes. They love to watch their sons and daughters play a game of soccer or baseball, and they celebrate when their kids score! I hope you sometimes make your parents jump for joy. This doesn't mean you have to win a prize; it also gives your parents great pleasure to see you do something nice or good. It may seem as if your dad is going to pop a shirt button the way his breast swells with pride.

That's exactly what the apostle Paul was talking about when he thought of his spiritual input into the lives of Christians in Philippi. He was already looking forward to the day when he would stand before the Lord, feeling proud that he worked so hard with them, encouraged them to serve the Lord, and helped them when they were not sure how to live.

I am sure you appreciate it when others show concern for you. But have you ever thought how happy you can make the Lord by helping your friends?

What is your input into the lives of others? Will it make the Lord proud of you?

10 February

Stand Firm When You're Carrying a Burden

A man cannot be established through wickedness, but the righteous cannot be uprooted (Proverbs 12:3).

In spite of living in a world that seems to offer instant answers to problems and to encourage us to satisfy our desires at any cost, there is really only one way to find real answers in life: to do God's will.

If things start going wrong, we are so quick to blame God. "Why did God allow this to happen to me?" we complain time and time again. But if you sit down and think about it, you know that you, and you alone, are to blame for many of the things that happen to you.

What is your attitude towards life? Do you think playing computer games on a Sunday morning is more important than going to church like God's children should? Do you take more than you give back? Do you run others down to put yourself in a good light? Do you always tell the truth or are you a backbiter?

God promises that the person who does what He wants will stand fast and not be uprooted. So it might be a good idea to go down on your knees and confess that you often serve yourself instead of the Lord, and that is why your efforts fail.

In the New Testament we read about Zacchaeus, a dishonest tax collector, who brought his life in line with the Lord's will. Read the story again in Luke 19:1-10.

11 February

Honor Your Parents

"Honor your father and your mother, so that you may live long in the land the LORD your God is giving you" (Exodus 20:12).

"**H**onor you father and your mother," reads the fifth commandment. God asks you not only to obey your parents, but also to honor them. This means you must respect them and have a great regard for them. People in Bible times all wanted to live very long, and the fifth commandment promises that you will, if you honor your parents.

God Himself put parents over you. They stand in for Him in your life. That is why He expects you to do what they want you to, even if it is difficult. But parents are ordinary people – they sometimes make mistakes. Nobody's perfect. When this happens, you must be prepared to forgive them like God forgives you. Always remember that your parents love you very much and want only what's best for you.

The fifth commandment also tells you to honor all other forms of authority over you. You must obey the laws of the country and the rules laid down by the teachers at your school. Can you do this? Then the Lord gives His promise that He will bless you.

What does the Lord promise you if you obey your parents? (See Exodus 20:12.)

12 February

In Jesus We See What God Is Like

He [Christ] is the image of the invisible God (Colossians 1:15).

Have you ever wondered what God looks like? Some people think He is an old man with a long beard – too old to be in touch with today's world. Others see Him as a strict king with spies all over to see what we do wrong so He can punish us. Then there are people who think He is too nice to get mad; He's like a grandfather handing out sweets all day, and in whose eyes His grandchildren can do nothing wrong!

But God is not like this. How do we know? After all, no one has ever seen Him! The Bible tells us if we want to know what the Lord God is like, we must look at His Son, Jesus. And we can read in the Bible about things that Jesus did. Now we know a lot about God. We know He loves children and wants to help us. We also know He hates sin. He will do anything to get rid of sin. God felt so strongly about putting an end to sin that He worked out the plan of the Cross. Has anybody ever explained to you why Jesus had to die on a wooden cross?

On the cross God showed us how much He loves us and how much He hates sin.

13 February

Look at the Birds

"Look at the birds of the air. ... Your heavenly Father feeds them. Are you not much more valuable than they?" (Matthew 6:26)

Isn't it amazing how many different bird species there are in the world? Just think of all the sizes and colors, the way each builds its nest, and how they all make different sounds. The Lord is a great God to have made such a variety of birds!

We read a lot about birds in the Bible. The Lord doesn't take care of birds only, but also of you and me, Matthew says. If God can care for so many millions of birds that don't have minds like we do, surely He will take care of us. You are worth more than a bird, aren't you?

Yes, the Lord knows each one of us and He loves us. He promises to look after His children. Don't be afraid of bad things that might happen. Trust in the Lord. Like a majestic eagle or a hen spreads her wings to shelter her young, you and I are protected every day by the Lord.

The Bible says: "I know every bird in the mountains, and the creatures of the field are mine" *(Psalm 50:11).*

14 February

How Do You Run the Race of Life?

I have fought the good fight, I have finished the race, I have kept the faith (2 Timothy 4:7).

Down the road from us is a lady who has a nursery school. I know you are thinking, "I'm way past the nursery school stage!" But today I want to remind you of nursery school. You see, long ago you probably also went to one. This was before you could read or write. Now you are able to read this book. And if you had not gone to nursery school, you might not have been able to read so fluently.

Nevertheless, the lady at the nursery school has a "graduation ceremony" at the end of each year. She invites all the parents, and they usually arrive with their cameras and video cameras to take pictures of their children when they receive their "diplomas" for attending faithfully. This, of course, motivates them to attend even more regularly the following year.

And this is precisely what Paul is saying here. He is looking back on his life and explains to his young pupil, Timothy, that he faithfully ran the race of life and completed his ministry. Now all that remains is the reward that he will receive from the hand of God. Let me ask you this question: Are you running the race in such a way that you will also receive the prize from the hand of the Lord at the finish?

Lord, help me to run the race of life in such a way that I will get the winner's crown one day.

15 February

The Lord Gives Victory

The horse is made ready for the day of battle, but victory rests with the Lord (Proverbs 21:31).

In Bible days, horses were trained for battle, as today's verse tells us. Today, soldiers use tanks, and horses are trained for racing only. This is much better, isn't it? Anyhow, it doesn't matter how good the horse trainer is or how strong the machinery of the war tanks; in the end, it is the Lord who decides on the victory.

The same is true on the sports field. You can be the best athlete with the best trainer. But if you do not rely on the Lord when putting your talents to good use, if you don't ask the Lord to help your coach, you might as well forget about winning. This works exactly the same way on a spiritual level. You can make up your mind to steer clear of the devil. You can ask others to help you stay on the right track, but of one thing you can be sure: If the Lord does not hold your hand and lead you on the right paths, you can forget about a winner's crown for faithfulness.

There is one thing you dare not ever forget. Eventually storms may loosen your grip on the hand of the Lord. But if you allow Him to hold your hand, you can be sure of victory.

When the Lord takes you by the hand, He will see to the victory.

16 February

I Feel Like a Flop

*"Indeed, the very hairs on your head are all numbered.
Don't be afraid; you are worth more than many sparrows"
(Luke 12:7).*

"**I**'m useless. Nothing I do is right. There's always someone who does it better than I do."

Sound familiar? Welcome to the club. Everybody, especially children, at times struggles with a low self-esteem, and then everybody else seems smarter and better than you. This results in pessimism, and it gets to a stage where all you think about is your own appearance and conduct.

Stop comparing yourself to others, because there will always be someone more attractive, clever, or more popular. Instead, try the following:

- Compare yourself to Jesus, not your friends. He is the best example of a cool person. He always did the opposite of what society expected. Read what the Gospels say about Him.
- Learn to laugh at yourself. You're not perfect. So? Everybody makes mistakes.
- Enjoy life. A positive attitude makes you much nicer than a negative one.

What others think of you is important, but what God thinks of you is much more important. You are precious to Him. Moses was a man of God. The Lord trusted him enough to make him His friend.

17 February

How Obedient Are You?

"I warned you ... but you said, 'I will not listen!' This has been your way from your youth; you have not obeyed me" (Jeremiah 22:21).

There are two types of children: the obedient ones and the disobedient ones. The first group listen to their parents and teachers, but the second group think they know better and do what they think best. To which group do you belong?

In the time of the prophet Jeremiah, God's people wouldn't listen to Him. The Lord was very unhappy because they were so disobedient. He warned them time and time again, but when they still didn't listen, He punished them very heavily. Jerusalem and the temple were destroyed, and God's people were taken away in exile.

You can also make the Lord unhappy by not listening to His Word or Spirit. I'm sure you've heard a tiny voice telling you at times that you are busy with things you should not do. But sometimes you might turn a deaf ear to this voice! The Bible tells us we make the Holy Spirit who lives inside us unhappy when we sin. (See Ephesians 4:30.) So think twice before you do something that could hurt the Lord.

What should you do if you realize you have sinned? (See 1 John 1:9.)

18 February

Our Wonderful Lord Jesus

"Worthy is the Lamb, who was slain, to receive power and wealth and wisdom and strength and honor and glory and praise!" (Revelation 5:12)

Nobody has ever been expected to do what Jesus did! He was the Son of God and yet He had to live like a human child, to get tired and hungry, to suffer, and to die.

In many ways He was amazingly different than ordinary people. His birth was special because His mother was a virgin. His death was also special because He rose and came out of the grave, alive. He was the adopted son of a poor carpenter, yet He could feed five thousand people on bread and fish. His feet not only walked the dirt roads of Palestine, but He also walked on the Sea of Galilee. He healed hundreds of people without any medicine.

For three years He traveled all over, telling people about God and teaching them. After two thousand years, He is still the most well known person in the history of the world. Our calendar started at His birth, and thousands and thousands of books and songs have been written about Him. Beautiful churches and cathedrals have been built for Him, and He was the inspiration for the most wonderful works of art. People come and go, but Jesus lives on.

If someone should ask you how one honors Him, you can say:

Kneel down before Him, and glorify His name!

19 February

Why Did Jesus Have to Die?

For the transgression of my people he was stricken [punished]
(Isaiah 53:8).

Have you ever wondered why Jesus had to die on the cross? Well, the Bible tells us that God knew that we human beings would always do things that are wrong, and that makes Him very sad because sin keeps us separated from Him. Sin also makes us feel bad. So God made a plan. He said that the punishment for sin is death, but that if people were very sorry for what they had done, and they slaughtered an animal which died in their place, then they would be forgiven. That is why we read so much about sacrifices in the Old Testament.

But God knew all along that these sacrifices would not be enough – only a perfect Person could die in the place of sinners and allow them to be forgiven. So He sent His Son Jesus to die on the cross in our place.

Jesus never sinned, and when He was crucified He was the Perfect Lamb. He paid with His blood for all the sins ever committed on earth, past, present, and future. Ever since He was sacrificed, we don't need to slaughter animals any more to die in our place and be punished for our sins. From that day on, if people believe in Jesus and repent and confess their sins, God will forgive them, because:

Jesus paid the price for our sins with His blood.

20 February

High Mountains

O Lord, when you favored me, you made my mountain stand firm (Psalm 30:7).

There are beautiful mountains in South Africa. There is the huge Drakensberg mountain range in KwaZulu-Natal and in Mpumalanga. There are also high mountains in the south of the country like the Swartberg and Hex River mountain ranges. Their peaks stand tall and proud against the blue sky.

We read a lot about mountains in the Bible. The temple was built on the "mountain of the Lord" – in other words, on Mount Zion, in Jerusalem. Moses received the Ten Commandments from the Lord on a high mountain. Psalm 125:2 says that mountains surround Jerusalem, and in this way the Lord protected His children. (The mountains made it difficult for the enemy to invade Jerusalem.)

Mountains are not only beautiful and strong but also dangerous. There have been many mountaineering accidents in which mountain climbers were very badly injured. The Bible says the Lord wants to lead us safely over dangerous mountains. Psalm 121:1-2 says, *"I lift up my eyes to the hills – where does my help come from? My help comes from the Lord."*

Our problems often seem like dangerous mountains to us, but the Lord will keep us safe if we just hold on to Him and trust Him. The Bible says He will help us to walk safely, even on heights. (See Habakkuk 3:19.)

The Bible says: "Those who trust in the Lord are like Mount Zion, which cannot be shaken but endures forever" (Psalm 125:1).

21 February

The Free
Admission Ticket

"To him who overcomes, I will give the right to sit with me on my throne, just as I overcame and sat down with my Father on his throne" (Revelation 3:21).

I can't help wondering, as I'm sitting here writing these words, if you have ever won a trophy or some award for sports. Not that it really matters, because here Paul is talking about how all Christians will be winners one day when we sit with the Lord on His throne.

You see, to sit with God on His throne does not necessarily mean we have to be achievers in this world and win many awards. No, the award of everlasting life is something we get because Jesus has already won it for us, in our place! We all receive it free from His hand if we choose to accept His free gift.

To put it differently, the right to sit with the Lord on His throne is not something that can be earned. You cannot buy it, not with all the money in the whole world. You are given a free admission ticket to sit with Him on His throne! Have you accepted God's gift of eternal life?

Isn't it awesome that we can look forward to sitting with Jesus on His golden throne one day – by the glory of His amazing grace!

22 February

What If Everything Changes?

F.R.O.G. F.R.O.G. F.R.O.G.

God is our refuge and strength, an ever-present help in trouble (Psalm 46:1).

What would your reaction be if your life suddenly changed drastically? What if someone in your family died? Or your parents got divorced, or you got a new brother or sister? Or your dad lost his job?

Change in a family is one of the most difficult situations for children to handle. Everything that is familiar to you suddenly becomes uncertain. You feel as if the bottom has dropped out of your world.

How would you handle it?

Job's children died when a very strong wind suddenly swept over their house. When this happened, Job said, *"The Lord gave and the Lord has taken away; may the name of the Lord be praised"* (Job 1:21). Job had learned that the Lord remains a steadfast rock in the midst of change and uncertainty.

What would your reaction be? Try to handle it like this. Say to Jesus, "I don't like it at home any more. Everything has changed. Show me that You are still the same. Give me the strength to get through these difficult times."

If you still doubt God's presence, think of Job, who never turned his back on God and never stopped believing that there would be good times again.

23 February

Grannies Who Know the Lord

I have been reminded of your sincere faith, which first lived in your grandmother Lois and in your mother Eunice and, I am persuaded, now lives in you also (2 Timothy 1:5).

Timothy had a great plus in his life. His mother and grandmother loved the Lord, and they started telling him about the God of Israel when he was still very young. When Timothy heard about Jesus for the first time, he already knew that the Messiah would be born. So, it was easy for him to believe in Jesus and be a witness for Him.

I can remember my grandmother very well. She also started telling me about Jesus when I was still small. Just the other day my own mother showed me a letter from one of her grandchildren. "Thank you very much that you told me about Jesus, Granny," wrote Karen, my brother's daughter.

There are millions of children in the world who have never heard of Jesus. You can say "thank you" that you live in a country where you have been told about the Lord since childhood. If you also have a grandmother who loves the Lord and talks about Him, remember to thank the Lord for a grandmother like this!

What choice did Joshua make with his family? (Joshua 24:15)

24 February

Rules! Rules! Rules!

Everyone must submit himself to the governing authorities (Romans 13:1).

Mandy was fed up. Their youth group was going camping that weekend, and she had just heard that the youth worker had a long list of typed-out rules waiting. Just think of that! "Obey the whistle!" and "No talking after lights out!" and "No radios or cassette players." Please, who wants to go camping with so many rules to spoil your fun?

"What are you moaning about?" her elder brother asked as he joined her in the kitchen. Mandy started to unload on Chris. He had been on a lot of camping trips, and he just smiled.

"I know how you feel!" he said. "But let me tell you: a camp without rules is ten times worse than the strictest of army camps! The thing is, if you live alone on an island, you don't need rules. But with a large group like this it is chaos if there are no rules. What if all of the thirty campers want lunch when it suits them, go to bed when they want to, and listen to music when they feel like it? Do you really think anything will come of the plans made for the weekend?"

Later that evening Mandy thought about what Chris had said. That must be the reason why the Lord made rules for His children. If everyone did as he or she pleased, none of God's great plans for our lives would work out.

God made rules for our lives because He wants only the best for us.

25 February

The Truth

"I am the ... truth" (John 14:6).

The devil is the father of all lies. He is the one who managed to get to Eve in the Garden of Eden and tell her a lie. The minute she believed him, sin started ruling. Ever since that day, lying and cheating have been problems. These problems are inside a person's heart. They are heard from our mouths. They are seen in our deeds. We need help, because lies are like a sickness inside of us.

Jesus came to us to help us and to free us from lies. He says, "I am the truth." There is nothing false about the Lord. He speaks the truth and does the truth. He is the truth. And only God can set us free from the lie in our hearts. Just believe in Him, ask Him to live in your heart, listen to His words, and follow Him. Then you will also learn to love the truth. You will feel bad about lies. You will start speaking the truth and living the right way.

The Bible says: "Then you will know the truth, and the truth will set you free" *(John 8:32).*

26 February

Family Is Important

Keep me as the apple of your eye; hide me in the shadow of your wings (Psalm 17:8).

Do you sometimes thank your mother and father for the way they take care of you? You know what it means to you when someone thanks you, even if you have just done something small for them. Too bad that children sometimes forget to tell their parents what they mean to them. After all, they work hard every day to care for you and even give you more than you really need, don't they?

Actually it is the Lord who gives you parents, so that you don't have to live on your own. Have you ever thought what it would be like if you did not have parents? So we see that the Lord sees not only to your health and the opportunities you get. The Lord's care goes much further than that. He also provides food and clothing, parents, and a roof over your head.

I visited a children's home recently to see a young friend. I have often wished other children could come visit a place like this. I am sure they would change their tune when they saw the heartache of some children who don't have parents to care for them. If you saw these children, you would realize what it means to be able to say, "The Lord takes care of me!"

Lord, thank you so much that You care for me, and that I have parents who love me.

27 February

How Big Is Your Family?

"Isn't this Mary's son and the brother of James, Joseph, Judas and Simon? Aren't his sisters here with us?" (Mark 6:3)

Our family consists of my wife and me and our four children. I wonder how big your family is. Did you know that Joseph and Mary had at least seven children? There were at least five boys and two girls. Except for the Lord Jesus (who was of course the eldest), there were at least four other boys. This is easy to remember, because four of their names started with a "J" and one with an "S." From the text we gather that there were at least two girls, because they are mentioned in the plural. Unfortunately we don't know their names, because the Bible doesn't tell us.

How great of the Lord to give us families (even if you don't always think it's so great when your brothers or sisters tease you!).

But besides your parents and brothers and sisters, the members of your household, you also have other relatives. Have you ever thought what it would be like if you had no other family? Maybe you should especially pray today for children who are in homes and other institutions because they have no family.

Lord, today I especially pray for other children my age who don't even know where their parents are.

28 February

Do Something About Your Faults

"Daniel, servant of the living God, has your God ... been able to rescue you from the lions?" (Daniel 6:20)

Mothers often tell you not to be friends with some person or other because he or she has a bad reputation and will have a bad influence on you. What if you are the one that other kids are being warned against? Could it be that you are the ringleader who drags others down to your level?

Perhaps you are a Christian but you have habits and attitudes in your life that do not suit a person who calls himself or herself a Christian. What do people say about you? Check those that fit:

- "You're such a liar."
- "Don't tell her anything – she'll tell everybody."
- "He uses people to get what he wants."
- "She's so stingy."
- "You should hear her swear!"
- "He'll do anything for money."

Now don't just check one and forget about it. Take one "fault" a day and work on it. If, for example, you tell lies, then concentrate on telling fewer lies today or not telling one at all.

Why not use your influence today to show others the right way?

Daniel was a young man who had a good reputation. He never gave up his principles.

29 February

When Parents Have Favorites

Isaac, who had a taste for wild game, loved Esau, but Rebekah loved Jacob (Genesis 25:28).

With this favoritism, Isaac and Rebekah made a lot of trouble for themselves.

Sad to say, it still happens that parents make a bigger fuss over one child than another. If, for example, there are three boys and one girl in a family, chances are that the little girl gets more than her share of attention! To tell the truth, I was my grandmother's favorite because I was named after her!

It's a shame if there's a favorite in a family. If you are the one your parents are partial to in your family, you could speak to them and ask them to treat your brothers and sisters the same. If the favorite is one of your brothers or sisters, don't feel bitter about it. Rather, try to be such a star that your parents will see something special in you.

If you are hurting because of favoritism, just remember one thing: God is one hundred percent fair; He is never partial to anybody. In His eyes, all His children are equal, and He loves us all.

The Bible says that to God, all His children are the same. Why not underline Ephesians 6:9 and Colossians 3:25 in your Bible?

1 March

Jesus Will Come Back Again

"This same Jesus, who has been taken from you into heaven, will come back in the same way you have seen him go into heaven" (Acts 1:11).

That day when the angels told the disciples on the Mount of Olives that Jesus would come back to them, Jesus' friends were not surprised. Jesus himself had promised them that He would go to heaven to prepare a place for them there and that He would come back to earth to get them.

When is He coming? No one on earth knows. What we do know for a fact is that He will come! The Bible tells us that the sound of trumpets will announce His second coming. All His angels will be with Him, and all the people on earth will be able to see Him. Those who didn't love Jesus will be terrified. For them, there will be punishment for their sins. But the children of God don't need to be afraid. Jesus has already taken the punishment for our sins. We can sing and rejoice that day, because then Jesus will take us to live with Him forever.

The Bible also tells us that Jesus will not come before people who live in faraway countries have heard about Him. If we would like Jesus to come soon, then we must help so that all people are given the chance to love Jesus.

We must be ready at all times for Christ's second coming.

2 March

Jesus Is the Light of the World

"While I am in the world, I am the light of the world" (John 9:5).

Jesus said it himself: "I am the light of the world!" And wherever He went, He drove out the darkness. He made sin and heartache and fear and uncertainty disappear. Do you agree that these are the things that make the world seem dark? Whenever Jesus arrived in a place, nobody felt like sinning, and those who were afraid took heart again. It was as if someone suddenly put a lamp in a dark room!

One cannot see Jesus here on earth anymore, but He still wants to make the darkness go away with His light.

Is there darkness in your life? Are you afraid because you don't know what lies ahead for you? Are you unhappy because there are things in your life that are wrong and that you would like to change? Go to Jesus. Tell Him what is causing the darkness in your life. He will light a flame in you so that you can see things more clearly and understand them better. He will help to drive the darkness out of your life.

And when He has lit a flame in your heart, you can tell others how this light came into your life. With your flame burning brightly, you can bring light into the lives of others.

Where Jesus is, there is light!

3 March

Streams

F.R.O.G. F.R.O.G. F.R.O.G.

"Your God will come. ... " Water will gush forth in the wilderness and streams in the desert (Isaiah 35:4, 6).

Have you ever spent some time at a stream of water? To see the water flow past brings joy to one's heart. Water means life, because water makes plants and fruit grow, which supplies food for humans and animals.

The Great Karoo is a semi-desert region in South Africa. Very few plants grow there, because it gets very little rain. But after a mighty thunderstorm in the Karoo, there are streams of water everywhere, and very soon one sees green plants and even flowers!

The Lord says in the Bible that He wants to give His living water to people. Naturally He means rain that we need to live. But the deeper meaning is the Lord's blessing on everyone – in our hearts. Sometimes our hearts feel like a desert – parched and barren. And without the Lord in our lives, there is no living water for us. Jesus himself said He is the only One who gives living water. Whoever drinks His water will never be thirsty again. (See John 4:14.) What He means is that if we love and follow Him, it is as if there is water inside us that gives life. Eternal life!

The Bible says: "Whoever believes in me, as the Scripture has said, streams of living water will flow from within him" *(John 7:38).*

"You give them drink from your river of delights" *(Psalm 36:8).*

4 March

Appreciate Your Family

You have made known to me the path of life (Psalm 16:11).

In our psalm today, the psalmist says he is happy with the portion the Lord has given him; he is pleased with what he has received. (See verses 5-6.) In our verse, he says the Lord has shown him the path of life – in other words, shown him how to live. This goes for one's relationship with one's own brothers and sisters, too. In my church, a child suddenly died. When I spoke to the rest of the family after the funeral, the other children said how they missed the brother that had passed away. While he was still alive, his brothers and sisters never realized how important he was to them.

For this reason I want to call on you today to take time to appreciate the other members of your family – especially if you have brothers and sisters. It doesn't matter at all if they are older or younger than you. Cherish them and love them, for things can change so suddenly. Maybe you should get up from your chair or bed right now, give each of them a nice hug and tell them, "I really love you very much!" It can make a world of difference in your relationship. I know this is sometimes so much easier to do with members of other families – especially if it is a very special girl or boy in your class! This does not change the fact that one's own family and relatives are of the utmost importance.

Make an effort – now!

5 March

Important Enough to Die For?

"They neither serve your gods nor worship the image of gold you have set up" (Daniel 3:12).

How important is your faith to you? Important enough to do without certain things? Important enough to go against the stream?

Would you think it important enough to say to your friends:

- Sorry, I don't play sports on Sundays because we go to church.
- I don't watch this type of movie, because everything I find holy and pure is made cheap.
- I don't use language like this because I find it embarrassing and so do my friends.

This is not easy, but it is possible. People will make fun of you. But they are also going to watch and see if you can carry it through. And if you do, they will think twice about the influence of Jesus in your life.

Read the story of the three friends in a foreign country, Shadrach, Meshach, and Abednego, who were prepared to be thrown into a fiery furnace for the sake of their faith. (See Daniel 3.)

6 March

Are You Jealous?

Israel loved Joseph more than any of his other sons, because he had been born to him in his old age. … His brothers were jealous of him (Genesis 37:3, 11).

Can you believe it? Just like his father and mother before him, Jacob (Israel) also loved one of his sons more than the others. It was Joseph, the son who was born when Jacob was already old. He had a beautiful robe made for Joseph. Joseph's brothers were so jealous that they sold Joseph to a group of Ishmaelites, who sold him as a slave in Egypt. They then told their father he had been killed by some wild animal.

Fortunately this story has a happy ending, because Joseph was true to his faith in this foreign country and refused to disobey God. Although he landed in prison, in the end he was in the position to save his family as well as the people of Egypt from seven years of famine.

Jealousy is always wrong, but let's face it, it is so easy to be jealous! If you ever feel your parents are not being fair with you, think of Joseph's story. The Lord has a plan for all of our lives – including yours. And in the end, God makes things work out for those who love Him.

What advice does Peter have for people who envy others? (See 1 Peter 2:1.)

7 March

God Can Also Feel Sad

And do not grieve the Holy Spirit of God (Ephesians 4:30).

How do you feel when your best friend suddenly pretends not to know you? How do you feel when your dog doesn't listen to you and slips out through the front gate so that you have to go and look for him? How do you feel when your dad doesn't look up from the paper when you speak to him?

Yes, you feel hurt when someone you love takes no notice of you. Ask your parents how they feel when you are disobedient. The Lord feels the same about you. He cares about you, and if you don't want to listen to Him, it hurts Him.

Someone once told me about a little boy who didn't want to join in when his friends were being naughty. "Are you worried your dad will hurt you?" they teased. "No," he replied, "I'm worried I'll hurt my dad."

God says in His Word that He feels about us like a Father about his child. He loves us very, very much. If we are disobedient, His Spirit is deeply hurt. Do you do things that hurt Him? Do you pick fights at school? Do you swear or lie or cheat?

Remember:

If you sin, you not only break God's laws but also His heart.

8 March

The Way

"I am the way" (John 14:6).

There are many roads in our country that cover thousands of miles. Because we must go places, we need roads to take us where we want to be. Every road leads somewhere. When we go on vacation, we pack our bags, get into the car, and take a road that will take us to our destination. If we take the wrong road, we lose our way or end up in the wrong place. Some roads are so bad they can damage your vehicle. Others are dead-end roads and can take you no farther.

Jesus says He is like a road. He is the way to the Father. And nobody can go to the Father in heaven without going through Jesus. If we want to go to heaven, we must be on the right road – with Jesus. If we follow Him, He will lead us to the Father. We don't even have to search for the road. If we just keep our eyes on Him, He will take us to our destination Himself. He also wants to lead us on our daily path of life, so that we can avoid getting hurt by taking a wrong turn and ending up in a dead end.

The Bible says: "Teach me your way, O Lord; lead me in a straight path" *(Psalm 27:11).*
"In all your ways acknowledge him, and he will make your paths straight" *(Proverbs 3:6).*

9 March

Pray Every Morning!

In the morning, O Lord, you hear my voice (Psalm 5:3).

In today's psalm, David tells us what he did in the morning. This was written at a time in his life when he lived in fear because of all the enemies in his country, and he couldn't have slept very well at night.

Have there been times in your life when you had such a busy schedule at school that you were actually afraid of the next day? Then the advice the Bible gives us is good, isn't it? Ask the Lord's guidance before you leave the house. Tell Him everything that lies ahead for you this day, because David says the Lord hears your voice in the morning.

It is a very good idea to pray in the morning before you get started on everything you have to do, and not only at night when you thank Him for the day that has passed. It will also help you to discuss your schedule for the day with the Lord. The Bible tells us that God's Spirit lives in His children, so through His Spirit, He will help you plan according to His will.

Remember to speak to the Lord in the morning when your mind is still fresh.

10 March

You Are Precious

Keep me as the apple of your eye; hide me in the shadow of your wings (Psalm 17:8).

If you ever travel through Turkey, you will find reproductions of the "evil eye" in some form or other at every market stall and shop, even in the front of every bus and vehicle. The message it conveys is that the eye of evil is watching you, waiting to catch you everywhere and all the time. How fortunate that this is not true of the Bible. Our verse for today says exactly the opposite: *"Keep me as the apple of your eye; hide me in the shadow of your wings from the wicked who assail me, from my mortal enemies who surround me"* (Psalm 17:8-9).

From this we learn that the Lord wants to protect us every day. He is not interested in catching us or harming us but wants to protect us like something precious. Isn't it great to know that we are so precious to the Lord? He is not on the look-out to see if He can catch us doing wrong. No, the Lord is there to protect us in every minute of our lives and to take care of us.

Thank You, Lord, that You protect and keep me safe every minute of the day.

11 March

One Is Judged by One's Friends

A man of many companions may come to ruin, but there is a friend who sticks closer than a brother (Proverbs 18:24).

In Proverbs 12:26 we read that a wise person chooses his friends with care, because the wrong friends can lead one astray. These are the people who egg you on to do things you would never have done on your own.

Our verse also says the person who is everyone's buddy can have a problem, but a true friend will stand by you through thick and thin.

We are also warned in Proverbs against friends who only want to use us. (See Proverbs 19:1-7.) Watch out for the kids who want to be friends with you just for what they can get out of it. These are the ones who know you are good at math or always have money to spend.

If you are involved in a friendship that is doing more harm than good, think again. Don't just drop this friend like a hot potato, but go and think about the value of true friendship. Being everybody's best friend won't work. As the saying goes, "A friend to all is a friend to none." Two or three loyal friends who share your principles are worth more than the friendship of the whole school.

Use your head when choosing your friends. Watch out for those who use you. Don't do things to impress friends.

12 March

Treat Older People with Respect

"Rise in the presence of the aged, show respect for the elderly and revere your God. I am the LORD" (Leviticus 19:32).

It is so important to the Lord that His people should treat the aged well that He gives Moses this special message. Your relationship with the Lord always spills over into your relationship with other people, especially with those older than you. If you love the Lord, you will also love others. If you respect the Lord, you will treat others with respect, especially people who are older than you.

What do you do when you see an older lady (or gentleman) carrying something heavy? Or if you meet up with an older person in town? The Bible tells us to show respect for the elderly. This means that you will always be friendly and that you will help them when you can.

Older people are often very lonely. Do you know of an elderly person who lives near you? You might just go and visit one afternoon, and take them a bunch of flowers or a basket of fruit from your garden. Or, you could ask your mom to invite them over for lunch one Sunday. Then you will not only make them happy, but the Lord will also be pleased with you.

What happened to the children who made fun of the elderly prophet Elisha? (See 2 Kings 2:24.)

13 March

The Holy Spirit

"The wind blows wherever it pleases. You hear its sound, but you cannot tell where it comes from. ... So it is with everyone born of the Spirit" (John 3:8).

Here is a riddle: I slip through keyholes easy and free; I strip leaves from the branches of any tree; when I am angry I send the roofs flying; and when I die down no one knows where I'm lying. Who am I? Easy, isn't it? Of course – it's the wind.

The Bible tells us the Holy Spirit is like the wind. They are alike in many ways: You cannot see either of them. Just as the wind can make things move, the Holy Spirit can put a person in motion. Perhaps you didn't feel like going to Sunday school one day, but before you realized it, you found yourself sitting there with your friends. Could it have been the Holy Spirit that motivated you?

The Holy Spirit also helps to spread the seed of the Word, like the wind blows seeds all over the world. What is more, the wind is very, very strong. God's Spirit is just as mighty and can make us strong Christians who will not let Jesus down. Besides that, He can keep us from falling and hurting ourselves in the same way the wind keeps a kite or a bird in the air.

Let's ask the Lord to blow His Spirit through us, so that we can be filled with Him.

The Holy Spirit is like the wind.

14 March

The Helper

"The Holy Spirit, whom the Father will send ... will teach you all things and will remind you of everything I have said to you" (John 14:26).

What bothers you about the following story? A young girl is standing in a shop paying for the ice cream she has bought. The eyesight of the old man at the cash register is not so good any more, and he gives her a shiny quarter instead of the ten cents change she is supposed to get. She gives him a broad smile, runs outside and says to her friends, "How lucky can I get!"

If you know what the little girl did was wrong, then someone has taught you what stealing is. If you feel sorry for the old man, you are most likely someone who is more fond of people than money. And if you happened to be that little girl, what would you have done? If you belong to the Lord, you would give back the money. How do I know that? Because when we belong to Jesus, the Holy Spirit lives in us. And Jesus said that the Holy Spirit will remind us of everything that is written in the Bible. The Bible says we must not steal and also that we must love others as much as we love ourselves.

God's Spirit doesn't only teach us what is right; He also helps us to do what is right.

The Holy Spirit helps us to live the way we should.

15 March

Nice to All People

Let your gentleness [friendliness] be evident to all (Philippians 4:5).

There are so many people in this world, and we all need each other. It is awful when people on earth are mean to one another. Just think of all the wars there have been, with millions of people killing one another. It really is terrible.

The world would be a much better place if we could be friendly and gentle toward others. Paul tells his friends in Philippi to be friendly to all people. We must be on friendly terms with the cafe owner and the gas station attendant and the helpers in the supermarket and, oh, just everyone we meet, including our parents and teachers and friends.

Friendliness costs nothing, but it is worth so much. If we are nice to someone, the world becomes a better place. Just think how nice Jesus was to us by loving us first.

The Bible says: "All the believers were together and had everything in common. ... Praising God and enjoying the favor of all the people" *(Acts 2:44, 47).*

16 March

The Lord Is Quick to Help You

He mounted the cherubim and flew (Psalm 18:10).

The word cherub is sometimes used in the Bible instead of angel, and the word for more than one cherub is cherubim. If you read our verse in context, you will find that it is part of a description illustrating with what speed the Lord approaches to help the believer in need. It doesn't matter how bad the circumstances are that you might find yourself – nothing will ever be so far, so deep, or so impossible that the Lord cannot save you.

Can you remember how safe you felt when you were little and you saw the sea for the first time? How your dad took your tiny hand in his and the two of you went to the beach? Or how safe you felt when you walked to school the first day, holding your mother's hand? Well, this image from the Bible tells you that you will feel safer than this, even in your worst moments, because the Lord will be there very quickly to help you and to save you.

Isn't this great? I'm sometimes scared by all the dangers I have to walk through every day, and I'm sure you are too. But you have nothing to fear if you take the Lord at His wonderful word. He will rush to help you!

The Lord mounts a cherub and flies in to help you when you are in trouble.

17 March

Sometimes the Choice Is the Lord's

We love because he [God] first loved us (1 John 4:19).

We don't always choose our own friends. Sometimes Christ does this for us. It happens at times that we find ourselves in the company of people, and on the face of it, they don't seem to be the type we would make friends with at all. You don't always know why someone chooses you for a friend. It could be because you are considerate or because you said something nice to him or her.

If someone likes you, but you don't really feel the same way, try not to be unfriendly. Who knows – you could have been chosen to support that person and help build back his or her self-confidence.

If you think about it, Christ didn't choose us to be His friends because we are so friendly, good, or attractive, but because He loved us. He made friends with us for our own good. He is our example of perfect friendship. We must also live in such a way that others can benefit from our friendship.

Of course we will like some friends better than others. But be friendly and helpful so that you can make others happy just like Christ wants to see us happy.

Just think what you would feel like if you wanted to make friends with someone and that person gave you the cold shoulder.

18 March

Whom Do You Take After?

"'Like mother, like daughter.' You are a true daughter of your mother" (Ezekiel 16:44-45).

Has somebody told you that you have dimples like your mother or eyes like your father's? Children usually look like and take after their parents. In this part from Scripture, the prophet Ezekiel tells the story of God's unfaithful people. Although He looked after them and loved them, they turned away from Him time and again. The "daughter" that the prophet tells us about here takes after her mother – she is just as bad and as sinful as her mother.

It is too bad that, like King Ahaziah, a child sometimes walks "in the ways of his father and mother." (See I Kings 22:53.) Often you are not only like your parents physically, but you also do the things your parents do. If your parents are regular churchgoers, chances are that you will also go to church regularly. If, on the other hand, your parents never see the inside of a church, you will probably not feel like going to church on a Sunday either.

If you are the Lord's child, you ought to look like Him. You should talk the way He does, think the way He does, and do the things He would. If you manage to do this, you will become more and more like Him. Ask the Holy Spirit to help you.

What does Paul say of the church of the Lord in Ephesians 4:13? We must become ...

19 March

Are You a Rocket-Christian?

I can do everything through him who gives me strength (Philippians 4:13).

At a service held for children, the minister fixed a target to the pulpit. He gave ten children a piece of paper each to fold into a paper airplane. Then they all had a chance to aim at the target, but not one of them managed to hit it! The paper planes took off well, but then they would swerve suddenly, strike out in a totally different direction, and take a nosedive. Then the minister reminded everyone what a poor showing a paper plane made compared to a rocket. He said we need to be rocket-Christians, not paper airplane-Christians.

Do you know the difference? A paper airplane has no power in itself, while a rocket is driven by the power built into it. Maybe you can think of some more differences. If you want to be a rocket-Christian that stays on course and heads straight for the target, you need to give the Holy Spirit a chance to fill you with His power. As long as you rely on your own strength, you will often be off course. You may find that your good intentions come to nothing. You aim to do your homework diligently, but you don't. You decide not to sin again, but every time you backslide. Tell the Lord that from now on you would very much like to make use of the power of His Spirit in your life.

Make use of the power of the Holy Spirit.

20 March

The Best Friend

A man of many companions may come to ruin, but there is a friend who sticks closer than a brother (Proverbs 18:24).

It's nice to have a good friend. A good friend is someone who wants to be with you because he or she likes you. He doesn't like you only for what he can get out of you. She likes doing things for you. A good friend will laugh with you and cry with you. This friend understands you, listens to your stories and your jokes, and also shares the deepest secrets of your heart. If you have a friend like this, then you are very lucky.

The best way to make a good friend is to be a good friend. Start today and be a friend to someone, without expecting anything in return. If you keep doing it, you will have many friends. But you must first know each other a while before someone can be your special friend. You don't share your deepest feelings or secrets with just anyone!

Above all, you must accept the Lord as your friend. He would like you to share everything with Him. By all means tell Him about your dreams and fears, and share your heartache with Him. He understands and will never let you down.

The Bible says: "I no longer call you servants. ... Instead, I have called you friends" *(John 15:15).*

21 March

Is There a Perfect Family?

As for God, his way is perfect (Psalm 18:30).

You might say, "Now I don't understand this at all! The Bible says everything God does is perfect, and look at my family. We all have our faults. If this is perfection … "

Naturally the Bible doesn't mean that the family circle is necessarily perfect in every way, but the way it is put together is exactly what the Lord wants. The whole is perfect, even if the different parts which form a puzzle are not, isn't that so? You have to agree that some of those parts are quite dull and uninteresting on their own. When, however, they are all put together in the way it was meant to be, you will soon realize that the puzzle is not complete if even only one small piece is missing.

It's exactly the same with a family. If one member is taken away from the larger whole, it leaves a big gap, and there is no way you can patch it up. It is, of course, possible that the Lord can decide at a certain stage that He wants to change the structure of the family. This can happen in many ways, but mainly through weddings, births, or deaths. Death can be especially traumatic and sad. One thing, however, is as clear as the nose on your face: What God does is perfect!

Thank You, Lord, that Your work and way are always perfect!

22 March

When You Feel Lonely

"But I am a worm and not a man, scorned by men and despised by the people" (Psalm 22:6).

I once was asked to speak at a large family gathering. The events started off with a church service on the Sunday morning, and the organizers tried their very best to make every member of the family feel at home. Some of them had never even laid eyes on one another.

After the service, while everybody was drinking tea, I noticed a young man who was clearly feeling out of place. Nobody talked to him, and he also kept to himself. I moved over to him, but he was obviously not very talkative. Because I was also a stranger, I understood very well when he said out of the blue, "I feel like a good-for-nothing, like a worm and not a man!" It was only later that I remembered that this was from the Bible.

Perhaps you have also felt like this before when you were among strangers, especially at a party or some occasion where you didn't know anyone. So what are you supposed to do then? Don't let the feeling get to you. Walk over to someone with a friendly smile on your face and say "hello." You can even tell that person how you feel. Normally he or she will ask, "But why?" This will be your cue to say that you feel lonely and like a stranger, and this will break the ice. Then you can crawl out of your cocoon of loneliness.

If you feel as low as a worm, don't despair – things can only get better!

23 March

How Do I
Make Friends?

We love because he first loved us (1 John 4:19).

We all know that feeling of desolation when you don't have a single friend you can count on. Remember that first day at a new school when everybody was checking you out first before they would bother to talk to you or sit next to you during lunch?

Most of the time we make friends. But there are times that you feel you are never, ever going to make a friend again. Here are a few tips:

- Be yourself. A sincere person makes a sincere friend.
- Keep an open mind. Make friends with people of a different color, culture, or age.
- Get involved. Take part in different activities like sports and cultural events, or join in youth activities at your church.
- Talk to others and ask them to tell you about themselves.
- Listen. Everybody likes a good listener. Make eye contact, don't interrupt, and show that you are listening by repeating something the other person says now and then.
- Be patient. Friendships do not develop overnight.
- Try your best to be interesting and not a bore.
- Smile! A smile is an open invitation for people to make friends with you.

If you are as full of love as Christ, you will attract people, and they will want to be your friends.

24 March

Christening Sunday

"Before I formed you in the womb I knew you, before you were born I set you apart" (Jeremiah 1:5).

I love being in church when parents bring their children to be dedicated to the Lord, or baptized. Parents who love the Lord and who believe in Jesus as their Lord and Savior, bring their children to be prayed for in church, and to be blessed, just as the mothers brought their babies to Jesus when He was on earth. Parents do this because they want their children to grow up to know Jesus. They promise before the congregation to teach their children about Jesus from an early age, and they ask God to help them be good, Christian parents to their child.

God loves you so much that He wants you to be His child. He knew about you before you were even born, and He wants you to know Him and love Him as much as He loves you. He placed you in the family that you are in, and gave you parents who love and care for you. If your parents dedicated you to the Lord when you were a baby, then you should try to live up to the promises they made for you. But even if your parents didn't have you dedicated or baptized, you can still know Jesus and learn to live a holy life that will please Him, and that will show others that you are His child.

Ask your parents to show you photos of your baptism or dedication, and talk to them about the promises they made, and how you can live up to them.

25 March

Give the Holy Spirit a Chance!

So I say, live by the Spirit (Galatians 5:16).

Have you ever heard of Mendelssohn? He was one of the greatest composers who ever lived. One day he was listening to a church organist play the organ in a big church in Europe. "May I play the organ, please?" he asked.

At first the organist wouldn't hear of it, but eventually he gave permission for the stranger to play. When the organist heard the beautiful sounds coming from the organ, you could have knocked him down with a feather. Amazed, he asked, "But who are you that you play the organ so well?"

"My name is Mendelssohn," the famous man replied.

"To think I very nearly wouldn't allow you to play our organ!" was all the stunned organist could stammer out.

Give God a chance to manage your life, because then only the nicest qualities in you will come to the front. There are so many choices to be made every day: Should I take swimming lessons or join the tennis club? Should I do my homework now or leave it till later? Should I dodge that stupid guy or must I bear with him? If you ask the Lord to guide you with His Spirit, you will know what to do, and then you can become the person God had in mind when He made you.

The Bible and the Holy Spirit help us make the right choices.

26 March

Our Bodyguard

"[God] will give you another Counselor to be with you forever" (John 14:16).

Do you know the game where one tries to step on someone else's shadow? It can be great fun. But you will find out soon enough that you can't get away from your own shadow. As long as you are in the sun, your shadow is there with you, close by!

When Jesus was taken up to heaven, His disciples were sad. They wanted Jesus to stay with them forever. But while Jesus was on earth He could be in only one place at a time. So He promised His disciples that once He had left them, He would be with them in a different way: His Spirit would be with them forever, like a shadow following them around wherever they went. And every one of His children, wherever they might be, would have the Holy Spirit close by to teach them and give them advice and help them.

Do you need someone today to help you with school work or to give you advice about a friend at school? Do you need strength for a difficult task? Whatever your problem, the Holy Spirit is there, ready to help you right away.

The Holy Spirit is not a lifeless shadow, but a living body-guard!

27 March

The Bread

"I am the bread of life" (John 6:35).

If we want to be strong and stay alive, we must eat. When we eat, our bodies are given a refill of fuel or energy so that we are able to move and work and play. Without food we die. Bread must be the most familiar and most common type of food there is. In most places in the world, people eat bread. Even the very poor can survive on bread. Bread is the staple diet of millions of people.

Jesus said He is the bread of life. By this He means that we all need Him if we really want to live. And it is impossible to live forever if you don't have the bread of life; and that is Jesus Himself.

We take bread and we eat it. But Jesus can't be eaten! We accept Him in faith, which means we hear (or understand) that the Bible says He is like bread, and then we believe it (or trust in it) and we say, "Lord, I need you if I want to live. Be the bread of my life." If we do this, we will live forever.

The Bible says: "Why spend money on what is not bread? … Listen, listen to me, and eat what is good, and your soul will delight in the richest of fare" (Isaiah 55:2).

28 March

You Are Part
of a Community
and a Congregation

*I will declare your name to my brothers; in the congregation
I will praise you (Psalm 22:22).*

It's great fun being young! You don't have all the responsibilities that adults must carry, but you are an important part of a community and a congregation. Even if you sometimes feel you are under pressure and have too much to do, it still is fun! Can you think how boring your life would be without church activities, for example? At church, you get together with many other Christians and you enjoy it, don't you?

Your congregation may be part of a larger denomination and is also part of your community. In the same way, all other churches and groups are part of one great community – almost like the wedges of an orange. And you know, even if you are only a tiny piece of pulp in the orange, you are a part of the whole! You are not alone in the world, but you are also not the only important member of your congregation or community. All members are like the muscles of one body, where every single muscle – no matter how small – has an important and vital role to play.

Praise the Lord, wherever you may be.

29 March

Be a Real Pal

Carry each other's burdens (Galatians 6:2).

I once heard the word friend defined as "the one who carries my sorrow on his back." This is one way of describing friendship, but there are many others. Let's make a list of "friendship-friendly qualities":

- Loyalty: Friends are caring and trustworthy.
- Listening: Friends listen to what their friends are saying.
- Time: Friends find time for one another. They enjoy spending time together without necessarily saying or doing anything.
- Consideration: Friends try to understand one another and are there in times of need.
- Encouragement: Friends are not jealous of each other and encourage one another to try something new.
- Honesty: Friends tell one another the truth in a nice way and show when they're upset without being mean.
- Sense of humor: Friends have a good laugh together. They sometimes laugh at each other but more often with each other.
- Trustworthiness: Real friends know how to keep secrets.
- Sincerity: Real friends are sincere, don't pretend to be someone they are not, and don't mind sharing their feelings with each other.
- Forgiveness: Friends know when to say, "I'm sorry," and, "You're forgiven."

How many of these qualities do you have? And your best friend?

30 March

Decide for Yourself

*"Choose for yourselves this day whom you will serve. ...
But as for me and my household, we will serve the LORD"
(Joshua 24:15).*

The Lord invited you to be His child a long time ago. But there
is a catch – the fact that you have been baptized or that your
parents dedicated you to the Lord when you were a baby does
not mean you will go straight to heaven one day. You must
still give a personal reply to God's invitation. Your mom or dad
cannot do it for you.

God's invitation to you is something like an invitation to a
birthday party. The fact that you received an invitation doesn't
mean you will be able to go to the party. Only when you have
replied in person and promised your friend to be there can the
friend who invited you be sure that you will be at the party.

The Lord has already chosen you and invited you to be His
child. He loves you very much – so much that He sent Jesus
to die on a cross for your sins. He did all this so that you can
become God's child.

Have you made a choice for Jesus yet? Invite Him into your
life; don't put it off any longer.

*Are you quite sure that you have replied personally to
God's invitation? If so, on a front page in your Bible, write
down the date of your baptism or christening and the
date you gave Him your life.*

31 March

A Clear Conscience

Paul looked straight at the Sanhedrin and said, "My brothers, I have fulfilled my duty to God in all good conscience" (Acts 23:1).

What is a conscience? Some say it's an angel who whispers in your ear when you do something wrong. Others tell you it's the Holy Spirit who lives in you and lets you know when you do something God is not happy with. Learned people say it is a part of your brain that is programmed like a computer and which makes you feel uncomfortable when you do something which goes against what your parents or others have taught you.

Whatever the case may be, all of us have this built-in compass. Just like a compass shows a seaman where north and south and east and west are, our consciences tell us what is good and what is bad. If our parents brought us up according to the right and the wrong of the Bible, that helps our consciences to keep us on God's way. Whenever we stray from it, it worries us.

Paul could say that his conscience was still clear, sharp, and useful because of his obedience to God. If you keep making the right choices, even when it is difficult to do so, your conscience will stay pure and clean and it will be easier and easier to do what is right.

The Holy Spirit will help you to have a clear conscience, like Paul had.

1 April

Gossip

"Whoever spreads slander is a fool" (Proverbs 10:18).

When you gossip, or spread slander, you say something bad about another person behind his or her back. One way of doing this is to spread stories about someone. "Wait till you hear about this!" is often the beginning of something we have heard, and we spread the story without knowing if there is any truth in it. It usually is done to put someone in a poor light and give that person a bad name.

Why do we do this? Do we think it will make us feel better? Someone once said, "To talk badly of someone else is a dishonest way of singing your own praises."

The devil loves rumors. This is why we must make up our minds never to say something bad about anyone. And if you hear of something wrong a person has done, speak to that person about it. Don't go behind someone's back and spread nasty rumors. Only a fool does that.

The Bible says: "Whoever would love life and see good days must keep his tongue from evil and his lips from deceitful speech" *(1 Peter 3:10).*

2 April

The Bread of Life

"I am the bread of life" (John 6:35).

Remember that day you went to school and forgot your sandwich at home? Remember the hunger pangs gnawing away at your stomach during lunch? It's as if your body was shouting out, "I'm hungry!"

Spiritually, we are no different. Jesus tells us that only He can give us the life-giving spiritual bread. He is the bread. He breaks Himself to feed us. There's no need for you to suffer spiritual famine, because you can actually live in spiritual plenty. If you allow the Lord Jesus into your life and you are honest and sincere about it, you will never go hungry again. You can do it right now by saying this prayer:

Lord Jesus, I want to allow You into my life. Thank You that I never have to suffer spiritual hunger again.

3 April

Are You Fat?

"I have come that they may have life, and have it to the full" (John 10:10).

Some girls have this thing about being fat. They look at themselves in the mirror and think, "Yuck, I'm fat!" Sometimes boys worry about it, too, but we're not talking about that now. Of course nobody wants to be too fat. On the other hand, we don't want to be too skinny either.

There is one part of your life, though, in which you can be as fat as you like, and that is in your spiritual life. Jesus says that He came so that we could have life and have it to the full. So if it was possible for you to climb onto a spiritual scale, it would actually be very good if it shows you are overweight. The more you allow Jesus to rule over your life, the fatter you will become, and that is great!

Do you eat enough spiritual food? Do you go to church regularly? Do you go to places where people talk about the Lord Jesus? Do you read your Bible regularly? These are all ways of getting spiritually fat. Make use of them!

4 April

To Speak or Not to Speak

"A gossip betrays a confidence, but a trustworthy man keeps a secret" (Proverbs 11:13).

It's nice to know you have a friend you can tell something that no one else knows! And not one of you would dream of telling someone else the secret, right?

But sometimes – just sometimes – it becomes necessary to betray your friend's confidence, especially if you think your friend is hurting or if there's a chance that he might harm himself or someone else. It could be that your friend is being abused or someone is ill-treating her. Or what if he tells you that he feels like committing suicide or running away from home? Then you can be a best friend if you tell someone who can help.

So think carefully before promising never to tell, because one shouldn't go back on one's word. Instead say, "I am your best friend, and I will never talk to others about our secrets, but I can't promise before you tell me what your secret is."

Having secrets is nice, but it cuts both ways. Don't be a blabbermouth and blurt out everything that happens in your home. If your brother was punished or your mom and dad had a fight, it's got nothing to do with anybody else. Tomorrow you and your friend may have a quarrel, and the next thing you know, your friend may be making your family's private life common knowledge on the playground!

If nothing good can come of talking about something, then just keep quiet.

5 April

God Wants Fruit

"The fruit of the spirit is love, joy, peace, patience, kindness, goodness, faithfulness, gentleness and self-control" (Galatians 5:22-23).

A man once planted a fig tree. Three years later the tree had not borne any fruit yet. "Chop it down!" the man said to the gardener. Isn't this punishment a bit unfair? And yet it is the Lord Jesus himself who told this story. When a farmer feeds a tree and waters it and looks after it well, surely it's not too much to expect that it should bear fruit!

The Lord wants to see fruit in our lives as well. He gives us many things: food and clothes, a place to live, people who care about us, and opportunities to learn about Him. If He sees no good fruit on our trees of life, He is not pleased.

This reminds me of the little boy who brought his puppy to the vet. He was cradling the tiny lifeless body of the animal in his arms. "Doctor, something very important is missing here!" the worried little boy said. Could it be that all the good qualities a child of the Lord should have in his or her life can be missing? In our verse from Scripture for today, many fruits are mentioned that should be seen in the lives of the Lord's children. How many of these nine qualities are missing from your life?

Ask the Holy Spirit to make all the good fruit grow in your life so that you can make God happy.

The Holy Spirit helps us to live good lives.

6 April

Our Greatest Enemy

"Be self-controlled and alert. Your enemy the devil prowls around like a roaring lion" (1 Peter 5:8).

"Mom, is the devil for real?" Sophie asked her mother unexpectedly one night. "The children at school were arguing about it today. Jolene says people tell stories about the devil just to scare people."

"Well," her mother answered, "the Bible says the devil is real. And even if I have never seen him, I believe it. Why else would one see horrible things like fighting and swearing and stealing? God would certainly not make people do things like that. I believe it's the devil who whispers in someone's ear, 'Hurt that boy!' or 'Everyone for himself!' or 'Don't say you're sorry!'"

Her mother continued. "The Bible tells us that the devil and his helpers are always trying to spoil all the wonderful plans God has for the world. This is why there are so many horrible things on earth. The Bible also says, though, that the devil is like a dog on a chain. He can make a lot of trouble, but he can't go where he wants to. And one day he will be taken away out of the world. Then we will live in a new world where everything is good and beautiful."

We need never be afraid of the devil as long as we follow Jesus.

7 April

All New

If anyone is in Christ, he is a new creation; the old has gone, the new has come! (2 Corinthians 5:17)

A businessman wanted to sell an old house. He was worried that he would not get a good price for the house because it had been neglected and was in a very bad state. When he showed the house to the buyer he promised to fix it up a bit first. But the buyer said, "Don't go to any trouble. I'm not interested in the house at all. I'm going to pull it down. I want to put up a brand new building. Actually, I'm only interested in the ground it stands on."

Jesus has a new plan for your life and mine. He paid for us with His death on the cross. He wants to do something new with us. He is not interested in patching up an old, sinful life. It's worth nothing to Him. That is why He starts a new job inside our hearts. We will be like newborn babies. And He will build a new life in us, according to His plan.

The Bible says: "Put on the new self, which is being renewed in knowledge in the image of its creator" *(Colossians 3:10)*.

8 April

Good Friday

But he was pierced for our transgressions, he was crushed for our iniquities; the punishment that brought us peace was upon him, and by his wounds we are healed (Isaiah 53:5).

It is strange, when you think about it, that we call the day on which Jesus was crucified Good Friday. After all, you are not happy when someone you love very much dies. But the Friday on which Jesus died is a good Friday, because with His death on the cross He gave us life.

You know by now that every human being is a sinner. And because you are a sinner, you can never reach God on your own. God is holy and He hates sin. So Jesus first had to pay the price of your sin in full on the cross before you could become God's child. When Jesus died in your place, He paid for your sins once and for all. He died so that you can live. And what is more, He has already paid for your sins of tomorrow and the day after.

So when you sin again, all you need to do is tell God you are sorry. Jesus earned God's forgiveness for you with His death on the cross. And that is why we celebrate Good Friday. Have you thanked Him yet?

What did the people of the Old Testament do when they had sinned? (See Leviticus 7:1-5.)

9 April

Holy Communion

Then he took the cup ... and they all drank from it. "This is my blood ... which is poured out for many," he said to them (Mark 14:23-24).

The Jews celebrated the Passover thousands of years ago. The purpose of this feast was to commemorate the night that God brought the Israelites out of slavery in Egypt.

When Jesus and His disciples celebrated the Passover for the last time, He told them that He was going to be crucified. He then took bread and offered a piece to each of His disciples. He told them that when they ate the bread, they should think about how He died for them, so that their sins would be forgiven. Then He took the jug of wine and told them to drink from it. He told them that the wine was like His blood, which flowed on the cross so that they could be saved. Every time they drank the wine, they should think of Him.

When we eat the bread at Holy Communion, we think of how Jesus' body was broken for us on the cross. When we drink the wine we remember how His blood flowed for us, so that our sins could be forgiven. We celebrate Holy Communion because Jesus overcame death, and He is now with God in heaven. We think ahead to that day when He will come again.

Read in Exodus 12:1-14 about how God instituted the first Passover.

10 April

Easter Sunday – Jesus Is Alive!

The men said to them, "Why do you look for the living among the dead? He is not here; he has risen!" (Luke 24:5-6)

Jesus' disciples were very sad when He died. Joseph of Arimathea and Nicodemus asked the Romans for His body and buried Him in a garden near Golgotha. On the Sunday after the crucifixion a few women went to the grave and saw that the big stone had been rolled away from the grave, but Jesus' body was not there. Two men in bright clothes announced that Jesus had risen.

Then they remembered that Jesus had told them He would rise from the dead in three days' time. The women went and told the disciples immediately, and they all went back to the grave. All they could find there was the linen cloth Jesus' body had been wrapped in. The believers were so happy that Jesus was alive. Jesus himself appeared to the disciples and told them He was going back to heaven.

On Easter Sunday we celebrate because Jesus overcame death. Jesus died for us, but He triumphed over death and lives today. If you believe in Him, you will also live again after your death one day, and you will be with Him in heaven forever. One day Jesus will come again to get all His children so that we can be with Him forever.

What will happen when Jesus comes again? (See Matthew 24:29-31.)

11 April

Under the Influence

There was also a prophetess, Anna. ... She never left the temple but worshiped day and night, fasting and praying (Luke 2:36-37).

When I was still a little girl, we used to sing a song that started with the words: "I want to be like Jesus." How does one become like Jesus?

Mother Teresa (from Calcutta) used to say if you want to be like Jesus, you must be completely under His influence and be able to follow Him with all your heart. How does one do that? Follow these steps to be like Jesus.

- Learn about Jesus. Not just hearsay – you must have firsthand information. How regularly do you read your Bible? That is where you get to know Jesus.
- Think about Jesus. To become like Jesus, you must continually think of Jesus so that He can become part of your life.
- Live like Jesus. Jesus wants us to live in such a way that what we have learned about Him will show in our everyday lives.

One can be under the influence of many different things. Usually being "under the influence" means a person has had too much alcohol to drink. One can be under the influence of the wrong friends. Or you can be influenced so completely by Jesus Christ that you really mean something to others. What is your choice?

Read the story in Luke 2 of two older people, Anna and Simeon, and you will see how faithfully they waited for Jesus to come.

12 April

It Is a Good Thing That Jesus Went Away

"It is for your good that I am going away. Unless I go away, the Counselor will not come to you" (John 16:7).

I can still remember how I used to love when my grandparents visited. They lived on a farm and always brought lots of delicious things to eat. When they left, it was, in a way, just as nice, because then we would always find presents on our beds. Long after they had gone, we still played with our presents and enjoyed the cookies and sweets and other goodies.

The Lord Jesus said it was also a good thing that He went away, because then He could send the Holy Spirit in His place. The Spirit reminds us of Christ all the time. The Holy Spirit is God. The good thing is that He has been with us since Jesus went away, and He is omnipresent (everywhere). In His human form, Jesus could be only in one place at a time. I can understand very well why our Master said it was for our own good that He went away.

Say thank you for the Holy Spirit who guides and teaches us.

13 April

Are You Like Joel?

"I will pour out my spirit on all people. Your sons and daughters will prophesy" (Joel 2:28).

Pentecost is the time of year when we think of the wonderful way in which the Holy Spirit came to live in the church of Jesus Christ. This is described in Acts 2. In the Old Testament, the prophet Joel is usually called the pentecostal prophet, because he was the one who talked most often about the Holy Spirit that was coming.

When a person is open to the guidance of the Spirit, he is like a prophet filled with the Holy Spirit. John the Baptist and the Lord Jesus Himself were obedient to the guidance of the Spirit of God in their lives. When the Spirit is guiding you, you don't want to be in control of your life anymore, but you allow the Holy Spirit to take control of your life.

Joel is talking about young people who are like this in the verse above.

Are you one of them? Then you will also be like a prophet. This means that you will confess that Jesus is Lord and the King of your life, that you want to follow Him, and that you don't want to do anything that will make the Holy Spirit unhappy.

It is interesting to know that the name Joel means "The Lord is God." If you profess Him as the Lord and the King of your life, it is the best proof that you have the Holy Spirit in your life.

If you live like this, you are a pentecostal prophet!

14 April

Wilted Flowers?

"I am the vine; you are the branches. ... apart from me you can do nothing" (John 15:5).

It takes a long time to grow a beautiful rose. Once the rosebush is planted, the soil must send food and water through the roots and the stem and the branches, right up to where the rosebud starts forming. The rosebush will not be able to produce roses without the stem and the roots.

On the first day you pick a rose, it is beautiful and fresh and smells divine. But in a few days, it will wilt. It will die, and its fragrance will fade.

Jesus says we can be like a rose or a bunch of grapes – lovely and fruitful – as long as we are connected to Him. He is like a vine with its roots in deep, fertile soil. You and I are like branches that carry the fruit. But the minute the branch is not part of the vine anymore, it dies and is no longer of any use, just like a rose that has died.

How do we remain part of Him? We must read His Word every day, do what He wants, talk to Him, and ask Him to fill us with the Holy Spirit. We must cling to Him in our mind and thoughts. Then we will bear spiritual fruit and flower like a beautiful, fragrant rose!

The Bible says: "But the fruit of the Spirit is love, joy, peace, patience, kindness, goodness, faithfulness, gentleness and self-control" (Galatians 5:22-23).

15 April

You Are an Important Branch

"I am the vine; you are the branches. If a man remains in me and I in him, he will bear much fruit; apart from me you can do nothing" (John 15:5).

Behind our house we have a vine with long climbing branches. Every summer a whole lot of new branches appear, and very soon they cover the whole trellis. Our dog loves lying in the shade of the large vine leaves. More important however, are the grapes that grow on it.

Jesus says in today's verse that we are branches. If we remain connected to Him (the Vine), we bear much fruit. He also says it is not possible to bear fruit if we do not remain in Him, because without Him we can do nothing.

Today's Bible study teaches us that we must have an intimate relationship with the Lord Jesus. Then we can be sure of bearing lots of fruit. Do you think this is true of you? If you don't have enough spiritual fruit in your life, you must check on the bond between you and the Lord Jesus – how close are you? If you are connected to Him, you will bear fruit. The bunches of grapes in your life will be big and full. You see, Bible study isn't something we do just to learn more. It is meant to be an opportunity for you to get to know the Lord better so that you can bear more and more fruit. You don't want to be like our dog that lies in the shade under the leaves all day!

Make sure you are connected to the vine.

16 April

Are You a
Man or a Mouse?

"The LORD who delivered me from the paw of the lion and the paw of the bear will deliver me from the hand of this Philistine" (1 Samuel 17:37).

Have you ever fought a giant and won? I don't mean a real giant, but a giant of a problem you came up against in your life, which you eventually solved?

Maybe your giant was math, and you beat it with hard work and perseverance. Or maybe it was a bully at school whom you stood up to. Or perhaps you wrung the neck of the exam monster by studying harder.

In the Bible we read the story of a young boy who came face to face with a real giant. This is the story of David and Goliath. Hardened soldiers were trembling with fear at the sight of Goliath. The giant shouted at David, a boy who had the nerve to challenge him with a sling. David quite calmly took aim and hit the giant with a stone on the forehead. And the giant fell down dead, facedown on the ground.

How did David manage to do this? He had God on his side. While the Philistines fought with swords and sticks and spears, David fought in the name of the Lord. He knew that even a mouse can be brave if he has someone much bigger right behind him.

The Lord often uses people who are not necessarily the smartest or the strongest to do His work. All He asks of us is to be willing.

17 April

Grace

"If we confess our sins, he is faithful and just and will forgive us our sins and purify us from all unrighteousness" (1 John 1:9).

Do you know the meaning of grace? It is a word that is often used in church. Someone once said it is the most important word in our religion. The dictionary explains it as "God's mercy and favor towards mankind." Grace is God's goodness towards His children. We sin, but He is still good to us. He forgives us the moment we speak to Him about our sins and tell Him we are sorry. So, grace also means forgiveness.

I see grace all around me. Grace is when I hold my dog in my arms again after he has run away. Grace is when Mom brings me hot chocolate after I have talked back to her. Grace is Dad comforting me after I have scratched his car. Grace is when I invite a friend to my party even if that friend told stories about me.

When you have done something wrong, you expect to be punished for it.

What a relief to find that the person who has every right to punish you showers you with love! Yes, grace is a wonderful thing. It's not something we just naturally have. There must be a lot of love in someone's heart before grace enters. This is how much God loves us.

Amazing grace, how sweet the sound!

18 April

You Have a Choice

"Choose for yourselves this day whom you will serve"
(Joshua 24:15).

The Lord doesn't point a gun at you and say, "Do as I tell you!" He doesn't kick the door of your heart down the way some policemen do in television programs. The Bible says He stands at the door of your heart and knocks. You can decide if you want to let Him in. If you do, He will come into your heart and live there, and His Spirit will be your Counselor. He will be there to help you with any kind of problem. He will make your life fruitful and beautiful.

It may happen that people will tease you because you belong to the Lord. At times it will be difficult to do what the Lord wants you to. But you will have the strength to handle everything that comes your way, and one day you will be with God in heaven forever.

You can also choose not to serve the Lord. Then your life on earth might be easier – you can just go with the flow, do what you want, and have no place for the Lord in your life. But just remember that you will never become the person God had in mind, and what is more, you will miss out on everlasting life with God.

If you choose Jesus, there is a wonderful adventure in store for you.

19 April

Green Grass, Brown Grass

As for man, his days are like grass. … the wind blows over it and it is gone, and its place remembers it no more (Psalm 103:15-16).

In the rainy season the fields turn a lovely green. The seeds from the previous season's grass then grow, and all over we see the tall grass swaying in the wind. When autumn comes along, the color changes and the fields become brown with dry grass.

The Bible says you and I are like grass. One day we are healthy and lively, but it can happen that we suddenly get sick or something makes us age very quickly. There are children in many hospitals who are dying, almost like grass – one day sprightly and the next, lifeless.

The Lord says we must live every day to the full. *"This is the day the Lord has made; let us rejoice and be glad in it"* (Psalm 118:24). Every day is precious. Don't let it slip through your fingers. Let today be your best day. Go all out to live for Jesus today. Ask Him to help you give your best at school, when you play sports, or when you do your homework. Tomorrow we might be in heaven.

The Bible says: "Make the most of every opportunity" (Colossians 4:5).

20 April

Help for the Poor

The disciples, each according to his ability, decided to provide help for the brothers living in Judea (Acts 11:29).

Recently they decided to build a pool at our children's school. A building fund was established, and all the parents had to contribute towards it. Possibly you have had this kind of thing at your school too.

Today's verse tells us about a fund to help needy believers in Jerusalem. Christians from different congregations were asked to contribute towards this fund. Eventually they gave the money they had collected to Barnabas and Saul to take to the elders in Jerusalem.

Have you ever contributed towards a fund? Don't hesitate to help the needy, because the Lord smiles with pleasure when His children do this – especially if it will help the poor.

21 April

Show Me
the Right Way

How can a young man keep his way pure? By living according to your word (Psalm 119:9).

Have you read Psalm 119 before? Maybe you haven't, because it's the longest psalm in the Bible. It would be a pity if you haven't read it, because one part of it explains exactly how to stay on the right path.

In a world where we don't always know the difference between right and wrong anymore, we find the recipe for a good life in Psalm 119:9-16. This part tells us:

- To obey God.
- To treasure God's promises.
- To stay away from sin.
- To really think about God's laws, one by one.
- To rejoice in the law of God and not forget any part of it.
- To pray that God will help us do all this.

The Bible is a light on our way. It shows us how to live, so it would be good to learn as much as possible from it. If you don't know what is written in the Bible or where to find it, you have nothing to hold on to when you are doubting. If you read your Bible every day and underline and memorize your favorite verses, you are not going to be shaken by every storm of life that threatens.

Read the story of Simeon in Luke 2:25. He was faithful to God's law and believed God's promises.

22 April

Holy Communion
Is a Sign

"This cup is the new covenant in my blood, which is poured out for you" (Luke 22:20).

Have you heard your parents speak of communion and baptism as the "sacraments" of the church? A sacrament is another word for a holy sign. In Luke 22, Jesus says when He instituted Holy Communion, "This cup is the new covenant in my blood, which is poured out for you." It is His way of explaining to the disciples that the wine they drink at the table is the sign of His blood – His blood that flowed for us on the cross, so that we could be washed clean from sin forever.

When Jesus came, He restored the covenant that God made with his people in the Old Testament, the same covenant they broke time and again. In Old Testament times, only the Israelites were allowed to be God's people. When Jesus died for you, He made it possible for you to become one of God's people – He came to enter into a new covenant with everyone who believes in Him.

Because Jesus spilled His blood on the cross for you, you are part of the new covenant. And even if you are too young now to take part in Holy Communion, by all means thank the Lord for it!

What exactly does this new covenant mean? See how the prophet Ezekiel explains it in Ezekiel 36:26-28.

23 April

What Is Conversion?

"And everyone who calls on the name of the Lord will be saved" (Acts 2:21).

While a missionary in India was busy showing slides about the life of Jesus, a man in the audience started getting very agitated. When the picture of the cross showed on the white wall, he ran forward and called out, "Jesus, Son of God, come down from the cross. I am the one who should be there, not You!"

Once you understand why Jesus had to die on a cross, you cannot help feeling sad. He had to go through so much for us! But we shouldn't leave it at that. We must also do something.

We must repent. This means you must make up your mind to stop doing whatever you want to. You must tell God that you are sorry about your sins and that from now on you want to make Him happy. Then God will forgive you and His Holy Spirit will come and live in your heart. This is how you become the Lord's child.

Many people these days wear a necklace with a cross around their necks. Some pop stars wear it because they believe it will bring them luck. But whenever you see a cross, you must remember that you belong to the Lord. His children do what He says, even if they do it at a price. They don't live for themselves any more.

Jesus died on a cross so that we could become God's children.

24 April

Will You Help?

Then he said to his disciples, "The harvest is plentiful but the workers are few. Ask the Lord of the harvest, therefore, to send out workers into his harvest field" (Matthew 9:37-38).

A wheat plant is a very important plant. It is used to make bread and many other kinds of food. The seed is very small, and where it is sown, many wheat plants come up. There are millions of plants on one wheat farm. When the plants grow tall and ripple in the breeze, farmers know that soon it will be time for the harvest. The time then comes for cutting and gathering the crop. In the time of the Bible, the workers harvested the wheat, and then the grain was threshed (beaten out). It was very hard work.

Jesus says there are millions of people on earth who stand like wheat on the lands. He means they are ready to enter into His kingdom. They also must be "picked" or "harvested" like wheat. The Lord loves them, and He has prepared their hearts so that they can follow Him. But someone must help them. Just as workers gather the wheat crop, so you and I must gather people and bring them to Jesus. Are you prepared to help?

The Bible says: "`Whom shall I send? And who will go for us?' And I said, `Here I am. Send me!'" (Isaiah 6:8)

25 April

The Holy Spirit Is Your Guide

Paul and his companions traveled throughout the region of Phrygia and Galatia, having been kept by the Holy Spirit from preaching the word in the province of Asia (Acts 16:6).

We don't know why and how the Holy Spirit stopped Paul and his friends from going to Asia. It could have been through a prophet, a vision, a feeling inside, or anything else. We don't need to hear God's voice in our ears to know His will.

He leads us in different ways. If you want to find out what His will is, you can do the following:

- Make sure what you plan is what He wants and that His Word tells you that.
- Ask adult Christians to help you.
- Examine your own motives carefully: Are you doing what *you* want or what God wants?
- Naturally it doesn't help just to know God's will. We must also do it.

Do you do what God wills every day?

26 April

Paul Preaches in Athens

"For as I walked around and looked carefully at your objects of worship, I even found an altar with this inscription: TO AN UNKNOWN GOD. Now what you worship as something unknown I am going to proclaim to you" (Acts 17:23).

As Paul was walking around in the big city of Athens, he saw this altar for an unknown god. The people of Athens were so worried that they had skipped one of the many gods they believed in, that to stay on the safe side they built this one. Paul started talking to them about that unknown god. This, of course, doesn't mean that he approved of that god. He used the words on the altar as a starting point for his own testimony of the living God.

The God of the Bible is, of course, the only true God, and He is the one you and I believe in. And we don't have to build Him altars or bring Him human offerings. We know the Name of God because Jesus came to tell us His Name: the Father, the Son and the Holy Spirit.

You are lucky that you don't have to travel to Athens to meet God. Because His Spirit lives in you and works in your heart, God is with you, right now. So worship Him as the only true God.

Lord, I worship You because You are the only God. Thank You that Your name is recorded in the Bible and that I can see Your wonderful creation.

27 April

In Christ We All Are Winners

But thanks be to God! He gives us the victory through our Lord Jesus Christ (1 Corinthians 15:57).

What picture do you see in your mind when you think of a winner? Do you only see a sports hero or heroine holding up the trophy, or do you think of the hours and hours of practice, sacrifice, and pain that went before it?

If you think about it, you realize that pain and gain go together. The apostle Paul experienced this firsthand. He was the famous young scribe who "breathed murder" over the followers of Jesus and who, later on, gave up everything to follow Him. In his lifetime he traveled hundreds of miles on foot to preach the gospel. He went hungry and was often in prison. And still he sees himself as a winner because he was part of the winning team – Christ's team.

At the end of his life Paul could say, *"I have fought the good fight, I have finished the race, I have kept the faith"* (2 Timothy 4:7).

You can also be a winner without ever playing for the best team or finishing first in a race. If you are on Jesus' team, you are always a winner.

There is no gain without pain, but the victory is certain because Christ has already won.

28 April

Live by the Spirit

So I say, live by the Spirit, and you will not gratify the desires of the sinful nature (Galatians 5:16).

If you are a Christian, the Holy Spirit lives in you. You have the Holy Spirit, but does the Holy Spirit have you? You must have noticed that you still sin even though you are a Christian. Every day you must fight sin, because every person has it in his or her nature to be sinful.

Paul writes to the churches in Galatia that they must live by the Holy Spirit. It is not enough that the Holy Spirit lives in you; you must also allow Him total control of your life.

When you become a child of the Lord, the Holy Spirit gets into the "car of life" with you, but you still hold the steering wheel. Often the Holy Spirit tells you how to drive, and sometimes you listen and sometimes you don't. God wants you to hand over the steering wheel of your car to the Holy Spirit – to go where He leads you and do what He wants you to. God's will is more important than yours from now on. Are you willing to do this?

What are the acts of the sinful nature? (See Galatians 5: 19-21.)

29 April

The Bible Is a Sword

Take ... the sword of the Spirit, which is the word of God (Ephesians 6:17).

A few years back there was an article in a magazine about four Americans who crash-landed their airplane in the snow-covered Andes mountain range. It was a very moving story. In the end, only two of them survived the tragedy. They said they tried to fight depression and fear by reciting parts of the Bible to one another. Unfortunately, after four rounds, they realized that they couldn't remember any more verses by heart.

A different story is told of a group of Christians in Romania. At the time the Bible was a forbidden book in their country, and this congregation had only one Bible among all its members. So every member of the group was told to memorize one chapter. When they gathered for a service and they wanted to read from, say Ephesians, the person who had to learn that part had to recite it.

How far would you get if you landed in prison without your Bible? How many verses would you know to defend yourself against the attacks of Satan? Jesus set us an example. When He was in the desert and the devil tempted Him, He used the sword of the Spirit, the Word of God. He had no scrolls with Him, but the Word was in His head and in His heart.

Christians should be able to use the Bible as a sword.

30 April

Born Again

"No one can see the kingdom of God unless he is born again" (John 3:3).

"**M**om," Jean said, "my teacher says we must be born again if we want to go to heaven. But how can you be born all over again?"

"The grown man Nicodemus asked Jesus the same question once," Jean's mother replied. "I'm going to try to explain it to you. On September 15, 1988, you were born. Ever since, you have been part of our family. But you can also become part of another family – God's family. The day you decide that you want to be God's child, you are born again. Then a new life starts for you."

"Mom, do you think I am born again?" Jean asked.

Mother looked deeply into Jean's eyes. "Do you believe that Jesus died on the cross for your sins?" she wanted to know.

"Yes!" Jean answered.

"And do you want to be His child?"

"Oh yes!" exclaimed Jean, "very much!"

"Then tell Him you are sorry about your sins and ask Him to accept you as His child!"

There was silence in the dining room as Jean put her head on her arms, praying. Her mother had tears in her eyes. She was thinking back to the day she held Jean in her arms for the first time, and she was so happy to be present at her daughter's second birth as well.

Are you a member of God's family yet?

1 May

Are You Afraid
of God's Punishment?

"The Lord ... punishes everyone he accepts as a son"
(Hebrews 12:6).

Are you afraid God will punish you for everything you do wrong? If you are the Lord's child, you needn't be afraid. Jesus took the punishment for your sins. Still, you will find out that God doesn't allow us just to keep on sinning without putting a stop to it. He knows how sin can harm us, and that is why He is angry about our sins.

Has your dad ever been mad at your brother because he crossed the road without looking out for cars first? And did he punish him for being so careless? For the same reason, God sometimes disciplines us, so that we will learn right from wrong.

You also know that your dad will not stay angry at your brother! Soon he'll be on your dad's lap again, the tears being wiped from his eyes. The Lord also forgives us for being disobedient if we turn back to Him.

God's children need to be afraid of sin – not of God!

2 May

Watch the Ants

Go to the ant, you sluggard; consider its ways and be wise! (Proverbs 6:6)

Have you ever seen a sleeping ant? I know I haven't. Ants are always on the move. Now and again you will see an ant stop for a moment, but soon it is on its way again. And if you should open up an anthill, you will not believe your eyes when you see the ants scurrying about. Actually it looks like total confusion. And yet they are all going about their business and know exactly what they are doing. An ant's nest is very well organized.

The wise man of Proverbs tells us to study the ants so that we can learn to be wise. We can learn a lot from ants, but the most important lesson we learn is that they are not lazy. They do what they have to do in a purposeful way, concentrating on their goal only!

When the Lord made the earth and everything on it, He told the humans that they would rule over it. This meant they could grow and make use of all the plants and vegetation. They could name the plants and animals. So we see that the Lord gave human beings the order to work. When sin came into the world, people had to work even harder if they wanted food on the table. God does not want us to be lazy. He wants us to work hard, just like the ants.

The Bible says: "A little sleep, a little slumber, a little folding of the hands to rest – and poverty will come on you like a bandit" (Proverbs 6:10-11).

3 May

Paul's Strange Miracle

Even handkerchiefs and aprons that had touched him
were taken to the sick, and their illnesses were cured and
the evil spirits left them (Acts 19:12).

The miracles we read about here are rather strange! Just think – someone held an apron against Paul's body, put it on sick people afterwards, and immediately they were healed.

God allowed these strange miracles to happen to convince the unbelievers of who He was. Of course, the Lord can make such miracles happen even today, but this is not His usual way of doing things.

Some people are forever looking for proof, watching out for strange happenings and miracles to take place. This is really not necessary, because the very fact that you can see or that the earth revolves around its axis in one day is already a miracle! So it really makes no difference if a miracle is ordinary or unusual. We don't have to see a miracle to believe in God. Actually it's the other way round. It's only when you believe in God that you notice the miracles that take place every day. You don't just take everything for granted, but you see the hand of God in it. No human being can make something happen if God doesn't want it to happen. This, then, is the reason why you and I, as believers, see the hand of God in ordinary, everyday things.

Ordinary, everyday things are also miracles!

4 May

I'm Scared of So Many Things

They were terrified. But the angel said to them, "Do not be afraid. I bring you good news" (Luke 2:9-10).

I once heard the story of a little boy who was afraid of the dark. His mother asked him, "Why are you scared? Jesus will look after you."

"Yes, I know," he said, "but I would rather have someone with skin around him."

Fear is a great drain on our energy. In the dictionary, we find no less than thirty-eight different phobias listed, from hydrophobia (fear of water) to arachnophobia (fear of spiders). Add to that all the fears that young people today face, such as school shootings or robberies, and it's hard to not be scared sometimes.

But the Bible says 365 times, "Do not be afraid." These were the first words the angels said to the shepherds and practically Jesus' last words to His disciples. So what makes us get the feeling the Bible is trying to tell us something about fear?

- Memorize Psalm 27:1 and say it out loud every time you are afraid.
- Write the psalm on a card and keep it next to your bed.

God gives us the assurance that He is more than someone with skin around him. He is everywhere and He is with you, even when you have reason to be afraid.

Get into the habit of putting your problems onto the Lord's shoulders.

5 May

Tell the Lord All About It

"If it were I, I would appeal to God; I would lay my cause before him. The lowly he sets on high, and those who mourn are lifted to safety" (Job 5:8, 11).

Job knew what it was to suffer. He lost all his possessions, all his children died, he became very ill, and to top it off, his friends and his wife turned against him. And still Job loved the Lord. It's very difficult to understand why these things had to happen to him. Job couldn't understand it either. He wanted God to give him the reason why he had to suffer so much.

Job's three friends had tons of advice for him. Eliphaz's advice is worth listening to. "Tell God how you feel, Job," Eliphaz said. "He can help."

Young people also have problems. Do you have things that upset you, and you don't know how to handle them? Tell God all about it. He loves you and wants to help you, even if it is in a way you don't expect. God doesn't always give us the answers we want to hear, but if we love Him and obey Him, He gives us what is best for us.

Read in 1 Samuel 1:15-20 how the Lord helped a woman who took her problems to Him.

6 May

Not Everybody
Knows the Right Way

"I am the way and the truth and the life. No one comes to the Father except through me" (John 14:6).

Is our religion really the only way to reach God? What about the Muslims, Buddhists, and Hindus? They do their best to live good lives. Some people say that just as there is more than one way to a mountaintop, so different religions are just different ways of reaching God. Perhaps there are children in your school who don't read the Bible but the Koran instead. Could it be that the secret of life is in that book in a different way, or is our Bible the only book of truth?

Jesus said there is no other way to God. He is the only One who can take us there. Other religions can be interesting, and you can learn from them. But no matter how hard you try, you can never satisfy God with trying to be good. We are simply too sinful to approach Him; it's as simple as that. Only those who believe in Jesus may approach God without fear.

All the other religions can show you where their leaders are buried, but Jesus' grave is empty. He is with the Father, and His Spirit is inside us to lead the way to the house of our Father.

Everyone must know about the living Lord Jesus, our Redeemer.

7 May

When a Donkey Talks

Then the Lord opened the donkey's mouth, and she said to Balaam, "What have I done to make you beat me these three times?" (Numbers 22:28)

In the Bible we read a very strange story. A man named Balaam wanted to take a message to someone, but the Lord told him not to. Balaam was traveling on a donkey, and while he was on the road, an angel suddenly stood in the way and stopped the donkey from passing. Balaam was very upset with the donkey and started beating it and shouting at it. Because Balaam was so disobedient toward the Lord, he never even realized it was the Lord trying to stop him.

While he was still hitting the donkey and shouting at it, the Lord suddenly opened the donkey's mouth, and the donkey talked to Balaam in a human voice! This was a miracle.

We learn from this story that we should listen when the Lord speaks to us. If we keep on doing what He doesn't like, it can mean big trouble for us. Let's listen to the Lord and do what He wants.

The Bible says: "To obey is better than sacrifice, and to heed is better than the fat of rams" (1 Samuel 15:22).

8 May

New Christians Who Burned Their Books

A number who had practiced sorcery brought their scrolls together and burned them publicly (Acts 19:19).

Ephesus was a beautiful city in Paul's day, but there was a lot of evil in the city. Many of the Ephesians made a profitable living from witchcraft. They even drove evil spirits out of people. The Lord used Paul to preach there, and because of him, many of these sorcerers became Christians. Jesus Christ is, after all, the only One who is able to change a person's life.

Before they became Christians, many of these people thought that magic words could make them happy or rich or could make their marriages work. Superstition and witchcraft were common and widespread. But God forbids these things very clearly in the Bible. You cannot have faith in God and play around with witchcraft. It is very easy to get caught in the web of these powers once you become interested in such practices.

The power of God is stronger and offers the only real security.

If you ever come into contact with superstition and witchcraft, learn from the Ephesians' experience and get rid of anything that can have a hold on you.

9 May

You Are an Important Heavenly Citizen

"Is it legal for you to flog a Roman citizen who hasn't even been found guilty?" (Acts 22:25)

Paul was a Roman citizen, so punishment without a trial was not allowed. Consequently, the soldiers stopped beating him when he asked the commander the question above, because it was against the law to punish a Roman citizen before he had been found guilty of a crime.

Paul was a Roman citizen by birth, while the commander had bought his citizenship. Many people in the Roman Empire bought their citizenship in those days, and this was also a source of income for the government. Someone who was a Roman citizen by birth, however, was seen as a "more important citizen" than one who bought his citizenship.

You must never forget that you are a heavenly citizen. No matter what people think or say about you, God always keeps an eye on you. Even when they seem to be getting the better of you and you can't see that God is doing anything about it, keep in mind that God does see, and He will make all things right on Judgment Day. Always remember, it is far more important to be a heavenly citizen than to be a citizen of the world. This should make you feel good, especially when you feel life is unfair.

Remember, you are an important heavenly citizen.

10 May

The "Can't Wait" Generation

You intended to harm me, but God intended it for good to accomplish what is now being done, the saving of many lives (Genesis 50:20).

We live in "instant" times. Everything is done quickly and easily. If you want hot chocolate, you put the milk in the mug, put the mug in the microwave, and in a minute you have a steaming mug of hot chocolate. Need money? Slip the card into the slot, and lo and behold, you have cash in your hand. And at McDonald's, you wait only minutes for a hamburger!

This is all very well, but it makes us very impatient with life. We want everything today, to experience everything now. It's no wonder that we have nothing to look forward to, and even little kids can say what we read in Ecclesiastes: *"There is nothing new under the sun."*

We don't have the time or the patience to wait. If God does not answer our prayers immediately, then He is not the God for modern youth. We want results, and we want them now!

Yet, waiting is often worthwhile. Just think how long Joseph had to wait before God used him to save his people. The Lord looks at things differently; in His eyes a thousand years can be like a day. The plan for your life spans many years, not just the here and now. The world says: "Seize the day." God says: "Be strong and take heart and wait for Me."

The next time you go shopping, be patient and don't be in too much of a hurry.

11 May

Sometimes God's Answer Is Different

"He performs wonders that cannot be fathomed, miracles that cannot be counted" (Job 5:9).

Have you ever prayed to do well in an exam and then your grade was worse than ever, or for someone to get well and it didn't happen? At such times it's easy to think that the Lord doesn't really hear what you say and doesn't listen when you pray. But God always answers your prayers – you just don't always get the answer you want.

God also gave Job an answer he didn't expect, allowing him to experience what is written in the verse above: "[I] perform wonders that cannot be fathomed, miracles that cannot be counted." It just isn't possible for us to understand with our tiny human brain the things God does. Because He is God, we dare not demand answers from Him.

God takes Job on an expedition in nature and shows him all the wonderful things He created. Then Job realizes that God is almighty, that He does not have to answer all his "why?" questions. When Job makes peace with the Lord, God changes his circumstances and blesses him more than before.

Byron Edwards said something to this effect: "True prayer always receives what it asks for – or something better."

Read Job's touching confession of guilt in Job 42:1-6. What happens after this? (See Job 42:10.)

12 May

The Bible Cannot Be Destroyed

"Heaven and earth will pass away, but my words will never pass away" (Mark 13:31).

A man called Voltaire lived two hundred years ago. He was a very talented and learned man, but he didn't believe in the Bible. One day he held a Bible up in the air at a meeting and said, "Let me tell you something. In a hundred years' time no one will believe in this book any more and it will be found only in museums."

What came of this prophecy? Today Voltaire lies buried in a lonely graveyard, and his books can scarcely be found in museums. But in the house where he used to live in Geneva, Switzerland, thousands of Bibles are stored to be sent to neighboring countries. The Bible Society bought Voltaire's house, and they use it as their office!

Not only is the Bible the bestseller of all books through the ages, but its message has also had a tremendous influence on its readers. Millions of people can testify how they started believing in the Lord Jesus by reading the Bible. Do you read it regularly?

The Bible cannot be destroyed because it is the Word of God.

13 May

The Book of All Books

I rejoice in your promise like one who finds great spoil [treasure] (Psalm 119:162).

Josh watches with great interest as George crams the last things into his backpack. He is jealous because George is on his way to Africa to take part in a missionary outreach. "Every dog has his day," he thinks to himself. "Just wait and see. One day I'll also do the things my brother is doing now."

George has almost finished packing. "Let's see, now I still need a roadmap, a lamp, a mirror, a poetry book, some letters, a sword, and a few storybooks!" he says.

Josh eyes the small space that is still available in one of the side pockets of the bag. "Must it all go in there?" he asks in disbelief.

"Yep!" says George, taking his Bible from his desk and fitting it neatly into the space in his bag. "That's it!" he says. "Now I'm ready for the trip! Africa, here we come!"

Josh goes along to see George off. All the young people in the team are in good spirits, singing cheerfully as the bus drives off: "Our light is bright, shining for the nations, a bright and shining light to bring joy to the world!" When he gets home, Josh remembers what George said about his Bible. He thinks about it and then realizes that a Bible can be all of those things his brother said he still needed. He is thrilled to think that the group of young people will take the Book of all books to those who have not even seen it yet.

The Bible is a precious treasure.

14 May

The Good Shepherd

"I am the good shepherd" (John 10:11).

Have you ever seen a sheep? Sheep are not the cleverest animals. They walk around and graze wherever they want and are easy prey for wild animals like wolves and jackals. Sheep are very easy to catch or steal.

Sheep need help. They must be looked after. That's why farmers fence them in or get herdsmen or shepherds to look after them.

Jesus said we humans are just like sheep that need help. He didn't mean we are as stupid as they are! But He knows that people so easily get caught by Satan and his lies. Jesus says that is why He came, to help us like a good shepherd. He will take care of us and look after us, give us life, and see that we always have enough. All we have to do is trust Him and follow Him.

Sheep don't have a choice whom they follow, but you and I do. Let's choose to follow Jesus.

The Bible says: "The LORD is my shepherd ... He guides me in paths of righteousness" *(Psalm 23:1, 3).*

15 May

Who Is Your Master?

For sin shall not be your master, because you are not under law, but under grace (Romans 6:14).

If you have a dog that belongs to you, you are its master. The same goes for any other pet you may have, such as a parakeet or a fish. You can make your pet do what you want because you are its master. Paul warns us that sin must not be our master.

If you look carefully at what the apostle writes, you see that he says the unbeliever is "employed" by sin. Sin is his master, and he is a "slave to sin." (See Romans 6:16.) In the case of the believer, God takes over the control. When you are a believer, you are obliged to be in God's service – ready and willing to do what He wants you to, because He is your Master. Like a good slave you obey your Master and you want to do what He tells you to. You belong to Him. After all, He bought you with the blood of His Son.

Aren't you glad you belong to God? Then don't forget to thank Him.

16 May

When Your Parents Make You Unhappy

"You are my Son; today I have become your Father"
(Psalm 2:7).

Your relationship with your parents can be pain or pleasure. For a lot of children, it feels mostly like pain. Many children are ill-treated by their parents in different ways.

James' stepfather is always belittling him. Anne's mother thinks nothing of it to slap her at the drop of a hat, while Sheila's mom makes it no secret that the younger sister is her favorite.

What do you do when your parents treat you unfairly? Remember your heavenly Father's love for you.

- He sees: *The eyes of the Lord are everywhere, keeping watch on the wicked and the good* (Proverbs 15:3).
- He cares: *Cast all your anxiety on him because he cares for you* (1 Peter 5:7).
- He comforts: *The Lord lifts up those who are bowed down* (Psalm 146:8).
- He heals: *He heals the brokenhearted and binds up their wounds* (Psalm 147:3).
- He is righteous: *O righteous God ... bring to an end the violence of the wicked and make the righteous secure* (Psalm 7:9).

If a grown up is ill-treating or abusing you, speak to someone you trust. If you have a friend whose parents are abusing him or her, speak to someone now.

17 May

"Why" Questions

"If the LORD is with us, why has all this happened to us?"
(Judges 6:13).

The nation of Israel suffered a lot in the time of the judges. The heathen nations destroyed their crops and stripped their lands bare. The Israelites just couldn't understand why these things were happening to them, the people of the Lord. "Why do all these things happen, if the Lord is with us?" Gideon asks the angel in the verse above.

Today many things happen that we don't understand. In almost every newspaper, we read about people being attacked and murdered, about children being kidnapped, and about people hurt in car accidents. I'm sure you also sometimes wonder how God can allow these things if He loves the human race.

All these horrific things that happen in the world are never God's will – they happen because of sin.

Suffering show us we can do nothing without Him. In the Sermon on the Mount, Jesus reminded people how blessed those people are who realize how dependent they are on God.

It is only when we cannot do anything about our circumstances ourselves that we turn to God. And luckily He is always prepared to help!

In what wonderful way did the Lord help His people in Judges 7:21-23?

18 May

The Bible Is
a Story Book

"Remember the former things, those of long ago; I am God, and there is no other" (Isaiah 46:9).

Can you still remember the things that happened to you before you started going to school? Not really? Ask your grandparents how much they remember about the time they were still at school – they probably won't remember much either. Isn't it strange how so many things that happen to you can be forgotten rather quickly?

God doesn't want us ever to forget what He did in Bible times, because through these stories we get to know Him. He made sure that His works were written down in the Bible, and He also made sure that it would still be there for us after all these years so that we can learn a lot about God even now when we read the Bible stories.

Which Bible story do you like best? The story of Daniel, perhaps? It teaches us how God looks after His children. Perhaps you like the one of David and Goliath where we learn that the size of your enemy is not important, just as long as you have God on your side!

How about reading some Bible stories again, in the Bible or a children's Bible, and see how many things you can learn about God?

Bible stories tell us how God works with His children.

19 May

Free Indeed!

He has sent me to bind up the brokenhearted, to proclaim freedom for the captives and release from darkness for the prisoners (Isaiah 61:1).

It's great to be free; to be able to walk around and go wherever you want. Prisoners in jail say the worst part of it is being locked up in a building all day long. They can't go for walks in the open air or sit in the sun.

The Bible tells us that people who don't know the Lord are prisoners. They could just as well be in prison because they are imprisoned by the devil. They are imprisoned by sin; they are not free. Without knowing it, they are the devil's prisoners.

How wonderful, then, that Jesus came to save and free people. Jesus' name means "Redeemer" (Savior). Yes, He is the One who comes to cut people loose, to set them free, to save them. He gives freedom to the prisoners kept in the prison of sin.

Let's ask Him today to deliver us from evil, and then you will also be free to live with Him. Let's tell the devil we're not interested in his prison of sin.

The Bible says: "So if the son sets you free, you will be free indeed" (John 8:36).

20 May

The Bible Is the Sword of the Spirit

Take the helmet of salvation and the sword of the Spirit which is the word of God (Ephesians 6:17).

The Bible is such a wonderful, powerful book that Paul calls it "the sword of the Spirit." This means that the Holy Spirit uses the Bible's words like a sword in battles against the devil. Jesus also did this. When the devil tempted Him, He used the Word of God to defend Himself. (See Matthew 4 and Luke 4.)

If you are a Christian, you are also a soldier in Jesus' service. That is why you should know the Bible. It's a good idea to use a daily devotional like this one, but never neglect the Bible itself. The easiest way to get to know the Bible is to use it every day.

That is why Bible study is so important. Let me give you a very simple tip to become familiar with the Bible. Try reading a whole chapter every time you read the Bible. Always try to find something in that chapter you didn't know or something that means a lot to you. Underline it in pencil. In this way you can remember it better and also find it if you want to read it again. It's almost like having a bookmark – it's easy to see where you have already underlined and then you know where you have already read. This is a much quicker way of getting to know the Bible than reading here, there, and everywhere.

Get to know the sword of the Spirit and use it.

21 May

The Bible Is a Library

"Do not think that I have come to abolish the law or the Prophets; I have not come to abolish them but to fulfill them" (Matthew 5:17).

When was the last time you visited a library? I find all those books quite awesome! Actually, the Bible with its sixty-six separate books is a library on its own.

This library has two rooms. In one room we find the thirty-nine Old Testament books. In the other room are the twenty-seven books of the New Testament. Each of those books has its own "personality." Did you know that between thirty and forty people worked on the Bible under the leadership of the Holy Spirit? They wrote it over a period of roughly one thousand years, and yet they don't contradict one another anywhere! The reason for this is, of course, that the Holy Spirit guided them.

Just think in what a wonderful way and over how many hundreds of years the Bible came into being, and you must already realize that it is an amazing book! This is one reason why you should have great respect for the Bible. You must look after your Bible because in it are the words of God.

The Bible is your most valuable possession; don't ever forget that.

22 May

War or Peace
with Your Parents?

Children, obey your parents in everything, for this pleases the Lord (Colossians 3:20).

Do you realize that even though you are still a child, you have the power to make your home either a battlefield or a place of peace? If you want to declare war against your parents, do the following:

- Ignore the Bible's instruction to obey your parents. (*"Children, obey your parents in everything, for this pleases the Lord"* Colossians 3:20.)
- Repay their generosity by refusing to be thankful. (*"If a man pays back evil for good, evil will never leave his house"* Proverbs 17:13.)
- Don't respect them. (*"Cursed is the man who dishonors his father or his mother"* Deuteronomy 27:16.)

Instead, make peace with your parents, and then your home will be a place where everyone can be happy. So if you want to make peace with your parents, do the following:

- Don't talk back when they ask you to do something.
- Be thankful for everything they give you.
- Treat them the way you want to be treated.
- Honor your father and your mother, even if you don't always agree with them. They are, after all, your parents.

The Bible tells the story of Absalom, who turned the whole country into a battlefield because he didn't honor his father (See 2 Samuel 18:9-14.)

23 May

The "So That" Answer

"Neither this man nor his parents sinned ... but this happened [he was born blind] so that the work of God might be displayed in his life" (John 9:3).

Jesus' disciples wanted to know why a man was born blind. They assumed that the man or his parents must have done something wrong. But Jesus told his disciples that the man was blind so that the good work of God could be seen in his life.

The American writer and artist named Joni Eareckson was paralyzed in a diving accident when she was a teenager. She firmly believed that God would make her walk again, but this didn't happen. It was only later that Joni realized God had also given her a "so that" answer to her why questions. The fact that she was paralyzed gave her opportunities she didn't have before. She wrote books that encouraged a great many readers, and she founded an organization for people who were paralyzed. Now she knows why God let her have the accident, Joni writes, so that He could be glorified in the process and others could get to know Him because they saw Him in her life.

If you have a why question in your life today, listen carefully for God's "so that" answer. He allows things to happen so that you can be a better, clearer witness for Him among your friends.

What was Peter's "so that" answer to suffering? (See 1 Peter 1:6-7.)

24 May

The Bible Is a Textbook on God

All Scripture is God-breathed and is useful for teaching, rebuking, correcting and training in righteousness (2 Timothy 3:16).

Where will you go if you want the correct spelling of a word? To the dictionary, of course. And if you want some facts about a certain country? You visit the library or grab an encyclopedia. And what will you do if you want to know what's going on in the world right now, at this moment? You will buy a newspaper or switch on the radio or TV. If you have a computer, you can hunt for this information on the Internet!

Well, if we want to know more about the Lord, we must read the Bible. We can learn everything about God in it – what He is like and how He wants us to live.

There will always be people who say things about God that make us wonder. Some say God is dead and that He is not interested in us. Others say that all of nature is God; He is not a separate being. If you want to know if there's any truth in what they say, you must look for the answers in your Bible. People who know the Bible know a lot about God. And the more you know about Him, the more you love Him.

The Bible teaches us everything there is to know about God.

25 May

The Bible Is a Letter from God

For everything that was written in the past was written to teach us, so that through endurance and the encouragement of the Scriptures we might have hope (Romans 15:4).

Who doesn't like getting a letter? Junk mail and window envelopes are no fun, but a letter or a postcard is very special. It's good to know someone remembered you and cared enough to write you a letter. Sometimes you can be so pleased about a letter that you read it over and over again.

The Bible is a letter to you, and it comes from God. In it you will find important information, encouragement, and advice. Just think how disappointed you would be if you should find out that a letter you wrote someone is lying around somewhere on a shelf, unread and covered in dust!

Some people don't think it's possible to read the Bible from cover to cover. Are you one of them? Then start with the Gospel of Matthew, read Paul's letter to the Philippians next, and then read the Acts of the Apostles, Psalms 1-24, and the Gospel of John. Take time to think everything over and try to apply it to your own life.

Just remember: You will never understand or enjoy the Bible on your own. Ask the Holy Spirit to help you.

Read the Bible and remember that this is God's way of speaking to you.

26 May

Lush Green Leaves

He is like a tree planted by streams of water, which yields its fruit in season and whose leaf does not wither (Psalm 1:3).

There are many lovely trees with glossy green leaves. It is only when winter comes, and it is cold and miserable that we notice the bare branches. Then we realize how beautiful a tree really is when it has leaves. If bugs start eating at the trunk of a tree or its roots, then the leaves wilt, and this is a sign that the tree is dying. When a tree doesn't get enough water, its leaves get dry and shrivel up, and eventually the tree dies.

Many people are like sick or dying trees. Their lives are bare and ugly. They don't have "leaves" or "fruit." The Bible says there is only one way that we can be like a beautiful tree with green leaves: If the Lord is in our hearts. If we believe in Him, follow Him, do what He wants, and stay close friends with people who believe in God, then we will be like a tree with glossy, healthy leaves.

The Bible says: "On each side of the river stood the tree of life, bearing twelve crops of fruit. ... The leaves of the tree are for the healing of the nations" *(Revelation 22:2).*

27 May

Where Does Everything Come From?

In the beginning God created the heavens and the earth (Genesis 1:1).

At first there was nothing. Then God created everything that exists. How magnificent our God is. He created everything out of nothing! This means that there wasn't even clay or anything the Lord could use to create the earth. God simply spoke everything that was created into existence.

You might find it interesting to know that there are many religious stories told by other religions about the way the earth was created. In all these stories, however, the gods have clay or some material to start their creation with. The Bible tells a completely different story, namely that God also made the very first clay!

Isn't our God amazing? Just think how your mom makes a cake. She creates it by mixing all kinds of different ingredients, and finally she bakes the cake. The establishment of heaven and earth, however, was different. God had no ingredients to start with; He created it all out of nothing. The book of Genesis tells us all about it. It tells us that God was the source of everything that was created.

Thank the Lord that He was so fantastic to create everything that exists, out of nothing.

28 May

The Youth of Today

"Let the little children come to me, and do not hinder them, for the kingdom of God belongs to such as these" (Luke 18:16).

"The youth of today are lazy, have bad manners, have no respect for authority, and feel nothing for the elderly." "Our children are spoiled and rude." Do these statements sound familiar? Or have you heard this: "There is no hope for our country if today's youth become tomorrow's leaders, because this generation is reckless and selfish."

Wow! These are serious accusations. Do you know that the very same remarks were made thousands of years ago? Some of the first accusations against young people were made by Socrates around 400 B.C., and some were also made by an Egyptian teacher about 200 B.C.

On the other hand, it might not be such a bad idea to do a bit of soul-searching. Which of these statements are true of the youth of today?

Yes, all of us, from the oldest to the youngest, are guilty of selfishness and disobedience in one form or another. But Jesus died for us and for all the children before us and after us. We are not better or worse off than the youngsters of those times. We are just very privileged that we know the greatest Friend of all times, Jesus. He loved children so much that He even said grownups had to be like children if they wanted to enter into the kingdom of heaven.

All people are sinful; we are saved by the grace of God.

29 May

The Holy Spirit Came at Pentecost

Suddenly a sound like the blowing of a violent wind came from heaven. ... They saw what seemed to be tongues of fire that separated and came to rest on each of them. All of them were filled with the Holy Spirit (Acts 2:2-4).

After His death and resurrection, Jesus promised that He would send the Holy Spirit to earth in His place when He returned to His Father in heaven. His disciples had to pray together in Jerusalem until the Holy Spirit came.

On the day of Pentecost, fifty days after the crucifixion, the disciples and followers suddenly heard the sound of a powerful wind. When they looked up, they saw something like flames settling on each of them. It was the Holy Spirit's way of showing them that He was now with them.

All the believers that were there were filled with the Holy Spirit, and they started speaking in foreign languages, so that all the people in Jerusalem could hear the good news in their own languages. Thousands of people were converted that day.

Today we still celebrate Pentecost, because we are so happy that the Holy Spirit came to the world to live in His children forever. Some churches have special pentecostal prayer meetings. Ask your parents if you can go with them to these prayer meetings this year.

On the day of Pentecost we say thank you for the Holy Spirit.

30 May

Pentecostal Festival

The Spirit of God lives in you (Romans 8:9).

There's an old song that goes: "Don't you know, don't you know: You're a temple! You're a temple of the Holy Spirit!" Before the day of Pentecost, children of the Lord couldn't sing this song to one another. God's Spirit didn't live in them yet. Only a few very special people had God's Spirit in them before this.

But early one Sunday morning, several weeks after Jesus was taken to heaven, God sent the Holy Spirit to Jesus' friends where they were praying together. He came with the sound of a very strong wind so that they could hear it and in flames of fire so that everybody could see. And from that day on, the lives of those people were never the same again.

The Holy Spirit made them brave and wise. The very same disciples who ran away when Jesus was captured now talked about Him openly.

The Holy Spirit will also fill you if you allow Him. Then with your heart overflowing with joy, you, too, will be a powerful witness for Jesus. You must, however, allow Him to live in every part of your heart, which is His temple. Some people don't want God to live in their whole heart. They want to forget about Him sometimes. Tell the Holy Spirit today that He is welcome to turn your whole heart into a temple.

What did the Holy Spirit come to do on earth? (See John 14:26 and 16:8-13.)

31 May

Shine Like the Stars

Those who lead many to righteousness [will shine] like the stars for ever and ever (Daniel 12:3).

When somebody does very well at sports or excels at school or anything else, we sometimes say, "You're a star!"

The stars glittering in the dark sky form a beautiful sight. It was a bright star that led the wise men to the birthplace of Jesus. And Jesus is also called the bright Morning Star! (See Revelation 22:16.)

Through Daniel, the Lord said that if we lead people to God, we will shine like stars forever. To the Lord we will be like stars glittering in the dark. Before you can show someone the right way, you must first know it yourself. There is only one right way, and that is the way of Jesus Christ. We are taught this way in the Bible.

Let's tell people about Jesus, and let's lead the way to Him. Then we will always shine like the stars!

"Someone `like a son of man,' [was] dressed in a robe reaching down to his feet and with a golden sash around his chest. ... In his right hand he held seven stars" *(Revelation 1:13, 16).*

1 June

It Was a Miracle!

The Israelites went up out of Egypt armed for battle (Exodus 13:18).

It has been calculated that more than two million people took part in the Exodus out of Egypt! This is quite awesome, don't you agree? Poor old Moses and Aaron must have had their hands full, trying to get everyone organized.

The Israelites were slaves in Egypt for more than four hundred years. When the Lord decided to set them free, He gave Moses the job of leading them out of Egypt. Moses was already eighty years old at the time. Imagine him standing there, facing Pharoah, demanding that his people be allowed to move out. The Egyptian king didn't want to at first, but then the Lord sent ten devastating plagues. At last he was finally forced to give in.

The book of Exodus (which means "going out") tells us how the Israelites left Egypt and all about the forty years they traveled around in the desert. Moses organized everything very well when they moved from place to place and set up camp there. The Israelites didn't always listen to him, though. They sometimes forgot that the Lord had appointed him and that he had authority over them. Remember, the Lord also appoints leaders over you. Perhaps you are a leader in some way yourself. Never forget that both leaders and followers have to obey the Lord.

Are you a leader?

2 June

You Must Be Holy

"Be holy because I, the Lord your God, am holy" (Leviticus 19:2).

If you page through the book of Leviticus, you will read rules, rules, and more rules.

The rules in the book of Leviticus were given to lead the people to God. The Lord wanted – then and now – for people to live holy lives. The word holy means set apart (for God). It's not necessary for us anymore to follow a whole set of rules to be holy. If you believe that Jesus Christ is your Redeemer, you are already holy.

An important rule that is repeated often in the book of Leviticus is one about the forgiveness of sin. The people of the Old Testament needed to bring offerings and sacrifices because the blood of animals helped to pay for the sins of the people. Since Jesus came, these offerings are not necessary anymore. When His blood was shed on Golgotha, He became the last offering in the place of all of us. So if you believe in Him, God forgives your sins because Jesus was sacrificed. Every Christian should show gratitude by living a life set apart for God.

Can people tell from the way you live that you have been set apart for God?

3 June

If I Were a Rich Man ...

"You still lack one thing. Sell everything you have and give to the poor, and you will have treasure in heaven. Then come, follow me" (Luke 18:22).

Once upon a time there was a little boy who lived in an ordinary little house in an ordinary part of town (maybe even on the wrong side of the tracks), with ordinary furniture and an ordinary (old) car, with his or her very ordinary parents and brothers and sisters.

He couldn't handle his very ordinary circumstances. He so badly wanted to be rich and have everything his friends at school had: bicycles, CDs, computers, cool clothes, and nonstop access to the Internet.

Children often think that possessions and status are the most important things in life, and they blame their parents if they don't have a lot of things. They forget that their parents know and understand how they feel. Most parents would do anything to give their children what they want. But if there's not enough money, then there's not enough money! Children must remember that the most important things in life are not things. How are you doing with what you have?

Paul wrote to the young man Timothy: "For we brought nothing into the world, and we can take nothing out of it" (1 Timothy 6:7).

4 June

When Is
Someone a Christian?

The disciples were called Christians first at Antioch (Acts 11:26).

What would you say if you had to give a definition of a Christian? The first Christians were given this specific name because they believed in Jesus Christ. So we can say that every child of God is a Christian. Do you know who God's children are? We find the answer to this question in John 1:12: "To all who received him, to those who believed in his name, he gave the right to become children of God."

Two words are important here: receive and believe. To receive Jesus means to choose Him, to invite Him into your life as your personal Savior. It means that you love Him, obey Him, and serve Him. It means that you don't do the things you want to do anymore but what your Bible tells you to.

To believe in Jesus is to know for sure – even if you can't see it – that Jesus is the Son of God and that He died on a cross so that you can be God's child and have eternal life. If you believe all of this, then you are a Christian, but that doesn't automatically make you a disciple. In the course of this book we are going to see what it means to be Jesus' disciple.

There is a good definition of faith in Hebrews 11:1. Underline it in your Bible.

5 June

Our Daily Bread

"Man does not live on bread alone, but on every word that comes from the mouth of God" (Matthew 4:4).

"**G**ood night, Mom," Kate said as she came out of the bathroom. "Please wake me up at about seven tomorrow."

Mom replied, "I thought you wanted me to wake you earlier now so that we can read something from the Bible together."

"Aw, does it really matter if we skip just one morning?" Kate said. "I'm tired tonight. We can catch up some time this week."

Kate's mother didn't say anything. The next morning she woke Kate up at seven o'clock, but Kate went right back to sleep. When she eventually started to get dressed, it was one big rush to finish in time. She ran into the kitchen to snatch a quick breakfast. But the table wasn't laid. There was also no sign of the sandwiches her mother usually made her for lunch. She stared at her mother who was paging through the newspaper.

"I thought it wouldn't matter if we skipped breakfast one day. I was really tired this morning. We can make up for it some time later this week," her mother said, stifling a yawn.

Kate got the message, loud and clear. "Can we read the Bible together this afternoon after volleyball practice?" she asked softly.

"Sure," Mom answered, slipping a sandwich into Kate's school bag.

Both your spirit and your body need nourishment every day.

6 June

The Bible Is Like a Mirror

How can a young man keep his way pure? By living according to your word (Psalm 119:9).

How many times a day do you look in the mirror? If you're a girl, definitely more than once! But even boys look in the mirror at least once a day. You look in the mirror to check on your hair and to make sure everything is in place.

Has it ever occurred to you that the Bible is like a mirror? It's true. When you read it, you realize that some things in your life are not in place. Perhaps you read the parable of the Good Samaritan, and suddenly you realize that you are exactly like the priest and the Levite in the story. They were too busy to help a poor man in need. And you realize you also are often too busy to pay attention to someone who is suffering.

When you look in the mirror and you see something about yourself that's not quite right, you fix it right away, don't you? Let's use the Lord's "mirror" regularly, and ask Him to help us fix everything that is wrong in our lives.

God's word reflects, like a mirror, everything that is wrong in our lives.

7 June

The Cloud over You

He guided them with the cloud by day (Psalm 78:14).

When the Israelites were in Egypt, they were slaves. They worked very hard and had no freedom. Then the Lord sent Moses to bring them out of Egypt. They had to travel through the desert where the heat of the blazing sun was so bad it was dangerous. But every day the Lord sent them a large cloud that traveled with them. Actually, the cloud guided them. Sometimes the cloud came to a stop, and then they also had to stop. As soon as the cloud started moving again, they had to pack up and go. The cloud protected them from the heat of the sun and gave welcome shade.

Even today, the Lord wants to guide us. Although there are lovely clouds in the sky and they sometimes give us welcome shade from the sun, He no longer uses them to lead us. He uses the Holy Spirit now. He lives in us and leads us according to the Word of God. All we need to do is follow where He leads, like the Israelites followed the cloud; then we will arrive safely where the Lord wants us to be.

The Bible says: "Those who are led by the Spirit of God are sons of God" *(Romans 8:14).*

8 June

The Church Building Is a Sign

"You will have these tassels to look at and so you will remember all the commands of the LORD, that you may obey them ... by [not] going after the lusts of your own hearts and eyes" (Numbers 15:39).

There is no better teacher than the Lord! He understands us so well. He knows we will remember so much better if we are given an outward sign that we can see.

In the Old Testament, He told the people to sew tassels on their clothes. Every time they saw these tassels they were to think about His commandments. This would help them not to think about or give in to sinful things.

Have you ever thought that a church building is also a sign of the Lord? The building reminds us of Jesus and what He did for us. So don't look at a church as just another building. It is made of bricks and mortar, but at the same time it is an important sign to everybody who looks at it. Of course it's true that God does not live in a building, and yet a church is the place where God can be served in a special way. That is why we also call it "the house of the Lord."

Next time you are in church, think about Jesus and what He did for you.

9 June

Why Must We Die?

For as in Adam all die, so in Christ all will be made alive (1 Corinthians 15:22).

One thing in life we know for sure is that eventually every one of us will die; there's no getting away from it. If you read the newspapers and watch the news, you see that many people die every day.

Why? Why did God make us just to die again?

Well, this was not exactly what God had in mind. The Bible tells us that God made human beings to live in peace with Him without having to fear death. It's too bad that Adam and Eve were disobedient, and the punishment for their sin was death. So, death is our enemy.

Job calls death the "king of all fears." We are all afraid of dying or that someone we love will die. But in a way, for Christians, death is a blessing in disguise, through Jesus Christ. He came to earth to defeat death, because He was dead and came alive again. He overcame death. He obeyed His Father till His dying moments so that we need not fear death. He counteracted Adam's disobedience, and now we can look forward to life after death.

Even if we don't like thinking about death, for Christians it is the door to a new life.

10 June

What Does a Disciple Look Like?

"If you hold to my teaching, you are really my disciples"
(John 8:31).

The Greek word from which we get the English word "disciple" can be translated as "follower." Therefore, when we say that someone is one of Jesus' disciples, we mean that they follow in Jesus' footsteps. Once you have accepted Jesus as your Savior, your whole life should be lived for His glory and to honor Him.

Disciples are willing and prepared to show how much they love Jesus by the way that they think and talk and act. They live the way that Jesus said we should, and follow His example. As you read through the Bible you will learn about how Jesus loved and worshiped the Father, and how He loved and cared for people. He was prepared to die for the people He loved.

It isn't always easy to be a disciple. It means laying aside your own ideas about how to live your life, and letting God lead and guide you in all things. Sometimes other people might not understand that you want to do the things of the Lord rather than the things they want to do, but the joy of serving Jesus is greater than anything the world can offer us. Are you prepared to follow in the footsteps of Jesus every day of your life, to follow where He leads you, and to do what He tells you to do in the Bible? Then your life will have purpose and meaning and be filled with the joy of the Lord.

Read in Matthew 4:18-21 how Jesus chose His first disciples and what they gave up to follow Him.

11 June

How Should We Pray?

We do not know what we ought to pray for, but the Spirit himself intercedes for us (Romans 8:26).

A teacher tells the story of a twelve-year-old boy who told her he had never prayed. He wanted to know how it's done. I'm sure you've prayed often, but how would you answer this young boy's question?

She told him, "Praying is talking to the Lord. Even if you are not sure what to say when you're talking to such an important person, the Lord will understand what you want to say. Think about the Lord when you pray and tell Him everything you would say if He was right there with you. Because the truth is, He is there with you and He hears every word you say."

"You can tell Him that you love Him and would like to know Him better. You can thank Him for everything He gives you. You can also say you're sorry about all the things you do wrong, and then you can pray for others and for yourself. You may ask Him anything you like, and you can be sure that He will take you seriously. The Lord will grant your request unless He has a very good reason not to. And whatever His answer is, you can be sure there's a good reason for it."

The Lord is pleased when we talk to Him.

12 June

One Big Family

There before me was a great multitude that no one could count, from every nation, tribe, people and language (Revelation 7:9).

There are billions of people all over the world. Each one of us is different. Cultures and nations differ from other nations or cultures. Some people have dark skin, others have light, and just think of how many different languages they speak!

The Lord loved the world so much that He sent Jesus to save people from their sin and from hell. Everyone who believes in Him will live forever and become part of His big family. So the Lord has children in South Africa, China, Japan, America, Europe, South America – all over the world.

All God's children are brothers and sisters, and they must care for one another and love one another. Even if they look different, their hearts look the same – they belong to the Lord. Let's love each other just as much as the members of the early church that we read about in Acts. They accepted and helped one another.

The Bible says: "Love one another. By this all men will know that you are my disciples, if you love one another" *(John 13:34-35).*

13 June

To Whom Does Your Heart Belong?

Love the LORD your God with all your heart and with all your soul and with all your strength (Deuteronomy 6:5).

Our text says you must love the Lord with all your heart, all your soul, and all your strength. Jesus called this the first commandment. (See Matthew 22:37-39.) This means that believers want to belong to the Lord with all they have and all they are.

When you read on in Deuteronomy 6, you will learn that it is the duty of parents to speak to their children about the Lord. If your parents do this, you are very fortunate. But not all parents believe in Jesus or talk to their children about these things. If this is your situation, you must be strong. If you are a believer, you have a personal responsibility to live like a child of the Lord, especially towards your parents.

Our love for Jesus needs to show in our lives. You see, just reading the Bible is not good enough; you have to do what you have learned from it. If you belong to the Lord with all your heart and all your soul and all your strength, there's no way it won't show in your life. How do you think others "read" your life? Do they see you as someone who truly loves the Lord with all your heart and soul and strength or not?

It might be time to make a few changes in your life. You can do it today.

14 June

The Day the Sun Stood Still

"O sun, stand still over Gibeon, O moon, over the Valley of Aijalon" (Joshua 10:12).

The Bible makes a point of telling us about the miracles that God performed. The day the sun stood still is a good example. The book of Joshua is all about the way the Israelites conquered the Promised Land.

One day Joshua and his men fought against five Amorite kings. The Lord encouraged His people not to be afraid of the enemy. "I have given them into your hand," the Lord told Joshua. The battle took a very long time, so Joshua called on the Lord to help them. It was then that the Lord made the sun stand still, giving them more time to fight. In addition, the Bible says that the moon also did not move until Israel had conquered the enemy. Joshua and his army soon found out that it was the Lord who was fighting the battle for Israel.

This is an example of an unusual miracle. To believers like you and me, however, the sunrise or new buds appearing on a plant are also miracles. Yes, the miracles have not stopped. Just keep your eyes open, and you will see miracles taking place around you day after day.

We worship a God who performs miracles!

15 June

When Mom and Dad Get Divorced

"Therefore what God has joined together, let man not separate" (Mark 10:9).

"D ivorce granted!" These words echo in courtrooms countless times each day. Divorce is one of the most heartbreaking things a child can experience. Probably the parents of many of your friends are divorced. Perhaps your parents are divorced.

How does a kid learn to live with this painful situation without making things even worse?

- Accept the fact that it is not your fault. Nothing you did or said led to the divorce.
- Don't complicate matters. It's a difficult time for you, but your parents are finding it even more difficult. They have to accept that their marriage failed, and they must prepare the children for it. Important decisions must be made, like where to stay and what's going to happen to the children.
- Don't bottle up your feelings. Tell someone you trust how you feel. If you're angry, say so. If you're sad, cry. Don't shut your parents out. They worry about you. Your attitude is not going to change the situation.
- Support a friend who is in this situation. Be a shoulder to cry on when your friend is sad.

Make up your mind now that one day your marriage will not end in divorce.

16 June

Characteristics
of a Disciple

"If anyone comes to me and does not hate his father and mother, his wife and children – yes, even his own life – he cannot be my disciple. And anyone who does not carry his cross and follow me cannot be my disciple" (Luke 14: 26-27).

A disciple worth his or her salt has three characteristics:
- A disciple is prepared to give her own interests second place.
- A disciple is prepared to carry his cross and follow Jesus.
- A disciple is prepared to give up all her possessions.

Is the Lord the most important person in your life? Or are there still other things, like your schoolwork or sports, that are more important to you than the kingdom of God?

To carry your cross means that you will be prepared to suffer on His account and that you will be a witness, even if your friends sometimes make fun of you because you are not prepared to do the things they want you to.

A disciple's possessions are not everything to him. He is prepared to contribute to the kingdom of God.

Now you know the three characteristics of a disciple – do you think you will pass the discipleship test?

Why couldn't the young man pass the discipleship test? (See Luke 18:22-24.)

17 June

Do You Have to Kneel When You Pray?

Three times a day he got down on his knees and prayed, giving thanks to his God, just as he had done before (Daniel 6:10).

Elaine carried her teacher's bag to the staff room for her. "Do you think it's necessary to kneel and close your eyes and fold your hands when you pray?" Elaine asked her teacher. In class they had read the story of how Daniel regularly knelt in prayer at the window facing Jerusalem. The teacher had also told them that Muslims bow and pray five times a day, facing the direction of Mecca. Buddhists sit in the lotus position when they go to the temple to meditate about life.

"No, I don't think God minds," the teacher replied. "But it might make a difference to you."

"In what way?" Elaine wanted to know.

"Well, your thoughts follow your body's example. If you lie back in a chair while you pray, it makes no difference to the Lord. He's not lazy or disinterested. But you might be lazy, and your mind might wander. It might have an influence on what you tell Him and also what you hear Him tell you. In any case, we must remember that God is holy, and if you kneel before Him, you show Him the necessary respect. But this does not mean you shouldn't talk to Him when you're sitting or lying down or walking down the road!"

We kneel when we pray to honor God.

18 June

Pray in Jesus' Name

"My father will give you whatever you ask in my name"
(John 16:23).

Many people believe that prayer has some kind of magic power. Muslims each have a rosary, which is a string of ninety-nine beads. Every bead on the string represents one of Allah's names. They believe if they have this string of beads with them when they pray, their prayers will have special strength. This reminds me of the little boy who said the Lord's Prayer fifty times, hoping this would give the Lord enough reason to make his dog better.

When Jesus tells us to pray in His name, it doesn't mean that "in the name of Jesus" are magic words. We can't pray for anything we like and then just say "in the name of Jesus" to make our wishes come true! That would make prayer the same as when a magician says "abracadabra" before he pulls a rabbit out of his hat. Remember, Jesus is not a magician. The Bible tells us to pray in His name because we are too sinful to stand before God with our requests.

The only reason we may approach God is because Jesus paid for our sins. Like one little girl put it, "I was naughty so I went and hid behind Jesus!" To hide behind Jesus when we pray is to pray in His name. Then we need not be shy, or afraid of God.

Because you ask in the name of Jesus, God hears your prayer.

19 June

It's Okay to Disagree

Barnabas wanted to take John. ... but Paul did not think it wise. ... They had such a sharp disagreement that they parted company (Acts 15:37-39).

Paul and Barnabas were friends. They worked together. They enjoyed each other's company, traveled together, and shared many good times. Of course they differed. Each had his own tastes, and they sometimes disagreed on matters. The verse above says that in one matter they disagreed so sharply that each went his own way. Perhaps they were still friends, just not best friends anymore.

Because we each have a unique personality; we also sometimes disagree. It's OK. We can be friends with someone without agreeing about everything. But if we disagree, we must disagree in love. Actually we should agree to disagree! If we get angry with each other just because we don't agree about something, then the devil wins.

The Bible says: "As iron sharpens iron, so one man sharpens another" (Proverbs 27:17).

20 June

The Lord Uses Ordinary People

"My clan is the weakest in Manasseh, and I am the least in my family" (Judges 6:15).

Many of us think the Lord chooses brave heroes to serve Him. You might get the same idea when you read the book of Judges. We are told about the courageous men and women who led the Israelites when they conquered the Promised Land.

Fortunately the Bible also tells us about Gideon. The Lord wanted to use him to save Israel out of the hand of the Midianites. It was then that Gideon spoke the famous words of the verse above. By saying this, he wished to make it very clear that he did not come from an important family and that he himself was just a plain and simple person.

As soon as the Lord took Gideon into His strong hand, he suddenly became a courageous hero and a good leader. Perhaps the Lord wants to use you in the community where you live or in the school you go to. Then you must make sure you are available – even if you think you are not important enough. Be thankful that, as an ordinary person, you don't have to rely on your own strength. If the Lord wants to use you, He will give you the strength you need. Just be available.

Be available if the Lord wants to use you.

21 June

A Good Strategy

Do not be misled: "Bad company corrupts good character"
(1 Corinthians 15:33).

It's not easy to say no to friends when they are asking you to do things that are wrong. But remember, you're on your way to adulthood. If you want to be an adult with healthy values and a bright future and not ruin things by making stupid mistakes, then you need to start practicing making the right decisions. Here are a few hints:

- Make a list of things that are important to you. Write down what you believe. For example, "Because I respect my body, I will never take drugs, no matter what my friends decide."
- Always be true to yourself. True friends will never force you to do anything that is against your principles.
- Let your no be no, and your yes, yes. You don't owe anyone an explanation.
- Remember, prevention is better than cure. Avoid situations that can get you into trouble. If you know that a certain group's parties tend to get out of hand, then stay away from them.
- Look critically at your group of friends. If the friends you hang out with are bugging you all the time to do things you don't want to, it could be time to make new friends.
- Birds of a feather flock together. Make friends with kids who think like you do.
- Pray. Jesus promised to give good things to those who ask. Make use of this offer, and ask Him to open your eyes to the kind of person who would be a good friend for you.

Birds of a feather flock together.

22 June

Disciples
Think Differently

To be made new in the attitude of your minds; and to put on the new self, created to be like God in true righteousness and holiness (Ephesians 4:23, 24).

Disciples not only live differently than ordinary people, but they also think differently. All sin we commit starts in our thoughts. If the thought of doing something you shouldn't comes into your mind, you have not done anything wrong until you decide to do it and act on that.

To be a disciple, you first need to get your thoughts right. Focus your thoughts on *"whatever is right, whatever is pure, whatever is lovely"* (Philippians 4:8). Also, you need to recognize the wrong thoughts immediately, and concentrate on not paying attention to these thoughts.

What do you think about when you're alone? Would it be OK with you if all your friends could read your thoughts? Even if people can't do this, the Lord knows exactly what goes on in your mind. If you want to be Jesus' disciple, start with your thoughts and teach yourself to think only those thoughts that will please the Lord. Ask the Holy Spirit to purify your thoughts, so that from today on, they will be thoughts suitable for a disciple.

With what does the writer of Proverbs compare your thoughts? (See Proverbs 27:19.)

23 June

Pray for Others

I urge ... that requests, prayers ... be made for everyone (1 Timothy 2:1).

The Bible teaches us not to pray for ourselves only. Other people also need our prayers. Little children usually pray only for themselves. Once, a little girl was asked to pray for her friends, so she prayed, "Lord, help my friends to be good friends to me." Later on, one learns to care for others as well and to pray for them.

Here's a nice way to remember who to pray for. Use your right hand, and let each finger remind you of someone you want to pray for. The thumb points to you. So you pray for those close to you: parents, brothers and sisters, family, and friends. The pointer finger reminds you of someone who shows others the way. So you pray for pastors, church leaders, teachers, and missionaries. The middle finger is the tallest. Now you pray for important people: the leaders of our country, for example. Then follows the weakest fourth finger. When you look at it, you can remember people you know who are sick, those who suffer, and those with problems. Your prayers for them can make a difference. The pinkie is the smallest finger. This reminds you of yourself, so now you pray for yourself.

Who knows – with this plan, you might pray great joy into someone else's life one day!

Don't pray for yourself only!

24 June

Two Are Better

Two are better than one. ... If one falls down, his friend can help him up (Ecclesiastes 4:9-10).

Do you know the song that says, "He ain't heavy, he's my brother"? The story goes that the songwriter composed this song after seeing a little boy carry his brother (who was much bigger than he was!) who had been hurt. When you care for someone, you don't mind doing things for him or her. That is what's so good about having a friend and being a friend – two are better than one. If one is in trouble, the other can help. If something heavy has to be carried, two have more strength to get the job done. If your friend doesn't know what to do, you can give advice.

People were not made to be alone and do everything alone. We need other people. We must not be too proud to ask others for help, and we must always be willing to help others.

The Bible says: "Carry each other's burdens, and in this way you will fulfill the law of Christ" *(Galatians 6:2).*

25 June

Make Your Choice!

"Where you go I will go, and where you stay I will stay. Your people will be my people and your God my God" (Ruth 1:16).

The book of Ruth tells a wonderful story. One thing that stands out is Ruth's loyalty towards her mother-in-law. Actually, it is quite a sad story. It's the story of a husband and wife who moved to another country with their two sons. There was no food in their own country because of a drought and famine.

After a while, the father died. Then later, the two boys, who married foreign women, also died. So the only ones left were the mother and her two daughters-in-law. Eventually the old woman decided to go back to her own country. When they had been walking for a while, she asked her two daughters-in-law if they wouldn't prefer staying with their own people, and she tried to send them back.

It was then that Ruth spoke the words of our text. We learn an important lesson from Ruth, that of loyalty towards your family, especially those who are closest to you. Are you loyal towards your family? Would you be prepared to stand by them in a crisis? You should sort this out for yourself right now, because when you are already in a crisis situation, it's too late to try to make up your mind.

Make sure where your loyalties lie.

26 June

Between Muscle-Mania and the Potbelly Brigade

Therefore let us leave the elementary teachings about Christ and go on to maturity (Hebrews 6:1).

If you want your body to be in good shape, you must exercise regularly. The writer of the letter to the Hebrews says the same is true of a Christian's spirit. On a scale of spiritual activity, there are two extreme poles. At one end you get Christians who are satisfied with their spiritual lives. They are the middle-aged guys with the potbellies.

At the other end you find those believers who are faithfully building their spiritual lives. Somewhere in between these two poles is the great majority, who exercise now and then but not very enthusiastically.

Draw a straight line on a sheet of paper. At one end draw a guy with big muscles, like a real power machine. At the other end draw someone with a paunchy stomach, someone from the potbelly brigade. Now draw yourself somewhere on the line. Do you have strong spiritual muscles, or are you taking it easy spiritually? Our verse says we must go on to spiritual maturity – that is, to get in shape and develop spiritually.

Where are you on the scale of spiritual fitness?

27 June

Against the Stream

Then Elijah said to them, "I am the only one of the LORD's prophets left, but Baal has four hundred and fifty prophets" (1 Kings 18:22).

Swimming upstream is not easy. You seem to be getting nowhere fast. It's much easier to swim with the current of the stream. You don't really know where you're headed, but the stream will eventually take you somewhere.

Someone who swims against the stream of society's values usually has a reason. A good reason for you to do this is if you've accepted God as your only Lord. Then, you will want to say no to the idolatry of fashion and fitness, the addiction to television or sports, and the worship of wealth.

In the Old Testament we read about the prophet Elijah who swam against the stream of prosperity and idolatry. Sick of the sinfulness of the people of God, he swam against the stream at Mount Carmel, where he faced the whole of Israel and scolded them for their sinful ways. Singlehandedly he stood before the four hundred and fifty prophets of Baal and challenged them to prove that their god lived. And he did all this while the wicked King Ahab and his wife Jezebel were planning to kill him.

If you want to go against the stream, you may lose a few friends but not your self-respect.

28 June

Disciples Keep Count!

"Suppose one of you wants to build a tower. Will he not first sit down and estimate the cost to see if he has enough money to complete it?" (Luke 14:28)

If your parents have just bought a new house or built one, then you know that you can't just buy any house you like. Before you buy, you must first make sure you can afford that house.

It's no good starting out as a disciple of Jesus and then throwing in the towel. Like someone who is buying a house, a disciple must also keep count carefully before deciding to become a devoted follower of Jesus, because this discipleship is not to be taken lightly. You can be sure that your journey will often be uphill, but you will have the Lord with you every step of the way!

God wants your everything; but then don't forget, God was prepared to give you His everything – He sent Jesus to suffer a cruel death on the cross so that you can live. Are you prepared to live for Him alone, starting now?

How will you manage to follow in Christ's footsteps? (See Hebrews 12:1-3.)

29 June

Bless Mom
and Bless Dad

Do not be anxious about anything, but in everything by prayer and petition, with thanksgiving, present your requests to God (Philippians 4:6).

It was time for bed, and Hilda was on her knees. "Lord, please bless us all. Amen." She took one leap, and was under the covers. But her mother had something to say.

"What do you mean when you say, 'Lord, bless us all'?" she wanted to know.

"Aw, Mom, you know!" Hilda answered. "I'm asking the Lord to be good to everybody and to take care of them."

"What do you want the Lord to do for them?" her mother asked.

"Well, I want the Lord to help Dad at work, and to make your headaches better, and to help Grandpa and Grandma to be happy in the nursing home."

"So, why don't you tell the Lord this?"

"Should I? But He knows everything already," Hilda said.

Her mother explained, "The Lord loves us, and He wants us to speak to Him. If we just say a few words, we often don't even think about the Lord or about the people we're praying for. Then it's just words. And anyway, if we ask for specific things, we can see much better how the Lord answers our prayers!"

"All right, no more quick prayers!" Hilda said and gave her mom a goodnight hug.

We must not rush when we pray.

30 June

Believe When You Pray!

But when he asks, he must believe and not doubt (James 1:6).

Someone once wrote a book about the wonderful ways in which prayers have been answered. They are all true stories, and it is really amazing to see how the Lord works. Some of the stories make you smile.

Listen to this one: A poor widow can't pay her rent. It's the end of the month, and the landlord is coming for the money today. What should she do? She decides to eat nothing all day and just read her Bible and pray. The Lord just might have mercy on her and help in some way! While she is still on her knees, the front door bell rings. "It must be the landlord!" she thinks. She keeps very quiet. The doorbell rings again and again, but she makes no move to open the door.

The next day at church, the minister asks the widow, "Where were you yesterday? I came to your house to bring you a check one of the elders asked me to give you!" She takes the envelope from the minister, and when she opens it, she sees that it is more than enough to pay her rent!

Do you also sometimes pray for something, but you can't believe the Lord can answer your prayer? Never underestimate the Lord. He gives even more than we ask for.

When we pray, we need to believe that nothing is impossible for God.

1 July

The Gate

F·R·O·G· F·R·O·G· F·R·O·G·

"I am the gate" (John 10:7).

In order to see a movie or a concert, you first have to pay for a ticket at the entrance. If you can't go through the gate, you miss everything. There are also doors at the entrance to our houses. We feel safe and comfortable inside, protected from the cold or dangers lurking outside.

There are two kingdoms in the world: the kingdom of darkness and the kingdom of light. All people are born in the kingdom of darkness. But Jesus came to establish a new kingdom: the kingdom of light. Before we can live there, we must first go inside. Now where do we find the entrance? Well, it is Jesus Himself! He is the door or the gate. If we believe in Him, accept Him as our Redeemer, and make Him the King in our lives, then it is as if the gate of His kingdom just swings open for us to walk in. Then we are not standing outside anymore. Then we are safe. Then we belong to Him.

The Bible says: "No one comes to the Father except through me" *(John 14:6).*

2 July

The Lord Was Pleased with Solomon's Choice

"So give your servant a discerning heart to govern your people and to distinguish between right and wrong. For who is able to govern this great people of yours?" (1 Kings 3:9).

Go back to the verse above and read again what Solomon asked of the Lord. In the next verse, the Bible says that the Lord was pleased that Solomon had asked for this. He wanted to listen for the voice of the Lord so that he could do what the Lord wanted him to.

Tell me, what would you choose if the Lord gave you the chance today to ask Him for anything you want? Would it be a request He would be pleased to grant you?

You see, in Solomon's case, the Lord was pleased with what the young king requested. So, God gave him much more than he had asked for. On top of it all, he was also promised a long life.

I want to suggest that you also ask the Lord for help to follow Him fully. One way to do this would be to pray for help to be obedient to Him, to your teachers, and to your parents. Of course it is not always easy. If, however, you ask the Lord to make you obedient, obedience becomes a way of life. And then it is easy.

Is it important to you to obey the Lord?

3 July

Listen with Your Heart, Body and Mind

"My son ... you are always with me, and everything I have is yours" (Luke 15:31).

There is no one so deaf as a person who will not hear. If you only pretend to listen, you might as well forget having a good relationship with anyone, especially your parents.

But if you decide to really listen, try the following:

- Pay attention when your parents speak. Listen to what they say and don't say. It's the unspoken messages that are often a stumbling block.
- Don't interrupt. First hear what they have to say before you reply.
- Put yourself in their shoes. What would you have done if you were in their position? Accept that your parents want only the best for you, even if it seems that they just want to spoil your fun.
- In one ear and out the other? Repeat what they have said to you so you are sure you understand.
- To have a proper conversation is not always easy but is definitely worth it. Your reward? A good, comfortable, open relationship with your parents in which you can discuss anything that bothers you in a mature way.

Read the parable of the lost son in Luke 15. The message we see in the father's words is quite clear: he loves his son without reserve – the way God loves us.

4 July

Disciples Are Hard-Working!

I went past the field of the sluggard [lazy person] ... the ground was covered with weeds (Proverbs 24:30-31).

The house and garden of a lazy person never look nice. When a house is untidy and a garden is overgrown with weeds, it's plain to see that the people who live there are not fond of working. One can also be spiritually lazy. You can sleep so late in the mornings that there's not enough time left for the Lord in your day. Disciples must make sure they are never lazy.

"A little sleep, a little slumber, a little folding of the hands to rest – and poverty will come on you" (Proverbs 24:33-34). Do you like your sleep? If you want to be a disciple, you will have to try, from now on, to get up a little earlier in the morning, or take time at night before bed, to make time for Jesus – time to talk to Him in prayer and time to read your Bible.

Why don't you ask your parents to buy you a book with daily devotions and use it every day. In this way you will get to know the Lord better, and also win a victory over spiritual laziness!

Do you think Jesus was also lazy at times? (See Luke 6:12.) How much time did He spend in prayer?

5 July

The Power of Prayer

The prayer of a righteous man is powerful and effective (James 5:16).

A world-famous nuclear scientist, Dr J. Courtland, once said that prayer is the greatest power in the universe. He knew everything about electric currents and atomic energy, yet as a Christian, he realized that the power of God is much, much stronger. And when we pray, we get to see God's power at work.

When you pray, your prayer goes to God. He sees everything on earth. He hears your requests and has the power to grant them.

It could happen that you pray for someone who is ill, and then God helps that person to feel better. Or if you pray for a missionary one morning, God might help him to feel much more positive about the difficult work he is doing. You can also ask the Lord to help you with a difficult task, and then you can experience the peace and strength that God gives you.

This powerful weapon that is always at our disposal is really worth trying. We don't even need to learn a foreign language or dress in special clothes or look for a priest to pray for us. (Some religions set a lot of rules for the way people should pray!) We can pray in the name of the Lord wherever we are, and He will hear us!

The Lord uses our prayers to do wonderful things.

6 July

If You Fail ...

The Lord turned and looked straight at Peter. ... And he went outside and wept bitterly (Luke 22:61-62).

Peter was an ordinary fisherman. Then Jesus came and invited Peter to follow Him. Peter was with Jesus for three years.

Peter wanted to follow Jesus, and he did. But Peter also had his faults. One of the biggest mistakes he made was thinking he would never make a mistake! He told Jesus he would never let Him down. But when the angry crowds came to capture Jesus, Peter ran away. Later on, he pretended not to know Jesus because he was scared they would capture him, too. Peter acted like a coward. He disowned Jesus.

But Jesus loved Peter, even though he had faults. Later on, Jesus went to Peter and encouraged him to follow Him again. "Feed my sheep," Jesus said to him. And he did. On the day of Pentecost the Holy Spirit came to live in Peter's heart, and Peter told all the people about Jesus. He did not try to hide anything anymore.

You and I also disappoint the Lord sometimes. We must just apologize every time we have sinned, like Peter did.

The Bible says: "If we confess our sins, he ... will forgive us our sins" (1 John 1:9).

7 July

Listen to the Advice of Older People

F.R.O.G. F.R.O.G. F.R.O.G.

But Rehoboam rejected the advice the elders gave him and consulted the young men who grew up with him and were serving him (2 Chronicles 10:8).

When King Solomon died, his son Rehoboam became king in his place. The people came to him and complained about the heavy taxes they had to pay. Rehoboam sent them away and told them to come back in three days' time.

During this time he asked the advice of older and experienced people who had served his father. They suggested that he should make the people pay less. Rehoboam was not satisfied with this advice and also asked his younger friends who grew up with him. They advised him to make the people pay even more. When they came back to the king in three days' time, he followed the advice of his young friends. Because they were now even more heavily taxed, a rebellion started, and the nation was divided.

Here we have an example of a young man who listened to the wrong advice. People with more experience usually give us better advice than inexperienced younger ones. Learn a lesson from this story, and don't make the same mistake. After all is said and done, your parents and other older people have a lot of wisdom.

Whose advice do you ask?

8 July

Don't Let Lies Scare You

I sent him this reply: "Nothing like what you are saying is happening; you are just making it up out of your head"
(Nehemiah 6:8).

Nehemiah was a builder and a famous leader of the people. He was one of those in charge of rebuilding the walls of Jerusalem. This project was certainly not without its problems. People tried in all kinds of ways to put a hole in their plans and to make Nehemiah and the men who were helping him the laughingstock of the town.

One way they did this was to spread rumors in letters about Nehemiah. In response, Nehemiah said to a certain letter writer: "Nothing you say is true. You are making up these stories." (See Nehemiah 6:8 above.)

There are many jealous people. When you are good in sports, do well in your schoolwork, or are liked by your teachers, don't be too surprised if rumors are spread about you as well – stories that people make up to hurt you. Don't let that bother you; instead, be like Nehemiah. His behavior made other people realize that he and his helpers were doing their work with the help of God. (See Nehemiah 6:16.) You can keep on doing the right thing in spite of the opposition of envious people. If you do your work according to the will of God, don't allow people who spread false rumors to scare you off.

The truth will always triumph over lies.

9 July

Keep Clear of the Devil

Satan rose up against Israel and incited David to take a census of Israel (1 Chronicles 21:1).

These days we hear a lot about Satan worship and demon possession. It can be frightening. How do you, a child of Jesus, handle this type of thing? The best you can do is to stay as far away as possible from those who are involved in these activities.

Unfortunately, demonic possession and Satanism have become popular in our modern culture, often because of movies and television programs with these themes. This makes children curious, and some kids want to find out more about it.

The Bible teaches that it is possible to be possessed by demons, but it so rarely happens that you don't need to worry about it, unless, of course, you are playing around with witchcraft, tarot cards, or other satanic stuff. Always remember, it doesn't pay to fool around with the devil. He is the father of lies (See John 8:44.) and has led cleverer people than you astray. So just stay away from everything that has anything to do with Satan. Instead, try to live close to Jesus in prayer and in your way of life so that Satan cannot get a hold on you.

Even great heroes of the Bible were tempted by the devil. King David brought great suffering on his country because Satan tempted him into disobeying God. Read about it in 1 Chronicles 21.

10 July

Choose the Right Friends

As iron sharpens iron, so one man sharpens another (Proverbs 27:17).

As you get older, you will realize that friends play a very important role in your life. Sometimes you may be pressured to do the wrong thing just so you're not the oddball in the group. That's when you need friends who help to keep you on the straight and narrow path and who warn you when you are meddling with the wrong things.

Choose the right friends – friends you can pray with and who enjoy doing Bible study with you. It is better to steer clear of those friends whose activities are not in line with your principles. And be prepared to share with others that you know the Lord. Your friends are going to watch you closely once they know you're His disciple, so make sure you set the right example with what you say and do.

What about your best friends? Do they help or hinder you in serving the Lord? And are you helping them to become disciples as well?

What did Andrew do after spending a day with Jesus? (See John 1:40-42.) Are you going to do the same?

11 July

Surprise! Surprise!

And my God will meet all your needs (Philippians 4:19).

"Lord," Susan prayed, "please let my parents say yes when I ask them about going to the beach with Grace and her folks! It's going to be so quiet and boring here at home!"

But her parents didn't want her to go. "Your cousin from far away is visiting," her mom said. "You can't go away." Susan was very upset. It didn't seem as if the Lord even heard her prayer.

A few days later, Susan and her cousin were sitting on the back porch of their home. Suddenly it struck Susan that she had not even once wished to be with Grace and her family. She and her cousin were having such a good time that she had not been bored for a moment.

See? Sometimes the Lord's answer to your prayer is not the one you bargained on at all. He sees what you need and gives it to you in His own way. People who work for Trans World Radio, a worldwide Christian radio ministry, tell how they feverishly prayed for enough money to buy sand for a new radio station they were building in South Africa. But they received no money to get started on the building. Then one night there was a violent storm. The next morning they saw what the flood, caused by the heavy rains, had "delivered" to their building site – a big load of building sand!

God sometimes surprises us with His answers to our prayers!

12 July

Where Do You Stand?

So do not be ashamed to testify about our Lord (2 Timothy 1:8).

Clifford grew up on a farm. When he was finished with elementary school, he had to go away to a boarding school. He shared a room with five other boys. He did not like being so far from his parents, but he was a child of the Lord. He knew the Lord would never let him down.

At home he was in the habit of reading the Bible and praying at night before getting into bed. The first night at boarding school, his roommates were joking and fooling around, and he was a bit hesitant about taking out his Bible. What if they teased him? He wondered if he shouldn't slip out and go read the Bible someplace else. But then he said to himself, "Nonsense! I'm a Christian, and the sooner these guys know it, the better!"

He bravely opened his Bible, knelt down by the bed and started reading. Then he closed his eyes and prayed softly. It became very quiet in the room. He felt like a goldfish in a bowl. After a while the other boys started chatting and joking again. Nobody said anything about him. But the following night when he went down on his knees again, three other boys took out their Bibles and did the same.

Enthusiasm for Jesus is contagious.

13 July

Shape Me, Lord

"Like clay in the hand of the potter, so are you in my hand"
(Jeremiah 18:6).

The Lord sent Jeremiah to the house of the potter. Jeremiah saw the potter at his wheel, shaping the clay he had in his hand, but it didn't turn out the way he wanted. So the potter had to start all over again.

The Lord told Jeremiah that Israel was like that clay. He wanted to shape them, but they were disobedient and wouldn't do what He told them to. They said that they would live the way they wanted to. (See Jeremiah 18:12.) They had to be reshaped, just like that bad pot the potter had to remake.

The Lord wants to shape you, too. He wants you to be a success. Only the Lord knows the plans He has for your life. Allow Him to shape you. Be good clay in His hand, clay that will not crumble. Tell Him to shape and make you just the way He wants. If we allow Him to do this, we will be beautiful, useful instruments for Him to use.

The Bible says: "'For I know the plans I have for you,' declares the Lord, 'plans to prosper you and not to harm you'" *(Jeremiah 29:11).*

14 July

The Orphan Who Saved Her People

Mordecai had a cousin named Hadassah, whom he had brought up because she had neither father or mother. This girl who was also known as Esther was lovely in form and features (Esther 2:7).

If ever a beauty queen had to be chosen in the Old Testament, it would certainly have been Esther! The verse above tells us that not only was she an orphan, but she also was very lovely!

Esther lived in a very difficult time in the history of her people. Powerful enemies wanted to destroy all the Jews. But Esther was very determined that the Jewish people would take their rightful place in the community.

Fortunately, her Uncle Mordecai helped her. He encouraged her and helped her not to give up. Their greatest opponent was a man called Haman. In the end, thanks to Esther and her uncle, the king had Haman hanged instead of Mordecai.

Religious Jews to this day still read the book of Esther when they celebrate the Purim festival. She is one of the greatest heroines in Jewish history.

It just goes to show you that when a young person sticks to the truth, the Lord takes that person by the hand in a very special way. Esther never planned to be a heroine, but her actions of faith made her one.

If God is for us, who can be against us? (Romans 8:31)

15 July

Talk If You Want to Talk

"So his father went out and pleaded with him" (Luke 15:28).

Children often complain that they cannot communicate with their parents so, here are a few helpful tips for good communication:

- Always be honest. Don't say what your parents want to hear, just to put an end to the conversation.
- Listen to your parents, rather than saying things like, "You never listen to me," or, "You don't understand." Instead say, "I don't understand," or, "Explain, please."
- Try to compromise. It's not a matter of who wins; it's a matter of finding the best solution for all concerned.
- Stick to one point at a time. Don't drag the past and the future into the argument. Solve one problem at a time.
- Don't shout. Ranting and raving will usually end all chances of any sensible solution, for parents and children alike.

Children today are actually very lucky, because they are given the opportunity to speak and reason with their parents. In the past, children were regarded as possessions, and they had no say, not even when it concerned their own lives. So use this privilege with responsibility.

Read the story of the lost son in Luke 15. His father gave him all the freedom he needed and welcomed him back with open arms when he returned with nothing.

16 July

Disciples Bear Fruit

"This is to my Father's glory, that you bear much fruit, showing yourselves to be my disciples" (John 15:8).

The only way to find out what kind of fruit trees you have in your garden is to look at the fruit they bear. A tree that produces apricots is an apricot tree, and a tree that bears apples is an apple tree – we all know that. And disciples are like trees – they are known by their fruit.

If you are a disciple, the fruit of the Holy Spirit must show in your life. In Galatians 5:22, Paul describes this fruit as nine qualities. The Greek word used here is translated as "fruit" – one fruit – like a bunch of grapes with nine grapes on it. So you can't choose which of these qualities you want; the Holy Spirit wants to bear all these qualities in your life. If one is missing, there is something wrong with the fruit!

Write Galatians 5:22-23 in your notebook or journal, and check each quality that you are still lacking in your life: *"But the fruit of the Spirit is love, joy, peace, patience, kindness, goodness, faithfulness, gentleness and self-control."* Then try to make every one of these qualities part of your life.

There is just one way that you will manage to produce this fruit of the spirit in your life – John 15:4-5 tells you what this way is.

17 July

Bumper Stickers

"By this all men will know that you are my disciples, if you love one another" (John 13:35).

"**C**an you believe that bumper sticker?" Nick exclaimed to his mother as they drove to school.

"Yes, bumper stickers on a car say quite a lot about the person behind the steering wheel," his mom replied. "Look at that one," she said, pointing at a car in front of them. "Soccer Is My Life! He certainly makes no secret of the fact that he's a soccer fan."

"Look there!" Nick said pointing to a small van with the words 'Mom's Taxi' stuck on the window. Judging from the children's heads bobbing up and down in the car, they could see clearly what the car was used for.

The rest of the afternoon Nick and his mom read all the bumper stickers they saw and then decided what these stickers told them about the owner of the car. Some Christians have a fish sign on their cars to show that they want to be fishers of people.

But today's verse gives us the very best way to show we are Christians.

When people see love in your actions, they will guess that you belong to the Lord.

18 July

Signs along the Road

I meditate on your precepts and consider your ways (Psalm 119:15).

Road signs give us certain information. There is a road sign that tells us there's a rest stop ahead. Others indicate a gas station where we can fill up the car. Then there's a sign to tell us that there is a hospital or a police station at the next exit. We need this information, because it helps to make our journeys safe and comfortable.

The Bible also provides a lot of information to make our journey through life easier. There are things we need to know about the right way to live, about how to be happy, and about how to behave so that we honor the Lord. The Bible tells us that Jesus Christ is Lord, that is, King of all. If we know Jesus is the King, then we know to follow Him. The Bible also says the Holy Spirit came to help and guide us every day. That is good news! Furthermore, the Bible says that all the Christians in the world are like one great family and that we need one another. That's good to know. We need to read the Bible every day so that we can become familiar with all the Lord's road signs.

The Bible says: "Show me your ways, O Lord, teach me your paths" (Psalm 25:4).

19 July

Like a Moth's Cocoon

"The house he [the unbeliever/the wicked] builds is like a moth's cocoon" (Job 27:18).

We have a mulberry tree in our garden. Every season when it's time for the silkworm eggs to hatch, all the kids who live nearby come to pick mulberry leaves. As soon as the search for leaves comes to an end, we know the time has come for the silkworms to start spinning cocoons. The next step is when a pupa forms inside the cocoon, and later on a moth comes out of the cocoon. The cocoon has been a temporary home for the moth.

This is exactly what is said in our verse. Unbelievers – those who don't serve the Lord – think they will be around forever. This is not true. This world, like the moth's cocoon, is just temporary. In a short while the moth comes out and flies away. Job understood this very well. Wicked people may think they are clever and know it all, but in reality they are foolish and shortsighted. They are like moths that live in cocoons for a short while. In the heart of the God-fearing person lives another dream: everlasting life with God.

Are you like a moth in a cocoon, or do you dream of everlasting life with God?

20 July

Discipline Means Love

He who spares the rod hates his son, but he who loves him is careful to discipline him (Proverbs 13:24).

Do you know how difficult it is for a parent to discipline a child? Because parents love their children, they don't enjoy punishing them. The Bible, however, makes it clear that parents who love their children will see to it that their children are disciplined, in love, when necessary. So you mustn't be angry with your parents for doing this. This is just proof that they love you.

The next time you are being disciplined, sit down and ask yourself the question: "Why am I being punished?" Then ask yourself a second question: "Is it because my parents love me, or not?" You will make the surprising discovery that they discipline you because they love you. Loving, God-fearing parents never punish their children without a good reason.

Punishment is never unfair if it is motivated by love.

21 July

This Crazy World

Woe to those who call evil good and good evil, who put darkness for light and light for darkness, who put bitter for sweet and sweet for bitter (Isaiah 5:20).

Suppose your math teacher marked an addition problem wrong that was really right and marked wrong ones as right. You would be totally confused! In our world, many people do whatever they think is right. If it feels right, they do it.

They think that it doesn't really matter much if something is right or wrong, as long as it gives them pleasure. They make and break the rules to suit themselves. They become their own little tin gods. How does this happen?

- This happens when the Bible is thrown out and people make rules without answering to God.
- It happens when people take from the Bible what they choose to, because it suits them.

Even if God chose you to be His child, He gave you the freedom to choose what you want to do. The smart choice would be to hold tight to everything you read in the Bible, because it "is a trustworthy saying" (Titus 3:8).

Isaiah lived in times very much like ours, when God's people forgot all about His commandments and started believing that good was bad and bad was good. Isaiah prophesied that they would be destroyed completely, because they ignored the Word of God. (See Isaiah 5:24.)

Not long after this, the Jews were exiled to Babylon where they were slaves.

22 July

Disciples Love Others

"By this all men will know that you are my disciples, if you love one another" (John 13:35).

If you wear a special uniform to your school, people can immediately tell which school you go to by the colors and style of the uniform. Jesus says that love is like a uniform for a disciple of Jesus. People must be able to tell by your love for others whether you are really His disciple or if you are just pretending to be one. None of us can manage by ourselves to love others the way Jesus wants us to. We are all selfish by nature, and we want what's best for us. We come first and the rest come second!

But Jesus asks you to love others just as much as He loves you. God's love is the kind of love that is prepared to give up everything for the other, with no strings attached. It's the kind of love that puts the other person first every time – an unselfish type of love that expects nothing in return.

Would you say your friends can see this type of love in your life? If not, ask the Lord now to give you this love in your heart, so that you can pass it on to others you meet.

What are the two most important things that God's law wants from you? (See Matthew 22:37-40.)

23 July

Light for a Dark World

F.R.O.G. F.R.O.G. F.R.O.G.

"You are the light of the world. ... People [do not] light a lamp and put it under a bowl. Instead they put it on its stand, and it gives light to everyone in the house" (Matthew 5:14-15).

Andrew was ashamed. His friends at school had told dirty jokes, and he had joined in laughing with them. Actually he hadn't enjoyed it at all. But it's not so easy to stand up for what's right. Last week at Michael's party, he was the only one who got up and left when they started showing a video that was not meant for children. As he left the room he heard: "Poor little mama's boy can't stomach blood and gore!"

That night when his mother comes to say goodnight, Andrew told her everything. "I should have been a brave witness for Jesus!" he said.

"Let's pray about this!" his mom said. "Lord, if Andrew's friends do things they shouldn't again, please give him the courage to do the right thing, no matter how difficult it might be!" Mom squeezed his hand. She switched off the light, and Andrew lay in the dark, thinking about what she said. Suddenly he saw a small flame in the doorway. Andrew could see his mom clearly. She was standing there with a match in her hand. "Remember, it takes only one small flame to light up a whole room!" she said before closing the door.

Be a light and show people the difference between good and bad.

24 July

Be a Magnet for Christ

"But I, when I am lifted up from the earth, will draw all men to myself" (John 12:32).

Jesus said these words a few days before He was crucified. He meant that through His crucifixion, people would see how much He loves them. Then they would love and follow Him.

Have you seen how a magnet draws a pin to it? The moment the magnet is brought close, the pin just about jumps up towards the magnet and clings to it so tightly that it is quite a struggle to lift it off the magnet again. If the pin sticks to the magnet for a while, it also becomes a little magnet in itself. One can pick up other pins with it. But if it is removed from the magnet, it loses its ability to attract pins after awhile.

We can learn a lesson from this, because the Lord attracts us to Him with His love. We understand what He wants to tell us with His death on the cross – that He loves us – and we humbly kneel at the Cross. If we will only stay in contact with Him, then we can also attract others to Him. But if we forget about Him and don't serve Him in church or don't spend time with Him in our quiet time, we will lose our connection and not be able to draw others to Him.

Stay close to the Lord; then you will draw others to Him as well.

25 July

Stand or Fall

Do not gloat over me, my enemy! Though I have fallen, I will rise (Micah 7:8).

Before you can walk, you must first learn to walk. First you crawl, and then you try to get up and walk. Before you can walk well you fall quite a few times. In the same way that you fall down physically, so you can also fall in your heart. Every time you make a mistake because you made the wrong choice, you fall spiritually. Sin is when you and I have failed because we didn't do what God wanted us to. Sin makes us fall.

There is no one in this whole wide world who doesn't sometimes fall spiritually. Just think of the characters of the Bible: Adam and Eve failed; Samson made a mistake; David fell for Bathsheba; Peter disowned Jesus; Paul killed followers of Jesus; Jonah didn't want to go to Nineveh. So we see that there were many of them who failed.

But there is hope for all those who fall. The worst fall is the one we don't want to get up from. The Lord helps us to get up. Micah says "Even if I fall, I will get up again." He says he failed but will start again. Christians don't stay down. They get up in Jesus' strength and try again.

The Bible says: "So, if you think you are standing firm, be careful that you don't fall!" (1 Corinthians 10:12)

26 July

Enjoy Your Youth

Be happy, young man, while you are young (Ecclesiastes 11:9).

Isn't it great that the Bible tells you to enjoy your youth? Perhaps you have thought grown-ups always want to put a damper on the joys of being young. This is not what the Bible does. The Lord wants us to be joyful while we are young, and enjoy our youth to the full. But just remember: God will expect you to account for everything you do, whether done in public or secret, good or bad. (See Ecclesiastes 12:14.)

You are now in a very special phase of your life. This is a time where you don't have to be stressed out about grown-up stuff. Enjoy life and find pleasure in it. But remember that you remain responsible for what you do.

This means that you can't do just anything you like when you are young. You ought to do what the Lord expects you to. Then He will have a smile on His face when He meets you in heaven. Do you live like this every day?

Enjoy your youth, and build your life on God's will.

27 July

How Do I Know What's Wrong or Right?

Asa did what was right in the eyes of the LORD, as his father David had done (1 Kings 15:11).

There are times when I wish that life was like a math problem, where there is only one answer and you can know it. How do you know if you make the right choices when you have to decide on a moral issue? Ask yourself the following questions:

- Am I being obedient to God's commandments?
- Who will benefit most from my actions: me or others?
- What will happen if everyone starts doing it?
- What will the consequences of my actions be? Good or bad?
- Did I decide with my emotions or use my head?
- Did I ask advice from someone with more experience?
- Will my parents be proud of what I am doing?
- Did I pray about the matter?

Apply the above questions to the following situations:

- Gossipping about another student in class.
- Saying racist remarks aimed at a classmate.
- Cheating on a test.
- Lying to my parents about where I was after school.

In the two books of Kings in the Old Testament, we read about kings who did what was right and many who did what was wrong. What were the consequences of their actions?

All of us sometimes make the wrong decisions, but fortunately God forgives us every time we ask Him to.

28 July

Disciples Grow

Therefore let us leave the elementary teachings about Christ and go on to maturity (Hebrews 6:1).

Have you ever tried to ride your bicycle backwards or to stand still without pedaling? Both of these tricks are impossible. The only way you can ride a bicycle is to move forward. The same is true about a disciple of Christ. A disciple must never stand still in faith – or worse, backpedal. Disciples grow spiritually and become stronger in their faith every day.

A disciple grows in three main ways:

- By studying the Bible.
- By talking to God in prayer.
- By fellowship with other believers. (This means doing things with other children of the Lord.)

Sometimes when people are first converted to Christ, they are very enthusiastic at the beginning, but later on they get lazy. Make sure that, from now on, you spend enough time in Bible study and prayer and that you and your friends attend the activities your church offers young people. Then you will notice that you are a growing Christian, and your love for the Lord will also grow.

Who knew the Bible very well, even as a child? (See Timothy 3:15.)

29 July

Not Always Easy

In fact, everyone who wants to live a godly life in Christ Jesus will be persecuted (2 Timothy 3:12).

When you belong to the Lord, you will sometimes have a hard time. Those who don't love Jesus might not like you. Hopefully it will never happen that people will want to kill you because you are a Christian, but without a doubt, there will be people who will want to hurt you in different ways.

We read the wonderful story of Stephen, the first Christian to die for his faith. How did he manage to keep so calm when the people came down on him like a pack of hungry wolves and dragged him out of the city where they stoned him to death?

What was his secret? He kept his eyes on Jesus and didn't look at the cruel faces of the people, because he knew he would be with Jesus after his death. Many Christian martyrs managed to forgive the people who wanted to kill them. The story is told that one of them, George Wishart, kissed his executioner before he was hanged. "To show that I forgive you," he said.

If your friends make fun of you because you are a Christian, pray for them.

30 July

Stop Signs

If you fully obey the LORD your God and carefully obey all his commands ... all these blessings will come upon you (Deuteronomy 28:1-2).

The Lord speaks to us through His Word. When we read the Bible, there are things the Lord wants to tell us. One thing is that there are certain things we are not allowed to do. If we go against His Word, then we are looking for trouble. We can very easily get hurt or our lives can even be ruined.

There are traffic signs on our roads. One sign is the red traffic sign that says STOP. If you ignore a stop sign, you can crash into another car, and someone can get hurt. There are also many stop signs in God's Word that we must observe. For example, the Bible says: "You must not steal," "You must not kill," "You must not commit adultery," and so forth. These are red lights that tell us: "Don't!" If you ignore these red lights in the Bible, you are heading for trouble.

The Bible says: "The L*ORD God commanded the man, ' ... You must not eat from the tree of the knowledge of good and evil, for when you eat of it you will surely die'" (Genesis 2:16-17).*

31 July

Have You Ever Been in Love?

Catch for us the foxes, the little foxes, that ruin the vineyards, our vineyards that are in bloom (Song of Songs 2:15).

One day you notice a guy or a girl, and suddenly you have butterflies in your stomach! Has it ever happened to you? The book of Song of Songs is all about these kind of feelings.

The Lord meant for men and women to love one another and eventually get married. It's too bad that we live in a time where people don't always keep this in mind. Sometimes young people live together as if they are already married when they're not. This is when the "little foxes" that the verse above talks about can ruin the vineyards of the relationship. While you are still young, you mustn't do everything grown-ups do, because your time for that has not yet come.

You must also watch out that you don't break the Lord's rules in small ways. Eventually this, too, can ruin the whole vineyard – your whole life can be ruined by irresponsible behavior. This is why parents warn their children against all kinds of misleading beliefs and practices. You might feel they are overdoing it, but they mean well.

It is very important that you watch out for the little foxes that ruin the vineyard, especially in the times we live in.

1 August

The Lord Is a Holy God

And they [the seraphs] were calling to one another: "Holy, holy, holy is the LORD Almighty; the whole earth is full of his glory" (Isaiah 6:3).

The fact that the Lord is a holy God means that He is a wonderful God, different from everybody else. And this is how the Bible presents Him to us.

The day the Lord called Isaiah to be a prophet, Isaiah thought, "Now I've had it!" Isaiah felt unclean in the presence of God. It was then that a seraph flew to him with a glowing coal in his hand and touched his mouth with it to show that Isaiah had been made pure. By the way, it's only in Isaiah 6 that we read about seraphs. They are beings that praise God night and day.

You must never doubt that God is the Holy One. Watch that you don't talk about Him as if He is just an ordinary person. He is the Holy God. So that's a very good reason to talk about Him with great respect.

Today, praise the Lord as the holy God.

2 August

Death Is Real

"But now that he is dead, why should I fast? Can I bring him back again? I will go to him, but he will not return to me" (2 Samuel 12:23).

Sometimes children fantasize about death. Do you sometimes pretend or dream that you are dead and then imagine what others would say about you then? You might even imagine seeing your family crying over you. But when you get tired of the game, you are your chirpy self again and take life up where you left off.

When death really walks in the door and takes away someone you love very much, then the game is over, and you are left with the stark reality of death. That person is never coming back again.

When someone close to you dies, apart from the terrible heartache, you also have many questions: Why? Where was God when it happened? How will I manage without that person in my life? It is important to ask these questions. The sad part is that some of them don't have answers. But what you know for sure is that Jesus is there to help you accept your loss and, eventually, to carry on with your life.

Read the story of King David. When his son died, he realized that death is final and that he must carry on with life, until the day he and his loved ones would be together again in heaven.

Death will not have the last word because Jesus overcame death.

3 August

Disciples Are Soldiers

For our struggle is not against flesh and blood, but against the ... powers of this dark world and against the spiritual forces of evil in the heavenly realms (Ephesians 6:12).

Every disciple of the Lord Jesus is fighting a war. This battle is not against people but against Satan himself. If you don't watch out for the devil, you can easily get caught in his snare. He's the one who wants you to sin. He tempts you to be disobedient, bad-tempered, and impatient. He prompts you to fight with your brothers and sisters, and he's happy when you're just plain impossible to live with.

The devil is going to try every day to get you away from the Lord. He knows you well. He knows just where your weaknesses lie, and it's just there that he's going to attack. Unfortunately you have no chance to win a battle against the devil – he's much too strong for you. So be thankful that Jesus has already won the battle for you when He died on the cross and rose from the dead!

Although the devil is a dangerous enemy and you must beware of him every day, he is an enemy behind bars. In Jesus' strength you can manage to fight him off, time after time!

God gives His soldiers a suit of armor to wear in the battle against the devil.

4 August

There Are Two Roads

"Enter through the narrow gate. For wide is the gate and broad is the road that leads to destruction, and many enter through it. But small is the gate and narrow the road that leads to life, and only a few find it" (Matthew 7:13-14).

In these verses, Jesus is inviting us to take His road. This means that we must choose. We can't simply shrug our shoulders and play deaf. Even if one decides not to choose at all, it's the same as not choosing the Lord Jesus.

In this world, there are actually only two types of people: those on the narrow road following Jesus, and those on the broad road not following Him. But then there are many people who have never had the opportunity of hearing about Jesus, so they don't know they have a choice. They also don't know where the road they are on will take them.

We must help people all over hear the good news, the news that tells of a road to heaven. Maybe you could invite a non-believer to a church youth meeting where that person can learn more about Jesus. Or lend a friend a nice book about Jesus. How about giving a Bible or a bookmark with a verse from Scripture on it to the gas station attendant, the mailman, or the homeless person on the street? In addition, you could also tell people what Jesus means to you.

We can help others choose Jesus' road.

5 August

Everyone Must Hear

"But you will receive power when the Holy Spirit comes on you; and you will be my witnesses in Jerusalem ... and to the ends of the earth" (Acts 1:8).

In Brian's church the theme for the week was mission work. All the speakers at their Sunday church services and prayer meetings stressed the importance of going out to nations that have not been reached before. Not every member of the youth group agreed. "Why must people go to Thailand or Peru if there's so much work to do right here where we are?" one kid said. Eventually there was quite an argument. At home Brian spoke to his dad about this.

His father said, "Imagine if your Sunday school teacher decides one Sunday to give everyone in the front row a piece of candy. After a while the same children each get a chocolate, and when they have finished that, she gives them each a lollipop. What would you think of that?"

"I'd be mad as anything!" said Brian. "That wouldn't be fair!"

"Well, do you think it's fair that we want to hear the good news about Christ over and over here in our neighborhood while there are people who have never even heard it once?"

"Does this mean that I will have to be a missionary in a faraway country one day?" Brian wanted to know.

"No," Dad answered, "This means you must be a missionary wherever the Lord puts you. At the moment your mission field is your friends at school!"

All people, near and far, need to hear about Jesus.

6 August

Dollars and Cents

For the love of money is a root of all kinds of evil. Some people, eager for money, have wandered from the faith (1 Timothy 6:10).

Money is important. It's almost impossible to survive without money. We need money to be clothed and fed, to have shelter, and for many other things.

Because we need money, it can become too important in our lives. There are people who live only to make money. That's when money can become a problem to them. They can become slaves to money – it's like being bound and tied up by it. Some people are such money-grabbers that they will even steal it.

The Lord warns us to be careful that money doesn't become our master. We must trust the Lord to provide what we need, and then we must thank Him for it. If we can earn something by doing an odd job or two, we must not forget that it is the Lord who gives us the ability to do the job.

The Lord wants us to put our money to good use and help others. We can buy them nice gifts or get a needy friend something he or she needs.

The Bible says: "And my God will meet all your needs according to his glorious riches in Christ Jesus" *(Philippians 4:19).*

7 August

Never Too Young to Serve the Lord

But the LORD said to me, "Do not say, 'I am only a child.'
You must go to everyone I send you to and say whatever
I command you" (Jeremiah 1:7).

Many children and young people think they are not old enough to serve the Lord. But this is not true. The Lord had already set Jeremiah apart before he was born (See Jeremiah 1:5). The Lord chooses some people for ministry even before they are born, and He calls others to serve Him after they're already grown, like the apostle Paul (See acts 9).

It makes no difference when the Lord lays His hand on your life to make you a new person in Christ. The lesson to learn is that nobody is too young to serve the Lord. The Lord chose to make Jeremiah a prophet. I don't know what the Lord has in mind for you, and maybe you are not sure yet either.

It really doesn't matter. As you grow up, it will become clearer how the Lord wants to use you in His service. In the meantime all you need to do is tell the Lord every day, "Lord, here I am! I am available." Wouldn't it be wonderful if every person in this country would say this? Needless to say, you can be one of them.

Tell the Lord today that not only is He a Holy God, but
He's also the God you want to serve every day.

8 August

Forgive and Forget

Bear with each other and forgive whatever grievances you may have against one another. Forgive as the Lord forgave you (Colossians 3:13).

Each of us at one time or another feels bitter about something someone has done – like when your best friend spread an ugly story about you or the time your parents blamed you for something you didn't do.

To forgive is not easy. Your pride has taken a blow, or you just cannot stand such unfairness. To forgive, however, is the only way to patch up a broken relationship.

If you find it difficult to forgive, just think how many times God has forgiven you. Think back to all the times you told a little lie, or when you made an unkind remark about someone, or when you didn't give your best for God. It's strange how small that one little sin of the person who wronged you seems when you compare it to all your sins against God. And God has forgiven you each time you repent.

Read the parable in Matthew 18:21-35 of the servant whose master cancelled the debt he owed him. But this same servant was not prepared to have pity on one of his fellow servants who owed him money. When the master heard about this, he made the servant pay back everything he owed him.

Jesus warns us that the same will happen to us if we don't forgive.

9 August

Disciples Have God with Them

But the LORD is with me like a mighty warrior; so my persecutors will stumble and not prevail (Jeremiah 20:11).

Israel, the people of God, won many of the wars they fought. They prevailed even against armies that were stronger than they were because almighty God was on their side.

In the New Testament we find the same message. Paul writes to the church in Rome: *"In all these things we are more than conquerors through him who loved us"* (Romans 8:37). There is nothing in this whole wide world that can separate God's children from His love. Even if Jesus' disciples are sometimes going through a hard time, one thing we know for sure is that if God is on our side, in the end, nothing will get us down.

God himself lives in you through His Holy Spirit. So, He is close to you every day to help and support you whenever you need it. When you need help, the mighty and powerful God wants to offer you His help. God is with you, and with God on your side, you are always on the winning side! Remember this the next time things go wrong.

What did Gehazi, Elisha's servant, see when the Lord opened his eyes? (See 2 Kings 6:15-17.)

10 August

The Unknown God

"Therefore go and make disciples of all nations ... teaching them to obey everything I have commanded you" (Matthew 28:19-20).

See if you can find Myanmar (Burma) on a world map. There are people in that country who keep a separate corner in their house free for "the God who must still come." This space is swept regularly, and every night they burn a candle there to the glory of this God. Fortunately there are missionaries now who are telling the Burmese that Jesus has already come.

Jesus wants people to know about Him and for all nations to worship only the one true God. He wants missionaries to go to distant countries and to every single island to tell the people who live there about God's love.

Paul was the first missionary who traveled all over the world to spread the good news about Jesus, God's Son. In Acts 17 we read how he arrived in Greece to preach the gospel. The Greeks of that time worshiped many gods. Paul was looking for a way to explain to the people of Athens that there is only one true God. Then he saw an altar with the words "To the unknown God" on it. "I know the unknown God," Paul told them, and in this way they also had the opportunity of learning about God.

Do you ever pray for missionaries?

People who worship idols must be told about the living God.

11 August

In My Own Language

"We hear them declaring the wonders of God in our own tongues!" (Acts 2:11)

Have you ever thought how wonderful it is to be able to speak a language? Others who know your language can understand when you want to tell them something. Thousands of languages are spoken around the world.

The Lord gave us each a language so that we can tell people how we feel and what we need. We can also do something for others by means of our language. We can encourage them, pay them compliments, or give them advice. One of the nicest things to say is "I care" or "I love you." And one of the nicest phrases in any language is "thank you."

So you see, you and I can use our language to say nice things. But we can also use our language to hurt others. Let's use our language to serve the Lord. Let's tell others about Him.

The Bible says: "If I speak in the tongues of men and of angels, but have not love, I am only a resounding gong" *(1 Corinthians 13:1).*

12 August

What Is Repentance?

"For I take no pleasure in the death of anyone, declares the Sovereign LORD. Repent and live!" (Ezekiel 18:32)

Sometimes people make repentance a very complicated issue. The prophet Ezekiel said it is God's will that people repent and live. In the Bible, repentance means to turn away from sin and turn to God and to bring your life in line with His will. You must cast aside sin, yes, but at the same time turn your head like a sunflower in the Lord's direction.

Paul could name the day and date of his conversion. Not all believers can do this. Timothy grew up in a home of believers, but he didn't know exactly when he was converted.

It would be nice to know the day and hour when you gave your life to the Lord. What is important, though, is that you can say today, "I belong to the Lord!" Can you honestly say it with total commitment? If you can, then others will see the change in you – at school, when you're playing sports, and in your attitude towards others. The life of a person who belongs to Jesus is different than that of someone who has not been converted yet.

Do you think others can tell from the way you live that you have repented of your sins? Take a good look at yourself and bring your life into line with God's will.

13 August

Silence Is
Also an Answer

"We do not need to defend ourselves before you. ... The God we serve is able to rescue us" (Daniel 3:16-17).

Can you imagine what a horrific experience it must be to be thrown into a fiery furnace? This is what happened to Daniel's three friends. To add to their dilemma, King Nebuchadnezzar asked them which god could save them. It was then that the three men replied with the verse that is our text today. They didn't find it necessary to defend themselves; they were steadfastly on the side of their God.

There are times when you need to defend yourself, like when you have to explain why you copied homework from a friend's book, or when you have to tell your dad how it happened that you drove his car into a wall when you tried your hand at driving. Irresponsible behavior needs an explanation.

But it's not always necessary to explain why you prefer not to take part in doing something wrong or joining a bad activity. You can be like the three friends, who did not even bother to give the heathen king an answer. They knew their God would save them from his power.

Do you know when to talk up and when to keep quiet?

14 August

Heads or Tails

When Joseph woke up, he did what the angel of the Lord had commanded him and took Mary home as his wife (Matthew 1:24).

One way to make a decision about something is to toss a coin and call "heads or tails" while it's coming down. If only it were as easy to make decisions about the things in life that really matter.

If you honestly don't know what to do about something, follow the next steps:

- Pray for guidance. (See James 1:5-8.)
- Discuss your problem with someone you trust and who is not going to give you the easiest way out. (See Proverbs 20:18.)
- Look for certain fixed principles in the Bible that can be applied to your situation. For example, treat others the way you want them to treat you.
- Of all your decisions, the most important one is the one in 1 Corinthians 10:31.
- Be obedient and do the right thing.

In Joseph's case in our verse today, the angel of the Lord told him very clearly what to do. He decided to listen to the angel and marry Mary, even though she was pregnant. Trust God for guidance.

Every decision has its own consequences. Before you decide, first think well about the effects of your decision.

15 August

Disciples
Always Look Up

*Let us run with perseverance the race marked out for us.
Let us fix our eyes on Jesus, the author and perfecter of
our faith (Hebrews 12:1-2).*

Disciples never take their eyes off Jesus. When you focus on your problems, it's easy to feel depressed and give up. But when you fix your eyes on Jesus, you know nothing will get you down. The God you love is almighty – nothing is impossible to Him. He has solutions to every one of your problems.

When Peter wanted to walk on the water to Jesus, everything was fine until he took his eyes off Jesus and saw how big the waves were. The minute he started getting scared, he started sinking. But luckily Jesus was there with him. He took his hand and helped him.

When the storms come in your life, remember not to keep your eyes fixed on your many problems. Look away from the problems, keep your eyes on Jesus, and ask Him to take your hand and help you. If you remember this, you will manage to complete the race of faith and receive the winner's crown at the finish line that God promises His children in heaven.

Why does God sometimes allow us to suffer? (See Hebrews 12:6-7.)

16 August

God Created All Things

In the beginning God created the heavens and the earth (Genesis 1:1).

From the dune they were sitting on, Edward and his dad had a perfect view over the sea. The sun was already low and they were drinking in all the beauty around them – the darkening sea, orange and purple clouds, the bright evening star. "Dad," asked Edward after a while, "why does Uncle Jack say that the world all just happened by chance, and that God didn't create it?" He had been thinking about this question all summer, ever since Uncle Jack's visit.

Dad picked up a handful of sand and let it drift through his fingers. "When I look at all the wonderful things around us, and see how perfectly everything in creation works together, then I can't help but feel sorry for people like Uncle Jack. I think it takes more effort to believe that all this happened by chance and for no reason, than to believe what the Bible tells us."

"I suppose some people don't want to believe the Bible because then they will have to live for Jesus," Edward said.

"That's it exactly," Dad agreed. "They'd rather believe any-thing, than believe that God created everything in the universe out of nothing, simply by speaking the words of creation."

As they got up to leave, Dad said, "God enjoys making things, and He wanted to create a beautiful world for us to enjoy, simply because He loves us so much."

God made everything according to a master plan.

17 August

God in Nature

Then the man and his wife heard the sound of the Lord God as he was walking in the garden in the cool of the day (Genesis 3:8).

Have you noticed that the first and last story in the Bible are set in a garden? God made human beings and let them live in the Garden of Eden. Here God and the man and his wife walked around together, as our verse says. And in Revelation 21 and 22, the last chapters in the Bible, we learn that the new earth will be like a garden by a river where God will make His home with His people.

Nature is a very special meeting place for God and His children. Jacob slept outside one night, his head resting on a stone, when he saw angels climbing up and down a ladder. Moses was alone on the side of a mountain when he saw God in a burning bush. Elijah was in a mountain cave when God came to him in the evening breeze. Many of the Lord's children and Jesus Himself made use of the silence of nature to make contact with God. Just think of John the Baptist in the desert and Paul in the wilderness of Arabia after his conversion.

It would be a good idea for us as well to find a quiet place in nature where it is easier to think about God than in a crowded home or a busy neighborhood. Isn't there a spot in your garden or in a nearby park where you could sometimes go to speak to the Lord?

The Lord would like to meet with us in nature.

18 August

More
Valuable than Gold

*Your faith [is] of greater worth than gold, which perishes
(1 Peter 1:7).*

Gold is worth a lot all over the world. Countries sell gold and use the money to buy something essential like food. Gold is also used to make jewelry and ornaments like rings, watches, earrings, or necklaces, and these cost a lot of money.

But there is something even more important than gold. This is our faith. When we believe in Christ, we give the Lord first place, because we accept that what He says in His Word is the truth. We trust Him, which is why we follow Him. We hear what He says, and then we do it. And He is so wonderful that He even helps us to believe in Him.

Believing is not always easy. So we must learn to believe more and more. Often it's easier to believe when we are having a hard time. When we have problems, we pray that the Lord will help us. In this way we exercise our faith. Faith is like a muscle. If we never use our muscles, they become weak, but when we exercise them, they become stronger all the time. Gold is put into a very hot fire to make it pure and shiny. In the same way, we must also go through a fire of suffering for our faith to become pure and strong.

*The Bible says: "In this you greatly rejoice, though now for
a little while you may have had to suffer grief. ... So that
your faith ... may be proved genuine" (1 Peter 1:6-7).*

19 August

Your Name Is Worth a Lot

*Then the L*ORD *said to Hosea, "Call him Jezreel" (Hosea 1:4).*

The book of Hosea tells a strange story. God told the prophet Hosea to marry a very bad woman. When people asked, "Why is the prophet's wife so wicked?" the answer was, "So she can be a sign to remind us of our bad behavior towards the Lord!"

Maybe just as strange is the fact that Hosea had three children with very different names. The name Jezreel means "God sows." When this little boy was running around the marketplace and people asked him, "Why do you have such a funny name?" he had to answer, "Because the Lord is going to sow His people and scatter them amongst the other nations." His daughter's name meant "not loved," and his second son's name meant "not my people." These children had symbolic names.

Have you ever tried to find out what your name means? And do you have a nickname as well? What does that name say about you? The Bible tells us that Jesus was very interested in people's names. He changed Simon's name to Peter, and called James and John "Boanergos." Look up Mark 3:17 to see what that means, and try to figure out why Jesus called them that! What name do you think Jesus would give you, if He were to give you a new name? It would be something that shows what kind of disciple of His you are! If you read Isaiah 43:1 you will find a special promise about your name!

Do you always behave like a Christian?

20 August

Just Do It

But Moses said to God, "Who am I, that I should go to Pharaoh and bring the Israelites out of Egypt?" (Exodus 3:11)

To stand up for your faith and speak openly about it is not always easy. Maybe your best friend swears by using the Lord's name when he feels strongly about something or when he is angry. You know your friend is a Christian, and you want to point out to him that he shouldn't do this, but you don't want to lose him as a friend.

At school is a girl of a different race who keeps to herself. You want to go and ask her to join in with your crowd, but don't want to risk losing your other friends. "I can't help it that I'm the only one who feels sorry for her," you think.

All of us at some time or other are guilty of looking the other way instead of speaking out. Yet the Bible and Christian history have many examples of people who were not afraid to stand up for their faith. Where would the church be today without Martin Luther who spoke up about church reforms? Or where would the Israelites be without Moses who spoke up to Pharaoh? Moses made the excuse that he stuttered. The Lord knows how nervous you are and how your hands sweat when you have to speak out against something, and He will not let you down.

To speak when you have to takes courage. Prepare yourself for this by memorizing Deuteronomy 31:8: "The Lord himself goes before you and will be with you."

21 August

Thinking of Others

He who is kind to the poor lends to the LORD, and he will reward him for what he has done (Proverbs 19:17).

We humans are all selfish by nature. When your mom offers you the plate with your favorite chocolate cake, and one piece is bigger than the rest, what do you do? (Be honest!) This selfishness, this love of self, is the main reason for most things we do wrong. If you want to be one of Jesus' disciples, you must learn to look away from yourself for a change and focus on others.

There are many people in your city, your country, and around the world who are having a hard time. There are people who don't have enough food to eat every day. What do you do to help? Is there perhaps a family near you who is struggling to make ends meet? Ask your mom if you can take them a basket of fruit. If someone you know needs food, give that person something to eat. When you help others who don't have as much as you do, it's just like lending to the Lord, says the writer of Proverbs.

Will you try to really see others from now on and do something to make life easier for them?

What beautiful promises does the Lord make to those who are prepared to help others? (See Isaiah 58:8-11.)

22 August

Do All People Know about God?

For since the creation of the world God's invisible qualities – his eternal power and divine nature – have been clearly seen (Romans 1:20).

Suppose you were born somewhere in India or Iceland or South America and you have never heard about God. Suppose you have never seen a church and don't know about books, let alone a Bible! Could you have guessed there is a God?

Let's pretend. You are a young boy or girl and you belong to a jungle tribe. You are absolutely fascinated by the beauty of the forests: the great variety of luxuriant plants, the bright colors of the birds, nests lined with the softest down to protect the eggs and baby birds, brightly colored butterflies hovering over green ferns, the tiniest bug stirring the carpet of leaves, the rivers and the waterfalls. Wouldn't you wonder who made it all? And wouldn't you have the greatest respect for the Creator of so much beauty?

No wonder that missionaries always find that most people groups have some form of religion! Aren't we lucky that we know about the true God? I think it's only people who close their eyes to the beauty of nature, or who don't want to believe in a Creator God, who overlook Him.

We get to know God from the Bible, but also from nature.

23 August

Like a Cedar

It will produce branches ... and become a splendid cedar. Birds of every kind will nest in it; they will find shelter in the shade of its branches (Ezekiel 17:23).

A cedar is a species of tree that grows very tall and has a sturdy trunk with many branches. Birds love building their nests in cedars.

In Bible times there were many cedars, especially on the Lebanese mountains. The temple that Solomon built was made of cedar wood, as were all his war chariots.

Because the cedar is such a strong and stately tree, the Bible likens a person who is strong and dignified to a cedar. In Ezekiel 31:3 we read that Assyria was as strong and important and as beautiful as a cedar of Lebanon. All the other trees were jealous of the beautiful cedar. (See verse 9.) Then the cedar became too proud, and God sent someone to chop it down. The cedar fell to the ground, broken.

The Lord wants our lives to be strong, upright, and beautiful like the cedar. But when that happens, we must not become high and mighty or proud.

The Bible says: "No tree in the garden of God could match [the cedar's] beauty" *(Ezekiel 31:8).*

24 August

The Farmer who Became a Prophet

"I was neither a prophet nor a prophet's son, but I was a shepherd, and I also took care of sycamore-fig trees" (Amos 7:14).

When you read the book of the prophet Amos, you find that he talks about birds being caught in snares, carts sagging under the weight of grain, the roaring of a lion in the bushes, a lamb being snatched from the jaws of a lion, and many more scenes from nature. You know immediately that it's a farmer speaking here.

This is how the Lord wants to use every one of us as His witness, wherever we may work. That means you, too! When you are playing a sport, when you are on the playground, when you give your opinion at home, do it as a witness of the Lord. Amos was a farmer. For a short while he was a prophet, but his whole life long he never stopped being a witness for the Lord.

If you read the book again and pay attention to detail, you will notice that Amos spoke out very strongly against the injustice of his times. This means that you and I are not to stand for injustice, ever. When your friend is being wronged in any way, help him. If you see your friends damaging the plants or gardens of other people just for the fun of it, stop them. Don't look the other way.

Be like a prophet wherever you are.

25 August

How Big is God's House in Heaven?

In my Father's house are many rooms; if it were not so, I would have told you. I am going there to prepare a place for you (John 14:2.)

It is really difficult for us to know exactly what heaven is like. The Bible gives a few word pictures to help us understand, but mostly it just tells us that we will live in heaven forever if we have given our hearts to Jesus. What we do know is that there will be plenty of room in heaven for everyone who loves God and worships Him. Jesus promised that He was going to prepare a place for us in heaven – and you can bet it will be a place that you will love!

When you go to visit your granny, she takes special care to prepare things just the way that will make you feel welcome. She puts fresh towels and new soap in the bathroom, and she might even put flowers in your bedroom – all because she knows her children and grandchildren are coming home!

It isn't important to know exactly what heaven looks like (we'll have all of eternity to find out!). What we really need to remember is that heaven is where God is. And Jesus is preparing a place for us there. When we go to be with Jesus, He will have our place all ready for us.

Jesus will come to take you to be with Him in heaven only when your place in the Father's house is ready, so you needn't worry that He will come at the wrong time.

26 August

Conflict Is Unavoidable – or Is It?

And the Lord's servant must not quarrel; instead he must be kind to everyone, able to teach, not resentful (2 Timothy 2:24).

Constant bickering and fighting in a family can drive anyone crazy. There are ways of solving this or avoiding it completely. How?

- Learn to keep your mouth shut.
- Don't poke your nose into matters that are none of your business.
- Take a back seat.

If you follow this three-point plan for zero conflict, no one can fight with you:

- Don't make a remark if it can lead to an argument.
- Don't gossip.
- Don't fight about stupid things. If someone wants the last of the ice cream, let him have it. So what if you can't watch your favorite TV program? Let it go. Granted, it's not always easy, but it beats fighting.

Abraham didn't like fighting either. When he and Lot started arguing about the grazing rights on a piece of land, he suggested that each of them go his own way. (Read the story in Genesis 13:8-9.)

It takes practice not to fight. Try it for a month and see the difference it can make in a family.

27 August

Disciples Like Giving

"Now, who is willing to consecrate himself today to the
LORD?" (1 Chronicles 29:5).

Disciples are people who like giving to the Lord – giving
their money and also their time and talents. The Bible teaches
us that God loves a generous giver.

In I Chronicles 29 David asks the people for gifts of gold,
silver, and other valuables for the building of the temple. And
they are more than willing to give. You will be surprised to
read in I Chronicles 29:7-8 what they were prepared to give
the king.

Unfortunately this cannot be said of most people. Maybe you
have heard adults grumble that the church is always collecting
money. Some people have a problem giving money for the
Lord's work, and a lot of money is needed for the kingdom of
God to grow.

Everything you have comes from the Lord. He gives you
parents, the house you live in, food, clothes, and also your
pocket money. It's a good idea to start giving now, while you
are still young. Put some of your pocket money aside for the
work of the Lord. Then you will find it much easier to give one
day when you are grown up.

Why was the widow's offering extra special to the Lord?
(See Mark 12:42-43.)

28 August

Nature's Songs of Praise

The heavens declare the glory of God; the skies proclaim the work of his hands (Psalm 19:1).

They say there is a tiny church in Ireland with stained glass windows – all but one. Through one of the windows you can see the landscape outside: a deep blue lake, green hills, bluish purple mountains, and the big sky. The beautiful words of Psalm 19 above are engraved underneath this window. Every time the members of the congregation look through that window, they realize that they are not the only part of God's creation that wants to praise Him!

Today, concentrate on everything that is beautiful in nature. Look away from tall buildings for a change, from electronic discoveries and human-made objects and really notice God's amazing creation: the sky, the clouds, the plants, the birds. Then pray: "Lord, thank You that You made everything so beautiful! Your power is breathtaking and Your creation awesome! How great You are!"

Some people never notice the beauty of nature. They never listen to the sound of the wind and the rain and the birds. They walk around with headphones and music on all day or sit at the computer or television for hours on end. These people cannot hear the messages the Lord wants to give them through His creation.

You are closer to God in nature than anywhere else on earth.

29 August

God's Footsteps

He has shown kindness by giving you rain from heaven and crops in their seasons (Acts 14:17).

"How do you know there is a God?" passers-by once asked an old desert-dweller.

He answered, "How do I know that a camel passed my tent at night? I see the footprints in the sand!"

We sometimes hear of almost unbelievable things happening in nature. The story is told of a female moth that was kept in a laboratory in Chicago. Several miles away from there a male moth of the same species was let loose. A few hours later the male arrived at the laboratory. It had covered the distance, braving pollution, noise, and traffic and was fluttering its wings against the closed window.

Every time you hear of these natural wonders, you realize that there must be Someone who put a lot of thought into everything and made it all. God has left His footprints all over so that we can find Him. Some scientists are blind to His miracle-working presence. They say it's simply a matter of coincidence. But if they are honest seekers and just follow the evidence that is found in nature, they will find the Designer and Creator himself. "He is our God."

Let's praise Him with the beautiful words of the old hymn "How great Thou art!"

The wonderful world of nature brings us to our knees.

30 August

Build Well!

"Therefore everyone who hears these words of mine and puts them into practice is like a wise man who built his house on the rock" (Matthew 7:24).

Lying on the sand and basking in the hot sun at the ocean is fantastic! Sand is also mixed with cement to build a house. But sand is not strong enough to use on its own. Have you seen how easily the waves break a sandcastle? A car also needs a good road or sturdy ground for it to move. Sand just gives way, and before you know it you get stuck in it. If you want to build a house, you can't do it on sand because it's not firm enough. A strong wind will blow your house down.

Jesus said we also need to build our lives on firm ground. The best place to build a house is on rock, because a rock is steady and strong. The Bible says Jesus is like a rock, a cornerstone or a strong rock, and you and I can safely build our lives on Him. Jesus says, "You and I should start doing everything together. Ask Me to help you with your schoolwork, or with your friends, or with your hurts, with everything. Do everything you do in My name, and let's do it together. Then you are building your life on a rock!" And then the structure of your life will remain standing.

The Bible says that you are a building, "With Christ Jesus himself as the chief cornerstone" (Ephesians 2:20).

31 August

The Day of the Lord

"The day of the Lord *is near for all nations" (Obadiah 15).*

When the Bible talks about "the day of the Lord," it refers to Judgment Day. This is a day that believers need not fear. This is the time when God will judge fairly between right and wrong.

In the times of the Old Testament, people believed that on the Day of the Lord, judgment would be passed on their enemies. Obadiah corrected them: judgment will be passed on everybody who ever lived, believers and unbelievers. So we see that if what we do is not what the Lord wants, we can very easily expect judgment against us.

The name Obadiah means "servant of the Lord." If you are a servant of God and you do what the Lord wants you to, then you really needn't be afraid of the Day of the Lord. It will be a joyful day you can look forward to.

Do you think your life always brings a smile to the Lord's face? Is your behavior going to please the Lord today, and every day from now on? If the answer is yes, you can go to bed with a smile on your face. If the answer is no, you must confess to the Lord that you have slipped up, and start living like someone who wants to look forward to the Day of the Lord with joy.

Are you looking forward to the Day of the Lord?

1 September

When Is Sin Sin?

Anyone, then, who knows the good he ought to do and doesn't do it, sins (James 4:17).

Some people have a very keen sense of right and wrong and think they have sinned long before they really have. Then there are those who find it very difficult to admit it when they have done something wrong. Some are very quick to blame others for their own sins. Think about Adam, who very conveniently put the blame on Eve.

If you come into contact with a temptation, you are not yet sinning. But if you give in to temptation, then you sin. Jesus himself was tempted by the devil, but He resisted temptation. When Cain was furious with his brother, he was not sinning. But when he decided to take out his anger on his brother, Abel, in a destructive manner, then he sinned. (See Genesis 4:7.)

The best advice is to steer clear of sin, because what person can "scoop fire into his lap without his clothes being burned?" (Proverbs 6:27). Instead, choose activities, friends, television programs, and books that will encourage you to do the right thing, instead of those that make you sin.

Sin starts with a wrong thought.

2 September

Jesus Is Sending You

Again Jesus said, "Peace be with you! As the Father has sent me, I am sending you" (John 20:21).

Just after Jesus' resurrection He appeared to His disciples. He asked them to go on with His work, making sure that His kingdom on earth would grow. He wants everyone in the world to hear the good news that he died and rose again so that if we believe in Him we will live forever and our sins will be forgiven.

One of the last instructions Jesus gave to His disciples was to go into all the world and preach the good news of the gospel to all people. His early followers were so excited by what Jesus did for them, that they wanted to tell everyone everywhere about Him. Just about every letter in the New Testament was written by a missionary or to a missionary. Eleven of the original twelve disciples of Jesus were all missionaries who traveled as far as they could to tell people about Jesus.

Jesus is still wanting to send missionaries into the world, because there are still millions of people who don't know anything about Him. A missionary is someone on a mission – and you can be on a mission to tell the people around you about Jesus!

Are you prepared to speak to your friends about Jesus?

3 September

Our Beautiful Earth

The LORD God took the man and put him in the Garden of Eden to work it and take care of it (Genesis 2:15).

Lillian is writing an essay on nature conservation. She enjoys an assignment like this because she loves plants and animals. It really makes her furious to hear of people who shoot elephants just for their ivory tusks, and she feels sad when rare plants are destroyed by forest fires. "How can people be so careless about our beautiful earth!" she writes. She did a lot of research on the topic in the library, and the things she read have her worried. "Is it possible that there will still be enough food and water for all the billions of people in the year 2005?" she wonders.

Her mother pops in to see how she's doing. "Isn't your essay finished yet?" she asks. "Remember it's your turn to water the garden this week!" Lillian is not at all crazy about this chore. As soon as her mom's back is turned, she slips out the back door, plants the little sprinkler somewhere among the shrubs and takes off on her bicycle.

It's already getting dark when she arrives back home again. The flower bed is drenched and the garden path is a river. She can see that her mom is not happy with her. "I read your essay!" she says. "It's good! In it you mention that the Lord put us in charge of His creation. But just remember, if we can't take responsibility for small tasks, we can never be trusted with the major responsibilities of nature conservation!"

We must take care of God's creation.

4 September

Be Careful!

Be very careful, then, how you live – not as unwise but as wise (Ephesians 5:15).

A danger sign along the road is there to warn you of something you must watch out for. It could be a sign to watch out for deer crossing the road or to warn us that there is a sharp curve ahead. Another sign says you can cross here but only if no other car is approaching. So you must be careful. If we ignore danger signs, we can be the cause of accidents.

The Bible also has danger signs. Sometimes the Bible says we are not allowed to do certain things. At other times it tells us about certain things we should take note of. When the Bible says "Be careful!" then we must take it to heart.

Examples of danger signs in the Bible are when the Lord says that money can become too important to us and that it can make us stray from the Lord. The Bible also warns us not to miss out on the grace of God (Hebrews 12:15) and to be careful how we live so we don't do stupid things. Let's read the Bible regularly, so that we know which things blink like the yellow street light, telling us, "Be careful."

The Bible says: "Son of man, look with your eyes and hear with your ears and pay attention to everything I am going to show you" *(Ezekiel 40:4).*

5 September

God Has a Soft Heart for Sinners

When God saw what they did and how they turned from their evil ways, he had compassion and did not bring upon them the destruction he had threatened (Jonah 3:10).

Sometimes we can't help thinking that the God of the Old Testament is cruel, and the God of the New Testament is a God of love. But this is not true. A great example of this is found in Jonah.

It's not important to find answers to questions like, "What kind of fish swallowed Jonah?" or, "How big was Nineveh really?" or, "How does one explain the vine that grew to give Jonah shade for his head?" No, all these issues are only examples to show one thing: God makes all kinds of plans so that people can repent and turn back to Him. He has loving eyes and a soft heart for sinners.

Our verse very clearly states that when God saw that the people of Nineveh had repented, He decided not to let the disaster He had planned come upon them.

You and I must be careful what we have to say about others. We should rather try to guide them in love to dedicate themselves to the Lord. The Lord does not want unrepentant sinners to lose the way to Him. The book of Jonah tells us about God's great love.

Have you told someone about God's love yet?

6 September

Jesus' Birthplace Was Prophesied

"But you, Bethlehem Ephrathah, though you are small among the clans of Judah, out of you will come for me one who will be ruler over Israel" (Micah 5:2).

Did you know the word Bethlehem means "House of bread"? In the Old Testament the small town of Bethlehem had been singled out as the place where God would provide spiritual bread for the world. This, of course, came true when the Lord Jesus Christ was born there.

What is surprising is that the prophet Micah lived more than seven hundred years before the birth of Christ. Already at that stage, God led Micah to make a prophecy about His Son, who was coming to this world. Perhaps Micah himself didn't even understand what he was saying, and the people of that time understood even less. We who are living long after the birth of Christ can now see that this was a prophecy.

At the time, nobody could have dreamed that the little town of Bethlehem would be the birthplace of the Messiah. This shows us how wonderful God is. To Him it doesn't count how important a person or a place is. He has His own rescue operation for this world. In this plan, Bethlehem had an important part to play, in spite of what people had to say about it.

Do you also think Jesus is the bread that gives life?

7 September

When a Child Is Missing

"Rejoice with me; I have found my sheep" (Luke 15:6).

Can you imagine what parents go through when their child is missing? Everything possible is done to find the child – talking to the police, neighbors, and school friends, and sometimes photos of the child are even put on milk cartons. Just think of the parents' relief when the child is found!

This is how God felt when the human beings He created ran away from Him. In Genesis we read how God looked for Adam and Eve in the Garden of Eden. He walked around calling, "Adam, where are you?"

In the New Testament Jesus tells us about the good shepherd who could not rest until he found his lost sheep. And how he rejoiced when he found it!

In heaven there is a "missing persons bureau," and it operates day and night, tracing runaways – runaway children who have been waylaid by Satan and who have fallen for his glib tongue and empty promises. And what joy there is in heaven when one sinner has been found and brought back home (Luke 15:7).

God is so set on finding lost persons that He moved heaven and earth to get you back. He sent His Son to this world.

8 September

Disciples
Make Disciples

"Therefore go and make disciples of all nations" (Matthew 28:19).

Jesus does not ask us only to be His disciples, but also that we make disciples for Him. Every time you talk to your friends about Jesus, you are obeying this instruction.

There are millions of people on earth who have not heard the good news. Every day 75,000 people die who have never heard of Jesus. Even if you are too young to go and speak to these people, you are not too young to start missionary work on your knees, praying for those who have never heard of Jesus.

"The harvest is plentiful but the workers are few. Ask the Lord of the harvest, therefore, to send out workers into his harvest field," says Jesus in Matthew 9:37-38. You can help pray that the Lord will send workers for the harvest. For people who have the Holy Spirit in their lives, it is a matter of great urgency to tell others about Jesus.

If you are a disciple, God also wants you to be a disciple-maker for Him. Are you ready, willing, and able?

Which one of Jesus' disciples was ready at once to go out and make a disciple? (See Acts 8:26-38.)

9 September

Everything God Made Was Good

God saw all that he had made, and it was very good (Genesis 1:31).

One afternoon when Kyle came home from school, his mother could tell something was very wrong. "What's the matter?" she asked as she sat down next to him.

"Mark wrecked my sailing boat; he smashed it to pieces!" Kyle answered, fighting back the tears.

"Surely not on purpose?" his mother asked, feeling very sorry for Kyle. She knew how many hours he had worked to build that boat.

"No, but he was just plain careless!" Kyle said. "He was swinging his golf club around in class and knocked my boat right off the shelf. I don't even feel like going to help the rest of my class with the river project this afternoon!"

Kyle's classmates had decided to clean up the town's riverbanks. They planned on getting all the garbage cleared up and then, accompanied by the school band, were going to take it to the dump. "It would be a pity if you decide not to help. The Lord will be very pleased if you manage to get the river as clean as it used to be! I think He feels about His creation just like you do about your boat!"

Kyle got up, and without a word started getting ready for Operation Clean Sweep. For the first time he understood how God must feel when he sees His beautiful world being ruined.

It makes the Lord sad to see His creation being spoiled.

10 September

What Is Man?

When I consider your heavens, the work of your fingers, the moon and the stars which you have set in place, what is man that you are mindful of him? (Psalm 8:4-5).

There is as astronomer who spends his quiet time looking at the starry sky. He traces the Milky Way, a faint band that seems to stretch across the sky. He remembers that the earth is in a solar system near the edge of the Milky Way, and that the center of the Milky Way is about 25,000 light years from the earth. He knows that the light from some of the stars he can see started shining when Jesus lived on earth, but hasn't even reached the earth yet! A light year is the distance light travels in a year, a staggering 5,88 trillion miles a year, or about 186,000 miles per second! The astronomer then reflects again on how vast the heavens are, and how small the earth is and how insignificant it seems to make us.

When he goes back inside, he kneels and worships God, overwhelmed once again by the thought that the mighty God, Creator and Ruler of the wide expanses of the universe, cares about each human being on earth. How amazing it is that Jesus says that even a sparrow is important to Him, and He knows exactly how many hairs are on your head.

When you look up at the stars and think about how immense the universe is, you probably also feel very small, but as you remember that God loves you, it should remind you of how special you actually are!

You are small, but God is mighty.

11 September

Our Safe Haven

They were glad when it grew calm, and he guided them to their desired haven (Psalm 107:30).

A harbor is a place of shelter for ships or boats. Even when the sea is rough and waves make the boats pitch and roll, it is calm and safe in a harbor. A seafarer knows his boat will be safe here, protected from the storms on the open sea. An old-fashioned word for harbor is "haven," and today the word haven means a place of safety or rest, a refuge.

Life is often stormy. Things happen that upset or hurt us. Parents sometimes have a stormy marriage, and this makes life difficult for their children. Seeing Mom and Dad fight hurts. Or someone we love very much might suddenly get sick and die. There are also storms in our hearts.

The Lord wants to protect us from the storms of life. He once stilled the storm on the Sea of Galilee. He tells us, *"Come to me ... and I will give you rest"* (Matthew 11:28). He is like a safe harbor, a haven in a stormy sea.

Why don't you give your pain and all your problems to the Lord today? If you do, you will be anchored in the harbor of His peace.

The Bible says: "He stilled the storm to a whisper; the waves of the sea were hushed" (Psalm 107:29).

12 September

What Gets You Going?

And whatever you do, whether in word or deed, do it all in the name of the Lord Jesus, giving thanks to God the Father through him (Colossians 3:17).

Philippa glanced at the stands before she took her position to dive for the start of the freestyle race. Yes, she smiled to herself, her classmates were sitting just where they were sure to notice her when she won! She pictured how they would cheer, and congratulate her for winning the trophy for the school team. She would be the school hero, for sure!

Philippa liked it when other people noticed her. She liked to get the badge for memorizing the most Bible verses, and she liked the way her teacher told everyone what a good student she was.

Philippa liked to impress people with all the things she could do well. When she prayed at night, she often asked God to help her do well so that other people would like her.

It's a good thing to want to do well in everything you do, because Jesus asks us to do our best. But sometimes we need to look at our hearts and think about why we want to do well. Trying to do well so that other people will be impressed and will reward us is not likely to impress God. We should be prepared to do our best even if no one else even notices, knowing that we do everything as if God was watching us – which He is. The best motive for doing anything is because it will please God. Then other people will look at the good things we do, and they too will glorify God!

Think about the reasons for doing the things you do.

13 September

Breaking Up

But after Uzziah became powerful, his pride led to his downfall (2 Chronicles 26:16).

The two friends had been inseparable, ever since they were little. They did everything together. He helped her with math, and she helped him with his projects. They went off on their bicycles in the afternoons and watched television together. And then one day, just like that, everything changed. He started avoiding her at school and talked to other girls during breaks. She was still crazy about him, but things couldn't go on like this, so she decided to break up with him. Painful, but unavoidable.

Breaking up with God is worse. When you withhold your love from Him, He is left with a love that is not returned. He will never break the bond of love with you, no matter how unfaithful you are. He waits patiently for you to come back to Him.

In 2 Chronicles 26:16-23 we read about King Uzziah who became just too important in his own eyes to remain faithful to the Lord. He insisted on entering the temple of the Lord and burning incense on the altar himself – something only the priests were to do. His life ended tragically. He became a leper and died alone. He was not even buried in the family burial ground.

God waits for us to come back to Him because He knows nobody else can love us the way He does.

14 September

Running to Win

Do you not know that in a race all the runners run, but only one gets the prize? Run in such a way as to get the prize (1 Corinthians 9:24).

Paul here compares your life as a disciple of the Lord with a race. This race should be run in such a way that you are sure of winning a prize at the finish.

If you are an athlete, you know only too well that there can only be one winner. But in the race of faith everybody can be winners! The prize is much more valuable than a cup or a trophy. The prize you win for completing the race of faith is everlasting life. And everyone who believes in Jesus can win that prize!

Just like there are rules in athletics, this race also has certain rules that one has to keep:

- Run for the goal.
- Be determined to reach that goal.
- Always do your very best.
- Don't ever give up.

If you are prepared to run like this, to be disciplined and purposeful in your discipleship, you can be sure that everlasting life will be yours one day!

What things can stand in the way of winning the race of faith? (See Hebrews 12:1-3.)

15 September

Christ Looks after His Church

"If their purpose or activity is of human origin, it will fail. But if it is from God, you will not be able to stop these men" (Acts 5:38-39).

In spite of being under constant siege by enemy attacks, the Christian faith has stood the test of time. In the verse quoted above, Gamaliel makes a prophecy that came true. Gamaliel was a wise old man who served in the Sanhedrin, the ruling council of the Jews in Jesus' time. When Peter and his friends were charged because they were preaching the gospel, he told the leaders, "If it is from God, you will not be able to stop these men."

And truly, nothing has been able to stop the good news about Jesus from spreading all over the world. Many people have tried in vain to stifle it. Christians were stoned to death; some were burned at the stake. Others were tortured and thrown to the lions. Even today, people are being sent to prison because they believe in Christ. Often Christians are insulted or made fun of because of their faith. Perhaps you have noticed that people avoid you or try to hurt you in other ways just because you want to take the Lord's road. But the Christian religion will never die; of that you can be sure!

The Lord is almighty, and He will make sure that His plans always work out.

16 September

Be Yourself

A wicked man accepts a bribe in secret (Proverbs 17:23).

In every group there is usually someone who takes the lead. It's normally the biggest or strongest boy or the one the girls or boys like best. If it's a girl, she's usually the prettiest or brightest or best at sports. Everybody wants to be this person's friend. To be in this person's good graces you may do all sorts of things that are not really like you at all. You start kissing up to them, almost like a puppy wanting its master to give it a pat on the head, and this is not right.

True friends meet each other halfway and on the same level. They are equal. One does not lord it over the other. They take one another just as they are. Behaving in a certain way simply to be popular or to find favor in somebody's eyes isn't healthy. A friendship like this will not last long.

Just be yourself and hold on to the Lord. Love Him and do what He wants. Be His friend, and He will also give you good friends.

The Bible says: "They make many promises, take false oaths and make agreements" *(Hosea 10:4).*

17 September

The Burden Bearer

How long, O LORD, must I call for help? (Habakkuk 1:2)

"I'm the better player. Why did he make the team?" "Why do I still fail some of my tests? I study so hard!" Maybe you've asked questions like these before. Sometimes it seems as if the Lord's children often suffer defeat while those who don't serve the Lord flourish.

We find this type of question in the Bible, especially in the first chapter of Habakkuk. In Habakkuk 2 we find something that surprises us. Here the Lord explains that He still has a plan for the world, even if it sometimes seems that He doesn't hear or doesn't see what is happening. In fact, He is still in control. In the end, He will be the Judge of all unrighteousness.

So it is not surprising that the prophet comes up with a confession of faith. In Habakkuk 3:17-18 the prophet says he will put his trust in the Lord, in spite of everything that is going on around him. He says, "Yet I will rejoice in the Lord, I will be joyful in God my Savior!"

So don't despair if things don't seem to be going the way they should. The Lord is still in control, and He is working on His plan for the world.

Believe in God and trust Him, because in time it will become clear that the Lord is on the throne.

18 September

I'll Pay!

I will pay it back – not to mention that you owe me your very self (Philemon 19).

Imagine if someone walks into your room and says, "Today I'm going to pay all your debts!" Will you be glad? What will you do? This is more or less what Paul does in his letter to Philemon. This is one of the four letters Paul wrote from prison, the other three being to the Ephesians, the Philippians, and the Colossians. It is a personal letter to Philemon, a leading Christian in Colosse, and it was written in the year 60 or 61 A.D.

Philemon's slave, Onesimus, ran away to Rome. There he met Paul and became a Christian. Now Paul is sending Onesimus back to his owner, begging Philemon to forgive and take him back. Paul promises to pay all expenses and to pay Philemon for any damages or debts Onesimus might have made.

Don't forget that Jesus also paid for your sins. Because of what He did, you and I are now free. Thank the Lord for this.

19 September

Heavenly Homework?

Jesus told him, "Go and do likewise" (Luke 10:37).

Children today have very busy lives. There are projects, assignments, tests, and exams. There are basketball games and music lessons and choir and drama – and always more homework! Make sure that you listen well so that you know exactly what to do.

But someone else has also given you homework: the Master. Every Sunday you are given an assignment, and you have a whole week to complete it. This devotional book that you are reading every day, together with your Bible, is your heavenly homework. You don't have to be very clever to do it; you don't need to know Greek or Hebrew to understand it. The test is in listening and obeying.

It's a shame that so many of us don't do our heavenly homework. How will we know what God's assignment for us is if we don't do our heavenly homework?

Read the parable of the Good Samaritan in Luke 10:30-37, and decide who obeyed the commandment to love your neighbor as yourself.

Homework might make us smart, but God's homework makes us better people.

20 September

Disciples
Are Enthusiastic

Never be lacking in zeal, but keep your spiritual fervor, serving the Lord (Romans 12:11).

People who reach the top and are successful in life are often not those who are the cleverest but those who are the most enthusiastic. At the beginning of their walk with God, most Christians are filled with enthusiasm for the Lord's work. Unfortunately that enthusiasm wanes as time passes.

In Jeremiah 2:2 God tells His unfaithful people that they don't love Him like they did in the beginning. In Revelation 3:16 the church in Laodicea is given the message that Jesus will spit them out of His mouth because they are lukewarm.

God doesn't want lukewarm, disinterested followers. He wants us to serve Him with total commitment, bubbling over with enthusiasm. He desires for us to be sincere in our excitement about being His disciples and for our love for Him to grow stronger every day.

You can do a quick test on yourself: Do you sometimes look for excuses not to go to church on a rainy day or for not taking part in church activities during a busy time at school? This is a warning sign that your enthusiasm is waning. Be careful that you don't become so fond of the world that your enthusiasm for the Lord is pushed into second place.

Which one of Paul's helpers turned back because he loved the world too much? (See 2 Timothy 4:10.)

21 September

Seek the Company of Other Christians

I rejoiced with those who said to me, "Let us go to the house of the Lord" (Psalm 122:1).

Louise's father is a bank manager. They move often because every now and then he is transferred from one town to another. Every time they hear the news that it's time to start packing again, they are sad. "Now we have to make friends all over again!" Louise complains when she hears they're going to start the new year in a new place, once again. "Rob was right when he said we're like a circus family, always on the move!"

Her mother also feels sad that they can't stay in this nice town longer. But she's not as upset as Louise. "Do you know what I've found out with all this moving around?" she says. "The Lord's people are all over. A different place and different faces, that's all! We'll quickly make new friends where we're moving, once we go to church there."

That night in bed Louise thinks about her mother's words. There's a lot of truth in what she said. In all the places they lived, she made very nice Christian friends. She will find out, first thing, where all the Christian children at school get together. She kneels at her bed and prays, "Thank you, Lord, that You are my best Friend and that You go with me wherever we move. Thank You that Your children are also in the town we're moving to, so I can make friends with them."

Make friends with girls and boys who love Jesus.

22 September

Serve the Lord
Because You Love Him

"I no longer call you servants. … Instead I have called you friends" (John 15:15).

It's Sunday morning, and there's football on TV. "Aw, Dad!" Tony begs. "Can't I please watch the football game today instead of going to church?"

He knows what his dad is going to say. "No, Tony, there are more important things than football, like going to church on Sundays!"

"Where in the Bible does it say that one must go to church every single Sunday?" Tony asks in a huff. But he has cooled off when he starts getting dressed. On their way to church, his dad hands him a note. He reads: "I want tennis balls for my birthday!"

This is not like his dad at all. If someone tells you what present you must get them, you don't feel like giving them anything at all. He wonders what his dad has up his sleeve. Just as they walk into church his dad says, "The Lord does not give us all the finer details. He wants us to serve Him because we love him, not out of a sense of duty!"

Now Tony understands. The Lord didn't write a verse that says: "You must go to church every Sunday." But if we do, it makes Him happy … just as happy as Dad will be to get a present he didn't have to ask for.

Serve the Lord because you love Him.

23 September

Hearts of Stone

"I will give them an undivided heart and put a new spirit in them; I will remove from them their heart of stone and give them a heart of flesh" (Ezekiel 11:19).

Have you ever stubbed your toe against a stone? Ouch! It hurts, doesn't it? Stones can puncture tires, and if your aim is off, can break windows. A stone is very hard. If you want to break a stone, you need a hammer or heavy machinery.

The Lord says many people have hearts like stone; they have hard hearts. What does He mean? This is a person who is too proud and is not able to forgive, or who is bad-tempered. This person believes only in himself, and everything he says is important. No one can give him advice; he is always right. He is stubborn, and his heart is as hard as stone.

It's the devil that makes people's hearts hard. He doesn't want us to love others or forgive them. He would much rather have us swear at them, insult them, or hate them and turn our backs on them. He has the hardest heart of all. He wants everybody to die.

But the Lord says He wants to give everyone a soft heart, one full of love. If we give our hearts to Jesus, He will make them soft hearts of flesh, full of love and charity for humanity.

The Bible says: "They made their hearts as hard as flint and would not listen ... to the words that the Lord Almighty had sent" (Zechariah 7:12).

24 September

A Bad Reputation

"Why do you do such things? I hear from all the people about these wicked deeds of yours" (1 Samuel 2:23).

Eli was a priest, and if his sons were in your school they would probably have been expelled long ago. These two young men did such wicked things that they really had a bad reputation. The Bible says that Eli often warned them, but they didn't listen.

Then there's the Bible story of the boy named Samuel. The Lord was very pleased with him, and everybody liked him. (See 1 Samuel 2:26.) Samuel was not like Eli's sons. He was an example to others.

In every school it happens that children form groups. Eli's sons and Samuel would not be in the same group. Think about your school. Which group do you belong with? How do the other students see you? How do you behave at school on the sports field? What is your attitude towards teachers?

You are not forced to belong to a certain group. You have a choice.

25 September

Do You Go
with the Flow?

If sinners entice you, do not give in to them (Proverbs 1:10).

Have you ever heard of the judas goat? His task every day is to lead hundreds of sheep to the slaughtering place. This goat mixes with the sheep, and then he takes the lead to the slaughterhouse. The sheep meekly follow him until he slips out at a side gate and they walk on to their death.

It's just as easy to influence young people when they are part of the crowd. Peer pressure can be negative or positive. It often happens that a whole class are achievers because they are encouraged by a diligent group in their class. Another example of positive peer pressure is when the whole class decides to help a sick friend stay up-to-date with schoolwork by sending a different student to him with the homework every day.

It's the negative pressure you should watch out for. It destroys your personality and makes you behave like a sheep in a flock. "But everybody's doing it!" is the war cry of this group. By the way, have you ever met "everybody"? There is no such person. Maybe today smoking is the "in" thing; tomorrow, it might be cheating on the exam. And what about a quick drink (of something strong) after school? Anything goes, as long as you're part of the group. Watch out! Following the crowd can be the first step in a wrong direction.

God gave you a mind of your own so that you can decide for yourself about right and wrong.

26 September

Disciples Are
Willing to Learn

Plans fail for lack of counsel, but with many advisers they succeed (Proverbs 15:22).

A person is shaped by the experience and insight of his or her role models. But when you are young, you don't always want to be taught. More often than not you are irritated by the advice of grown-ups and would much rather ignore it than take it. When my daughter was a teenager, she once told me to my face that she would prefer learning from her own mistakes, not mine!

Yet, disciples of Jesus should be prepared to listen to people who have more wisdom and insight into spiritual matters than they have. You can also help yourself grow by reading and studying the right books.

Make time to read Christian books. These can help you grow so much spiritually. There are many interesting Bible study courses for young people that you can use as a guide when you do Bible study. A daily devotional can also help you become spiritually stronger. Make notes when you read the Bible, and make use of the practical hints in your life. Learn to listen for the voice of God when you go to church, and it's really not a bad idea to listen to the advice of grown-ups who cross your path.

What did the Lord teach the prophet Isaiah? (See Isaiah 50:4-6.)

27 September

Sundays Are Special

Blessed are those who dwell in your house ... whose strength is in you (Psalm 84:4-5).

If there's one day a week the devil and his henchmen have no rest, it must be Sunday. He doesn't want people to go to church! On Saturday night he begins his preparations. If the Lord's children stay up late, they will be tired and listless in church on Sunday morning. Late parties and movies (especially ones in which the Lord is scorned) help a lot to put one off from going to church.

When church bells start ringing on a Sunday morning, "Operation Stay-At-Home" is put into action. "You're tired, sleep in today!" the devil whispers. "Go to the beach! Why go to church every Sunday?" And all the while he's also stirring up trouble among all the members of the family. Everyone is moody and irritable at the breakfast table. It's a mad rush to finish dressing in time, and someone is always late.

If, however, he doesn't manage to make them stay home, he uses other tactics. He turns them into church critics – people who have something to say about everything concerning the church. The minister is boring, the organ music is too loud, the members of the congregation are hypocrites, the singing is boring, and the sermon goes on and on.

Try praying about the church service before you go and keep an open mind in church.

The Lord wants to make every Sunday church service special.

28 September

The Fire Test

The fire will test the quality of each man's work (1 Corinthians 3:13).

Fire can easily burn down a whole house and leave nothing standing. Nothing can stop the power of fire. Gold is melted in a furnace to purify it. Iron is melted from stone in very hot furnaces.

The Bible tells us that our deeds will be tested with fire. The quality of everything we do here on earth will be tested. If we have done things that were not the will of God, the fire will burn them. Even things we did for the Lord, but with the wrong attitude, will be tested and destroyed by the fire.

How can we be sure that our lives and deeds will stand the test of fire? The Bible tells us to do things the way God wills. Everything we do must be to His glory, and we must do it because we are thankful for everything He does for us. We must not do things to be seen or as a means to an end, because then we are being selfish. What we do must be for the Lord and to glorify Him. We must build spiritually; then our building will not burn down.

The Bible says: "The crucible for silver and the furnace for gold, but the LORD tests the heart" *(Proverbs 17:3).*

29 September

Watch Your Tongue

The tongue is a small part of the body, but it makes great boasts. Consider what a great forest is set on fire by a small spark. The tongue is also a fire (James 3:5, 6).

Have you ever felt like biting your tongue after saying something negative about someone? You almost feel like grabbing at the words you have just spoken to try to take them back. Do you know the feeling? James does. He says this happens with the words you form in your mind and then pronounce with your tongue.

The tongue is a very small organ but very mighty! James uses various images to explain the functioning of one's tongue: the bit in a horse's mouth (James 3:3) and the rudder of a ship (3:4). Then the tongue is likened to a fire (3:5-6) and to a restless evil, full of deadly poison (3:8).

How do you use your tongue? Do you use it to the glory of God, or to light fires and cause trouble?

30 September

F.R.O.G.

F.R.O.G.

F.R.O.G.

Are You a Body without a Spirit?

As the body without the spirit is dead, so faith without deeds is dead (James 2:26).

"I've already been saved! Why do I have to keep doing good works?" Have you heard (or said) this before? James's answer in our verse is short and sweet. He says if your faith doesn't show in your deeds, you are dead, just like a body without a spirit.

This makes you think, doesn't it? Why not do a quick test to see how genuine your faith is? Think back to your actions yesterday or the past week. Do you think people will see you as a dedicated Christian judging by the good things you did? Don't keep them guessing any longer! Make up your mind to start doing good deeds because it glorifies your Father. *"Let your light shine before men, that they may see your good deeds and praise your Father in heaven."* That's what Jesus says in Matthew 5:16.

Is your light shining for Jesus?

1 October

Speak, Lord, I'm Listening

The LORD came and stood there, calling as at the other times, "Samuel! Samuel!" (1 Samuel 3:10).

"**W**here are your ears?" teachers and parents often ask when we don't listen to what they're saying. Sometimes it's difficult to pay attention because we're bored. Sometimes we don't want to listen because then it means we have to obey.

We like it much better when others listen to us instead. What we have to say is much more important. Even when we pray, we talk too much and don't listen enough. In church we think of lots of things, but not what the minister is saying. To tell the truth, we are so busy with our own thoughts that we don't have the time to listen.

In the Old Testament we read how God called Samuel. At first he didn't even realize it was God calling him. But when Eli told him it was God, his answer was, "Speak, Lord, for your servant is listening." Samuel listened with all his heart, and he did what the Lord told him to. Because he was prepared to listen and obey, he became one of God's most faithful prophets. Samuel was not afraid to bring God's good news, as well as bad news, to His people.

Next time you pray, say, "Speak, Lord, I'm listening."

2 October

Refined As Silver

"I have refined you. ... I have tested you in the furnace of affliction. For my own sake, for my own sake, I do this" (Isaiah 48:10-11).

I f you have ever visited a goldmine, you will know that there is only one way of getting gold or any other precious metals from the hard rock. This is done by crushing the rock that contains the gold ore and heating it at very high temperatures so that the gold in the rock melts and runs from the rock.

Just like precious metals are put through a process of purification, God sometimes purifies His children by putting them through a process of suffering. This is necessary to remove any sin that is still in your life, because as we all know, in times of crisis we spend much more time with God than in good times!

Christopher Reeve, who played the part of Superman in the movies, was paralyzed a few years ago when he fell from his horse. But he didn't allow this tragedy to get him down. Instead of feeling sorry for himself, he started collecting money for medical research on back and neck injuries.

If tragedy strikes in your life, you can also change that tragedy into a gem. Like Christopher Reeve, look around and see what you can do for others who are worse off than you.

People who suffer can be comforted by a beautiful promise in 2 Corinthians 4:17. What is it?

3 October

Your Church

Let us not give up meeting together, as some are in the habit of doing (Hebrews 10:25).

We all know that the church of God is not just bricks and mortar. It's the people who believe in Jesus who form the church. The building where we usually go on Sundays and where the preacher delivers his sermon, is only the church building, not the church.

Close your eyes and think of the map of the world. Let's pretend it's dark and every believer is a light. Do you see all the lights shining for Jesus all over the world? This is His church!

A tourist tells how impressed she was one night in Switzerland when they attended a church service there. It was in a small stone church that had no lights. Every member took along his own lantern and then put it down on one of the shelves they have for this purpose. At nightfall, all the lights moved towards the little building on the hill, and after the service, the people all carried their lights back home.

We shouldn't go to church only to get something from it. We must also take something along: praise and gratitude for the Lord, kindness and smiles for other people, and money for the work of the Lord. Only then will we too have something to take back home with us.

You can help your church shine like a light in a dark world.

4 October

Christ's Bride

You are no longer foreigners ... but fellow citizens with God's people and members of God's household (Ephesians 2:19).

The Bible often compares the church to a family or household preparing for the day that Christ, the Firstborn Son, will come. How can the church celebrate being together and get ready for His return?

One church decided to start a new program on Sundays. Each family has a regular "Sunday search." The rules are as follows: First, everyone searches for something the Lord wants to teach him or her. It can come to that person in the sermon, a song, a conversation, or a thought. Second, every person must find out what they can do to contribute to the Sunday service. Perhaps you can help someone who has difficulty walking, or you can talk with someone who is lonely. After the service maybe you can get a glass of water for someone who has a cough. In this way ties of love and friendship are formed. Third, at the dinner table that afternoon the family can share with one another what they have learned and in what way they made a contribution.

Everyone who takes part in the Sunday search says it works very well. People now have their antennae out on a Sunday to find out what the Lord wants them to do (and what there is to learn). Perhaps your family could take part in something like this at your church.

The church should show that they are God's family by caring for each other and obeying the Father.

5 October

When God Calls

The LORD ... stood there calling ... "Samuel! Samuel!" Then Samuel said, "Speak, for your servant is listening" (1 Samuel 3:10).

Samuel was still a baby when his mother dedicated him to the Lord. He started working for God as a little boy. He was an instrument in the Lord's hand. He had to learn to recognize God's voice. Eli helped him with that. It was also Eli who taught him to say, "Speak, Lord, your servant is listening." Even as a very young boy Samuel spoke to the Lord and listened to Him.

When Samuel grew up, he became a leader who guided and taught his people. Because he lived so close to the Lord, he knew the Lord's will and then told the people what He wanted. Samuel was a great leader in Israel.

Our country also needs leaders who can guide people the way God says. Maybe the Lord wants you to be a leader. Then you need to start listening to the voice of the Lord in your heart right now. He doesn't speak so you can physically hear Him, but He speaks to you through the Bible and through the Holy Spirit in your heart. If we know something is according to the Word of God and we are happy with that, then it is most probably the Lord speaking. Just tell Him you are listening, He can go ahead and speak. Who knows, maybe you will also become a great leader like Samuel.

The Bible says: "The Lord called to him in a vision, `Ananias!' `Yes, Lord,' he answered" (Acts 9:10).

6 October

The End of
a Crooked Road

Woe to them! (Jude 11).

Jude says that people who take the wrong road will come to a terrible end. He is talking about people who don't serve the Lord and who don't obey His commandments. He uses three images to describe people like this:

- They are like autumn trees, without fruit even at this late stage of the year, uprooted and dead (verse 12).
- They are like wild waves of the sea, their shame blown about like sea spray in the wind (verse 13).
- They are like wandering stars, flung from their orbits. Their place is reserved in the deepest darkness, where they will stay forever (verse 13).

So there can be no doubt about it. In the end God will punish those who are blatantly against Him and don't want to serve Him. Meanwhile you and I must let our testimony be heard loud and clear in contrast to this.

Do you know someone who wants nothing to do with God? Pray for that person.

7 October

Rainbow Nation

I have set my rainbow in the clouds, and it will be the sign of the covenant between me and the earth (Genesis 9:13).

South Africa is known these days as the "rainbow nation." It is a good description of a nation striving to be one, without anyone losing his or her own character. But this means that each citizen of the country must sacrifice something – perhaps a portion of pride that makes one think one is better than others, or an unwillingness to share with someone who has wronged you in the past.

The Bible tells us about a different kind of rainbow nation, the children of God's covenant. After the flood in Noah's time, God repeated His instruction to humankind to rule over the earth. Everything is here for us to make use of, but we must do so with responsibility. God gives His rainbow as a sign that He will never again send a flood to destroy the earth. Every time you see the rainbow, you are reminded of God's promise to His people. Read God's covenant with Noah in Genesis 9:1-18.

We are responsible for the earth and also for our country. Let's make it a rainbow nation who knows its Creator.

8 October

When the Lord Won't Listen

Even when I call out or cry for help, he shuts out my prayer (Lamentations 3:8).

Have you sometimes felt that you pray and pray but the Lord just doesn't listen? Sometimes it feels as if your prayer gets no farther than the ceiling! Jeremiah felt just like this. During the time he was a prophet, the people of Israel really suffered. They were being punished because they wouldn't listen to the Lord's warnings. Jerusalem was destroyed, and the Israelites were taken away in exile.

Jeremiah stayed behind with the people who were still left in Israel. Sometimes things looked so bad that he couldn't help wondering why the Lord was not answering his prayers.

But when Jeremiah remembered the Lord's faithfulness in the past, he felt better again. In the lovely verses of Lamentations 3:22-24, he confesses: *"Because of the LORD's great love we are not consumed, for his compassions never fail. They are new every morning; great is your faithfulness. I say to myself, 'The LORD is my portion; therefore I will wait for him.'"*

Why not make this lovely prayer your prayer the next time you feel the Lord is not listening?

What other man in the Bible had a similar experience to that of Jeremiah? (See Psalm 40:1-5)

9 October

Dead Religion

I will sing with my spirit, but I will also sing with my mind (1 Corinthians 14:15).

Many young people attended the youth service in the church auditorium. Everybody sang at the top of their voices, and some put their hands up in the air, swaying in time to the music. The band was great, and it was really something to hear everyone sing along.

Yet Ursula was unhappy afterwards. "What's wrong?" her father asked.

"Well, I'm not sure if the Lord was praised by tonight's service," she said. "Some of the boys were teasing the girls around them. And there was a lot of talking going on. Some even passed notes to one another. It could just as well have been a lot of heathens gathered around their stone idol."

Ursula's father cleared his throat. "Whoa!" he said. "Just a moment. Be careful of making a rash judgment. You don't know how many there really meant what they were singing. But I agree with you, if we sing to the Lord and our minds are on something else, it's not much different from the mindless rituals of other religions. In any case, I think it's breaking the third commandment."

"Right now I can't think what the third commandment is," Ursula said.

"It's the one that says you shall not misuse the name of the Lord!" her dad answered.

We must mean the words we sing to the Lord.

10 October

The Lion of Judah

"See the lion of the tribe of Judah, the Root of David, has triumphed" (Revelation 5:5).

If you lived in Africa, you would not have to travel very far to see wild animals. You could drive to a game reserve and see many kinds of animals. Many tourists come to Africa from countries all over the world just to see a lion. The lion is called the king of the animals because of its strength. There are few animals that lions are afraid of.

Jesus is called the Lion of Judah in the Bible, because He is the great King of heaven and earth. He is even stronger than the devil who tried to destroy the Lord's work. Nothing and no one is as strong and mighty as the Lord. Jesus came to destroy the devil's work.

When a big lion roars, all the animals in the area listen, and many tremble in fear. When the Lord speaks, we must also listen and be still, because what He says will happen. And one day all of us will stand before His throne, and we will have to tell Him if we did what He said.

The Bible says: "To him be glory and power for ever and ever! Amen." *(Revelation 1:6).*

11 October

F.R.O.G.

F.R.O.G.

F.R.O.G.

Light or Darkness

God is light; in him there is no darkness at all (1 John 1:5).

Have you noticed that even the tiny light of a match can be seen at night in a dark room? The apostle John uses the image of light to explain what God is like. No matter how dark the world is, God and His light will always be seen.

The wonderful part is, of course, that you and I who belong to Him are also God's tiny lights in the world. That is why we must let our light shine before everyone so that our Father in heaven is glorified. Don't ever forget that you are God's representative in the world.

So don't worry that your light might be too small and that it won't be seen. Just like the light of the match we talked about, your light will also be seen. When you are with people who don't believe in the Lord Jesus, your testimony will be at its brightest. It is at such times, more than others, that you must make sure you behave like a true Christian.

Let your light shine brightly. You can stand out like a lily planted in black mud; like a light in the dark night; like a city on a hill.

12 October

A Clear
Conscience before God

Whenever our hearts [consciences] condemn us … God is greater than our hearts, and he knows everything (1 John 3:20).

Do you sometimes get the feeling that your love for other Christians is not what it should be? Do you sometimes feel guilty because you are not able to feel the love you are expected to have?

Sometimes you have reason to feel guilty. But sometimes it is unfounded, if you are honestly trying to live like a true Christian! Then it is necessary to remember that God is bigger than your heart or conscience. This means if the Lord has forgiven you for something you confessed, give your conscience a rest. After all, God is bigger than your conscience, and He forgave you after you confessed your sin. Isn't it great to know that the Lord lives in you through His Spirit, and that His Spirit also activates your conscience when you do something wrong. Then you pay attention to your conscience and confess your sins. But once you have done this, you are free because your conscience is clear again before God.

Do you listen to the still, small voice of conscience?

13 October

Caught Up in
Your Problems

"Come to me, all you who are weary and burdened, and I will give you rest" (Matthew 11:28).

One of the easiest ways to catch a monkey is to make a small round hole in a calabash gourd, put seeds in it, and fasten it to a tree. Monkeys are very inquisitive, and it won't be long before one comes along and puts his hand in the hole to feel what's inside.

When he feels the seeds, he'll hold on to them and try to pull his fist back through the tiny hole. No go! But he won't let go of his goodies, and he'll hold on to them until he's caught. All he had to do to free himself was to open up his hand.

Humans are sometimes just as stupid. We are so worried about life and what is going to happen to us that we get hopelessly caught up in our situation. We see no way out.

Let go, and let God take over. Jesus gives us good advice in Matthew 6:33. He says, *"But seek first his kingdom and his righteousness, and all these things will be given to you as well."*

When you really have your back to the wall, God gives the escape route. Read the story of the twenty loaves in the prophet Elisha's time in 2 Kings 4:42-44.

14 October

Take Heart!

"I will refresh the weary and satisfy the faint" (Jeremiah 31:25).

When Jeremiah was a prophet, times were bad for the Israelites, and he often felt quite depressed. So the Lord made him a promise: He would give him strength when he was tired and encourage him when he was feeling low!

When the well-known scientist Thomas Edison started school in a small town called Port Huron in Michigan, he brought home poor report cards every term. His teachers let his parents know that he was "uneducable"; it was impossible to educate him, and he was too slow to keep up with "normal" children. At her wits' end, his mother decided to teach him herself at home. When he was ten years old, Thomas built his first chemical laboratory. By the end of his life, this child who was uneducable, patented more than 1300 inventions!

There's never a right time to give up. Perhaps you are also struggling a bit at school at the moment. Maybe you are in the depths of despair like Jeremiah was. Today's verse tells you it's worthwhile hanging in there. The Lord knows about your problems, and He wants to help you.

What can you do to thank the Lord that He is always prepared to help you? (See 2 Corinthians 1:3-4.)

15 October

Holy Communion

For whenever you eat this bread and drink this cup, you proclaim the Lord's death until he comes (1 Corinthians 11:26).

Paul was a very careless guy. He was always forgetting his book or his coat or his sports bag at school. So his mother thought of a clever plan. Every time Paul forgot something at school, she tied an extra knot in his tie. The children teased him about it, but he left the tie like that because it reminded him to remember important things.

What Paul didn't know was that the tie plan would also come in handy in Sunday school. It was Holy Communion one Sunday and afterwards their teacher spoke to them about the meaning of communion. He held up a badge and said, "The person who gives me the best reason why we celebrate communion can have this badge!"

This is when Paul thought of his creased tie. "Sir," he said, "we celebrate communion so that we won't forget what the Lord Jesus did for us. It's like when my mom ties a knot in my tie to remind me of things I mustn't forget." No one could think of a better answer and so Paul got the lovely pin with a cross and a dove on it.

How often do you think about the things Jesus did for you?

16 October

How Well do You Know God?

All the saints send their greetings (2 Corinthians 13:13).

"Hey, I know that guy over there," called Kathy excitedly as she finished her milkshake. "I've seen him on TV. And I read all about him in a magazine." Mom smiled as Kathy carried on talking. "Gee, I feel I know him so well that he could be my friend," she wound down at last.

"You do know a lot about him," Mom agreed. "But it takes more than that for someone to be your friend. You don't really know someone until you've spent time together enjoying each other's company." Mom took out money to pay for the meal they had just finished. "It's a little like some people's relationship with God," she added as they walked to the door. Just then the TV actor brushed past them, hardly even glancing at Kathy.

"I guess being friends works both ways," she said slowly. As they walked to the car park Kathy was quietly thinking about what her mom had said about knowing God. She heard lots about God at Sunday school, but she didn't really spend very much time talking to God, and sharing things with Him in prayer. She also didn't often read the Bible for herself to find out what pleases God, and what He doesn't like. That night before she went to sleep she spent longer than usual praying. "Lord Jesus," she said, " I really want to know You as my friend. Help me to spend time getting to know You. Amen."

How important was getting to know Jesus to Paul? See Philippians 3:7

17 October

Pray for Them

Respect those who work hard among you, who are over you in the Lord and who admonish you (1 Thessalonians 5:12).

The Lord calls certain men and women to work for Him full-time. These people know deep down that they won't be happy if they don't work for Him.

You can, of course, glorify the Lord in any job you do. If your father is a lawyer, he must do it as if he is doing it for Jesus. If your mom is an accountant or a housewife, she must also honor the Lord in her work.

But if you do the Lord's work full-time, you are busy with the Bible all day long, and you learn to share the Word of God with others. Then you pray for people, teach them from the Bible, visit the sick, and help others wherever you can. The Lord calls these workers of His to care for His children in the church. These workers are called ministers, pastors, evangelists, music ministers, counselors, and missionaries.

We should thank the Lord for these spiritual workers, and we should also pray for them often, so that they can help us to live for the Lord.

The Bible says: "Pray that I may proclaim it clearly, as I should" *(Colossians 4:4).*

18 October

You Are in Jesus' Family Photo

Pointing to his disciples, he said, "Here are my mother and my brothers. For whoever does the will of my Father in heaven is my brother and sister and mother" (Matthew 12:49-50).

If we took a photograph of a group of Christians today, we don't need a caption saying this is a specific football team, or these are the students in the seventh grade class. No, we can just write: "Family of Jesus Christ."

The reason for this is given in our verses for the day. Every one of us who does the will of the Lord in heaven is Jesus' brother, sister, and mother. The family bond is the bond of faith.

What makes this so wonderful is that no one can take your face out of the photograph if he doesn't like you. Jesus Himself guarantees this. I hope you can see your face very clearly in the family of God photograph. If you believe in Jesus, your face will definitely be there. And if you are there, He will point to you and say, "There is my brother or my sister!"

Say thank you that you may call Jesus your brother.

19 October

Weigh Your Words

"But I tell you that men will have to give account on the day of judgment for every careless word they have spoken. For by your words you will be acquitted, and by your words you will be condemned" (Matthew 12:36-37).

I once saw a movie of a little girl who was posssessed by the devil. It was a terrible movie that I would like to forget. One thing I simply can't get out of my mind is the steady stream of filthy language that flowed from this beautiful little girl's mouth.

Every time I hear children swear, this saying comes to mind: "What the heart thinks, the tongue speaks." It is truly shocking how many children think swearing is a part of everyday language. The kind of words that come from their mouths is even more disturbing. Out of respect for God, the Jews didn't dare even speak His name aloud, and now children are using it as a swear word.

In Ephesians 4:29 we are warned by Paul not to use bad language.

Swearing is crude, rude, ugly, and quite unnecessary. Nobody should be allowed to get away with it.

20 October

Can God
Forget about You?

How long, O LORD? Will you forget me forever? (Psalm 13:1).

When David wrote this psalm, he was really feeling very low. He was so depressed that he felt God had forgotten all about him.

What do you think the answer is to the question David asks here? Is it possible that God can forget about His children? Fortunately God is not like people. Often when everything is going our way, we forget about the Lord, which is exactly what His people, Israel, used to do so many times. But the Lord will never forget His children.

If you have a baby brother or sister, you know how well your mother cares for that baby. She won't forget to change the baby's diaper or feed it. And even if she did forget sometimes, the Lord tells the prophet Isaiah that He will never forget His children. Read Isaiah 49:15 and underline it in your Bible: "Can a mother forget the baby at her breast ... the child she has borne? Though she may forget, I will not forget you!"

We learn two things from today's devotion:
- Make sure you never forget about the Lord, and
- The next time you feel the Lord has forgotten you, just remember His promise in Isaiah 49!

What happens to people who forget about the Lord? (See Job 8:13.)

21 October

What about Dinosaurs?

God made the wild animals according to their kinds, the livestock ... and all the creatures that move along the ground. ... And God saw that it was good (Genesis 1:25).

There is no mention of dinosaurs and other prehistoric animals in the Bible. There are Christian scientists who say that God created the universe in six very long periods, and not literally in six days, and that dinosaurs had already died out by the time He made humans. Others say all the prehistoric animals died in the flood in Noah's time or directly afterwards. Whatever the case may be, the fact that they are not mentioned in the Bible is not at all strange. Only animals important to the history of Bible times are mentioned. You would be able to make a very long list of animals not mentioned in the Bible.

It's quite clear, though, that animals like dinosaurs did exist on earth. One learns a lot about these animals from fossils that have been excavated. God must be proud of us, His creation, who have found out so much about creation through research. After all, He told us to rule over nature and to conserve and work the earth. But He must feel sad if this knowledge leads to doubts about the truth of the Bible. One day in heaven we will see that there is no difference between the story that nature tells us about God and the story we read in the Bible.

Science does not contradict the Bible.

22 October

All Equal in Jesus

For there is no difference between Jew and Gentile – the same Lord is Lord of all and richly blesses all who call on Him (Romans 10:12).

There are many different cultural groups in the world: Greeks, Jews, Afrikaners, British, Chinese, Japanese, Americans, Mexicans, Germans, and many more. Each group has their own language and their own customs and habits. The members of the different groups don't look the same either.

People from different groups who accept Jesus are all the same to Him. He doesn't check to see which group you belong to. All He asks is that we all belong to Him. When someone belongs to Jesus, then that person is a new creature – that's what the Bible says. Then all people are equal. There are no more differences. It's not important to the Lord that they look different or that they have different customs. As long as they have all been forgiven and washed clean, their names are written in the Book of Life.

The Bible says: "Here there is no Greek or Jew, circumcised or uncircumcised, barbarian, Scythian, slave or free, but Christ is all, and is in all" *(Colossians 3:11).*

23 October

He Chose Us

But you are a chosen people ... belonging to God, that you may declare the praises of him who called you out of the darkness into his wonderful light (1 Peter 2:9).

If you belong to God, you are special in this world. Apart from that, you are also a member of God's family, and that makes you part of the church of Jesus Christ.

At the time Peter lived, Christians suffered a lot. Other people didn't think much of them. And then this apostle came along and told them of the high standing they and other believers had with God. This must have given them the strength and courage to bear all the persecution and insults. At least now they knew what God thought of them.

Don't you also find that thought encouraging? As a believer, you are a member of a chosen people; you belong to God. And why did God choose you and save you? To be a witness for Him!

Are you a good witness for the Lord wherever you go?

24 October

The Tax Collector in the Tree

When Jesus reached the spot, he looked up and said to him, "Zacchaeus, come down immediately. I must stay at your house today" (Luke 19:5).

Can you think what a stir it caused when the chief tax collector of Jericho climbed a tree because he was too short? Jesus was coming that way, and Zacchaeus very badly wanted to see Him. The minute Jesus noticed him, He spoke to him and said the well-known words of our text.

Zacchaeus was very happy that Jesus went home with him, but the people of Jericho were not. They saw Zacchaeus as a sinner because he often cheated when he collected money from them. On this day, however, a change took place in Zacchaeus's heart. He promised to give half of everything he owned to the poor, and if he had cheated anybody out of anything, he would pay back four times the amount.

Jesus said on that day salvation had come to Zacchaeus. That is, after all, why Jesus came: to seek and save those who are lost.

Zacchaeus could not have been a popular man in Jericho. Yet, Jesus chose to stay at his house, no matter what the people said.

No one is popular or unpopular in Jesus' eyes. He came to bring salvation to everyone – that means you, too!

25 October

Be Warned!

"He was a murderer from the beginning ... there is no truth in him. When he lies, he speaks his native language, for he is a liar" (John 8:44).

I know of someone who is so mean that he promises young people heaven on earth and then gives them hell on earth.

I know someone who sweet-talks young people with promises and then leaves them in the lurch. I know someone who starts whole organizations to get people into his clutches. I know someone who masquerades in all different disguises. He prowls around the world like a roaring lion, watching for innocent prey.

This someone is the devil.

I also know Someone else who says, "Don't be afraid. I am with you all the days of your life."

I know Someone who knocks at the door of your heart because He wants to come into your life and walk with you. I know Someone who has a whole army in the sky, at sea, and on land to protect you against evil. I know Someone who was prepared to die so that you can live.

Do you know Him, too?

Jesus, the Son of God, came to destroy the devil's work. (See 1 John 3:8.)

26 October

God Keeps His Promises!

"Praise be to the LORD. ... Not one word has failed of all the good promises he gave through his servant Moses" (1 Kings 8:56).

When your parents have promised you something and don't do it, you are not happy with them at all, are you? When you have promised to do something for someone, it's very important that you keep your promise. I'm sure you've broken some of your promises and that others have made promises to you that they also didn't keep.

God is different. He is true to His word. If things are going wrong for you, there is something you can do: remind God of His promises in His Word. King Solomon was right in saying what he did in today's verse. God kept every single promise He made to His people.

God is just as faithful today as in Solomon's time. He never breaks a promise. Here are a few promises to remember: He will protect you in dangerous times (Psalm 91:4); He is always with you (Joshua 1:9); He takes care of you every day (Matthew 6:30); He is there for you when you need help (Psalm 54:4).

See how many promises you can find in Isaiah 40-45, and 60-66.

27 October

Do Miracles
Still Happen?

"For nothing is impossible with God" (Luke 1:37).

Do you believe in miracles? And do you believe that the Lord can, now as in Bible times, do things that are impossible for people to do? God still does things today that cannot be explained by scientists. Many people will tell you that they were so ill that doctors had given up on them. Then friends prayed for them, and to everybody's surprise, they recovered.

Talk to any child of the Lord and that person will be able to tell you about a miracle in his or her life. Every baby that is born, every seed that germinates and becomes a tree, every caterpillar that changes into a butterfly is a miracle! But the greatest miracle of all is that the Lord can change a person's life.

A man once made fun of people who believe in miracles. "Has any one of you seen a miracle?" he asked his friends with a sneer on his face. One of them got up and pointed to himself, "Here is one," he said. His friends nodded. They understood what he meant, because they knew him when he was still a drunk and a loafer. They saw the difference Jesus made in his life when he gave his heart to Him. He became a good, hard-working man.

God's miracle-working power can change a person's life completely.

28 October

Warmheartedness

Be devoted to one another in brotherly love (Romans 12:10).

When you are warmhearted, it means you have filled your heart with love for someone, and then you open it up so that all that love is poured out. A warmhearted person is someone who is friendly and kind towards others. Warmheartedness reminds us of bright sunshine. The opposite of warmheartedness is surliness. Someone who is surly is like a cold, cloudy winter's day without a ray of sunshine.

The Bible says we must be warmhearted towards one another. The only way we can do this is to get rid of all the negative, bad thoughts we harbor in our hearts against others. We must ask the Lord to wash our hearts clean of sin and impure thoughts and to fill our hearts with love for others. Then we will be able to treat others with sincere and warmhearted love.

Warmheartedness reaches out to others. It wants to embrace and touch. It wants to comfort. It wants to be kind.

The Bible says: "But while he was still a long way off, his father saw him and was filled with compassion for him; he ran to his son, threw his arms around him and kissed him" *(Luke 15:20).*

29 October

Raised from the Dead?

Turning towards the dead woman, he [Peter] said, "Tabitha, get up" (Acts 9:40).

Marian is really upset. Her best friend died in a car accident. Her mother tries her best to comfort her and asks their minister to speak to her. Everybody assures her that she and her friend will meet again in heaven, but she can't help wondering why the Lord can't bring Susan back to life again if she asks Him earnestly. After all, it happened in Bible times. Think about Tabitha, for example. She died, and Peter prayed her back to life!

The minister explains, "Marian, miracles like this are few and far between. In the Bible only eight such miracles are mentioned. In the beginning of the Christian church God did wonderful things to establish His church on earth. The news of that miracle in Joppa spread far and wide, and many people started believing in Jesus because of it. These days we don't see things like that happening. But one day, when Jesus comes back on the clouds as He promised, thousands of these miracles will take place! The bodies of all God's children will be raised from the dead that day. Isn't it something to look forward to?"

That night Marian prays, "Thank you, Lord, that Susan is with Jesus, and her body will be brought back to life one day."

One day all the Christians who have died will be raised with transformed bodies.

30 October

Clay Jars Break Easily

But we have this treasure in jars of clay to show that this all-surpassing power is from God and not from us (2 Corinthians 4:7).

The other day my wife bought a beautiful clay pot to plant seedlings in. When we opened the trunk of the car at home, we discovered that the pot had fallen over and broken into pieces. We had to throw it away because it was useless like that.

Paul writes that believers who carry the treasure of the gospel in their hearts are like fragile clay pots that can easily break. He adds that the greatest power of all is from God. Yes, the power of the gospel in our hearts is of much greater importance than we are.

This doesn't mean that the Lord thinks you are unimportant. It is because you are so important to Him that He sent His Son into the world for you and for me. Through His Spirit, Christ came to live in your heart. It is this power in your heart that is stronger than anything else. But the Bible also makes it very clear that you are important to the Lord as well.

You are a clay pot with the message of the gospel in your heart. Thank the Lord for this.

31 October

Suicide Is a Dead End

"I have had enough, Lᴏʀᴅ," he said. "Take my life; I am no better than my ancestors" (1 Kings 19:4).

When a young person commits suicide, it is a tremendous blow to those left behind. You ask yourself what could have made the child so unhappy that he or she just couldn't face life anymore. The disturbing fact is that suicide is one of the main causes of death in children in the United States right now. Why?

The reasons given portray a sad state of affairs in society. Children break down because of:

- pressure to achieve,
- broken homes,
- death or loss of someone close to the child,
- sexual or verbal abuse,
- loneliness,
- depression.

If you are considering suicide, remember it's a permanent solution to a temporary problem that most likely can be solved. Hang in there! You can be helped. Go and speak to the person who is closest to you without delay.

Elijah, God's prophet, also reached a point where he wanted to die. But God spoke to him sternly and gave him another task to do. Read the story in I Kings 19.

People who have been in deep waters come out stronger on the other side. Don't give up. The good times are yet to come.

1 November

It's Great to Be Young!

Be happy ... while you are young, and let your heart give you joy in the days of your youth. Follow the ways of your heart and whatever your eyes see, but know for all these things God will bring you to judgment (Ecclesiastes 11:9).

Being young is really great! It's a time to do things with your friends, explore new places, and get to know new people. You can enjoy hobbies or sports you like and dream about your future and things you still want to do one day.

And this is the way it should be. The Lord wants you to enjoy your youth and to do the things you like. Just keep one thing in mind, though: the day will come when the Lord will expect you to answer for your deeds.

So be careful how you live. Avoid things that are bad for your health, like smoking or drinking. If you are sensible when you are young, you won't have to be sorry one day when you are old about things you should never have started with. And always remember that life here on earth is just a very small part of real life. Everlasting life will last much longer than the time you spend here on earth. So live your life in such a way now that you will live with God forever one day.

What is the most important thing a young person should remember? (See Ecclesiastes 12:13.)

2 November

Is the Bible Really True?

"Your word is truth" (John 17:17).

Suppose someone at school asks you, "How do you know the Bible is true?"

What would your answer be? You could say, "Because Jesus said so!" But then your friend could say, "And how do you know everything the Bible says about Jesus is true?"

A good answer to this would be, "If the Bible is not true, people would have packed it away a long time ago and forgotten about it! But the Bible has always meant so much to people who read it and took its message to heart that they wanted to tell others about it. That is why the Bible has been translated into more than two thousand languages!"

There is also other proof that the Bible is true. People who dug up old scrolls in the Middle East discovered papyrus scrolls thousands of years old. These texts prove without a shadow of a doubt that the Old Testament is true. And there are thousands of really old Greek manuscripts that have the same contents as the New Testament.

Moreover, many of the things predicted in the Bible have come true. All this makes us realize that the Bible is not just an ordinary book. Many people have tried to erase all signs of the Bible, but no one has been able to.

The Bible is a very special book and the Bible is true.

3 November

Stop Complaining

Do everything without complaining or arguing (Philippians 2:14).

Someone who is always complaining is a very unhappy person. And besides that, they also make those around them unhappy. When you complain, you are forgetting about the many things to be thankful for and those that make you happy. Complaining is a sign of unthankfulness.

The Bible tells us not to complain. We read about many people who complained. The Israelites complained to God that they didn't have decent food, and forgot how good the Lord was to bring them out of Egypt. The Pharisees complained because Jesus shared a meal with sinners and tax collectors, ignoring the fact that it was because He loved people so much that he wanted to be with them. The Israelites complained about Moses and Aaron being their leaders, and this made the Lord so angry that He wanted to put an end to the people of Israel (see Numbers 16:45).

The best way to overcome the tendency to complain, is to start thanking the Lord for good and wonderful things. Thank Him for the sun, thank Him for food, thank Him that you are alive, thank Him for your friends, thank Him for shoes, thank Him for water, thank Him, thank Him! There are so many things to praise the Lord for!

The Bible says: Give thanks is all circumstances ... (1 Thessalonians 5:18).

4 November

The Holy Spirit and Your Free Time

So I say, live by the Spirit (Galatians 5:16).

Waht do you do in your free time? Nowadays there are all sorts of things the Lord's children take part in that are not honoring to God. There's a lot of experimenting in risky things going on, and often children and young people have to pay a heavy price for it later.

When you do what Paul says, namely to let the Spirit of God rule your life, you will not waste your time doing what you shouldn't be doing. Like what? Spending time with anything or anyone that takes you away from the Lord and does not glorify Him. Sometimes you can get so caught up in these activities that it becomes very difficult to break free again.

For this reason it is so important that you allow the Spirit of God to control your life. How can you do this? You simply make a decision: "I want the Spirit of the Lord to rule over my life." Then you ask the Lord to help you. Have you done it yet?

You can do it right now. Pray and ask the Lord to rule your life through His Spirit.

5 November

Don't Make the Spirit Unhappy

And do not grieve the Holy Spirit of God (Ephesians 4:30).

Did you know that children can make their parents very unhappy? Every time you do something wrong it is like a sharp arrow in your parents' hearts.

You must never forget that the Holy Spirit has feelings. He can be unhappy, too. That's why the apostle Paul says we must not hurt the Holy Spirit of God. Every time you do something that is against the will of God, the Holy Spirit is sad.

Young people have often said to me, "Every time I want to do something bad, I hear a small voice whispering in my heart that I should not do it."

This is the voice of the Holy Spirit. And if you hear that voice, but you ignore it and go ahead anyway, then the Holy Spirit becomes very sad. This is exactly what Paul warns us against.

Next time you hear the voice of the Holy Spirit, start praying right away: "Spirit of God, thank You for warning me. Please help me not to do anything that I know is wrong!"

6 November

Rule Over,
Don't Destroy!

The LORD God took the man and put him in the Garden of Eden to work it and take care of it (Genesis 2:15).

God put so much trust in His creation, the human being. He trusted us to take charge of the earth. The Owner has only given us a lease on it, though. God expects us to treat His creation with care and give it back to Him in one piece.

Now, thousands of years after Creation, we have made a giant garbage dump of the earth. Countless animal species, insects, birds, and fish have already become extinct. But we just carry on without thinking. We have developed weapons that can blow up the earth by pressing a button. Aren't we clever?

If I were God, I would have said, "This is enough!"

As a matter of fact, the Lord did say this one time in Genesis 6:7, *"I will wipe mankind, whom I have created, from the face of the earth ... for I am grieved that I have made them."*

Before that day comes, let's clean up the earth, literally and figuratively.

7 November

Be An Example

Don't let anyone look down on you because you are young, but set an example for the believers in speech, in life, in love, in faith and in purity (1 Timothy 4:12).

Paul loved Timothy very much. People who study and explain the Bible believe that Paul led Timothy to Jesus. Because Paul didn't have any children, he thought of Timothy as his own son.

Paul tells Timothy that he should be an example to other believers even if he is still young. If you are a believer, your friends are going to watch you closely to see if you really do the things a Christian should. It's sometimes quite difficult to be an example! It's hard not to lose your temper, not to gossip, not to copy someone's homework, and not to do some of the other bad things that young people do.

Timothy managed to be an example, and so can you if you follow Timothy's recipe. You can ask the Lord to help you, starting today, so that what you say, think, and do every day will be an example to others – an example in love, faith, and virtue. Pray that your friends will notice and see Jesus in you!

Read in Acts 16:1-2 what other believers thought of Timothy.

8 November

Is There a Hell?

They will be punished with everlasting destruction and shut out from the presence of the Lord and from the majesty of his power (2 Thessalonians 1:9).

What terrible place is this? And who will be sent there, banished from the presence of God?

Can you think of a more awful place than where God is not? This is exactly what hell, or "everlasting destruction," is – a place where God is not. People who go there are those who didn't want to listen to God all their lives.

There are people who say to the Lord, "Leave me alone! I want nothing to do with you. I'll manage on my own!" If someone keeps on saying this to the Lord, eventually when the person dies, the Lord will in effect say to him, "Your wish has been granted. I am leaving you alone now. From now on you are without Me forever!"

No one knows where hell is or what it looks like there. But Jesus himself said there is a place like hell. God so badly wants people to live with Him in heaven after their death that He gave His everything to make it possible. He let Jesus, His only Child, die on a cross so that everyone who believes in Him won't go to hell but will live with God forever.

If you love the Lord and want to be near Him, you won't go to hell one day.

9 November

What Is Heaven Like?

"But store up for yourselves treasures in heaven ... where thieves do not break in and steal" (Matthew 6:20).

In the book of Revelation we are given a picture of heaven. The streets, it is said, are not paved with concrete; they are pure gold!

Here on earth money and gold are everything to some people. They will work their fingers to the bone for it; they will think up clever schemes and plans to get their hands on it. Yes, they will even become criminals or kill for it! But in heaven gold is just used for paving the roads, because in heaven with God, there are much more important things than gold or money.

What will be seen as treasures in heaven? Since we are going to be on earth only a short while and forever in heaven, it sounds like a good idea to start planning now for our heavenly home. Certain things will be left behind when you go to heaven, like your money box and your rollerblades and your sports trophies and certificates. But do you know what will be there with you? All the friends you won for Jesus. Won't it be fabulous to hear the story they tell there: "You cared about me and I could see that you loved Jesus. That's why I started following Him!"

Only the things I do for Jesus will be important in heaven.

10 November

Feeling Down?

"I have told you these things, so that in me you may have peace. In this world you will have trouble. But take heart! I have overcome the world" (John 16:33).

If you've lost heart, you see only problems. You feel you cannot go on. Everything looks dark. You've lost hope. There is a saying that goes: "Lost your money, lost something; lost hope, lost everything." While you still have hope in your heart, no matter how bad things may look, there might be a way out. But once you have lost hope, it's very difficult to see a way out.

The Lord is a major source of hope. He doesn't want us to lose hope while He is there for us! He is the great God who is almighty. He can do anything. He can even perform miracles if He wants to. All He expects us to do is trust Him. This means we believe and know that He will look after us and help. Often the Lord waits until we have almost lost hope to see if we really trust Him and will keep on believing.

When you start thanking Him and praising Him for all His help, even if you haven't received it yet, the courage and hope in your heart becomes stronger. Hold on to Him today!

The Bible says: "I will be with you; I will never leave you nor forsake you" (Joshua 1:5).

11 November

Rejoice!

Rejoice in the Lord always. I will say it again: Rejoice! (Philippians 4:4).

According to the Bible, joy is one of the qualities that must be part of a Christian's life. Cheerfulness and joy are not necessarily the same thing. Cheerfulness can sometimes be only skin-deep, like when you are enjoying yourself at a party. Joy goes deeper; there is joy in your heart because you have parents who care about you.

When there is joy in your heart because you know you belong to the Lord, this is joy that goes deep. The anchor of real joy is knowing you belong to the Lord. He is the source of genuine joy. And this is a kind of joy that no one can take away from you. Even in sad circumstances, you can still experience joy because you know you belong to the Lord.

So we see that the joy Paul is talking about does not depend on a feeling inside, nor on something special happening. True joy comes from Jesus Christ. This is why we can experience this joy in any circumstances.

Is Jesus the source of your joy?

12 November

Clothes That
Never Go Out of Style

Put on the full armor of God (Ephesians 6:11).

Do you know the story of the foolish emperor and his new clothes? Not wanting to offend the emperor, his subjects praised his lovely "outfit." The clothes were actually invisible, and without knowing it, the emperor paraded down the streets wearing nothing at all. As the saying goes, "Fine feathers make fine birds." And what a fool the emperor made of himself!

There is a description in the Bible of another outfit that is also invisible but that all good Christians need to wear. These "clothes" are invisible because our enemy is invisible.

First you get a lovely belt made of truth. A strong breastplate protects your heart, which has already been washed clean. Your shoes walk the path of peace. For accessories you have a shield to ward off the attacks of evil and also a helmet of salvation. With the sword of the Spirit, the Word of God, in your hand, you are dressed to take on the world. And what's more, this outfit will always be in fashion.

Once upon a time there was a young boy who wore this outfit, and he defeated a giant. Do you know who he is? (See 1 Samuel 17:31-50.)

Paul warns us to wear the full armor so that we will always be ready.

13 November

Are You Satisfied?

For we brought nothing into the world, and we can take nothing out of it. But if we have food and clothing, we will be content with that (1 Timothy 6:7-8).

Paul expected a lot from Timothy, his "true son in the faith." In this letter he tells Timothy that possessions are not important; he should be satisfied to have food and clothes. In Timothy's day children definitely did not have as many things and belongings as children have today. So maybe it was easier for Timothy to be satisfied with what he had than it is for you!

If all your friends have rollerblades or CD players, it can be hard to be content with what you have or don't have! But the Lord wants you to be satisfied with the things He gives you. So, if there are many things you want and if you find that you are jealous of your friends, stop and think again.

Perhaps that is just the right time to make a list of all the things you want to thank the Lord for. Learn to concentrate on the things the Lord has already given you rather than focusing on everything you don't have.

Make a list of everything you want to thank the Lord for.

14 November

Can the Stars Foretell the Future?

Let no one be found among you ... who practices divination or sorcery, interprets omens. ... Anyone who does these things is detestable to the LORD (Deuteronomy 18:10-12).

Have you noticed how many magazines and newspapers feature daily astrology readings? Some people believe we are all born under a certain zodiac sign based on star constellations. They say everybody born under the same sign will have similar characteristics. On top of that, they believe that fortune-tellers and astrologers can see what lies in the future for each star sign.

For example, they say if you were born between June 21 and July 22, then you are a Cancer. And you will, perhaps, get very bad news in the coming month. Sometimes they even give advice: "Move out of the neighborhood where you live." And people believe them and do all kinds of stupid things.

The Bible says believers must not have anything to do with this kind of thing. It is the devil's work. Satan will do anything to lure us away from God's path.

The Lord wants us to trust Him with our future. It's better to ask the advice of other Christian believers and get it from the Bible, not from fortune-tellers.

The Lord gave us His Holy Spirit to lead us into the future.

15 November

The Right Clothes

"They will walk with me, dressed in white" (Revelation 3:4).

We like wearing nice, clean clothes. If you buy a pretty dress or a new shirt, you can't wait to wear it.

Jesus told the story of a king who arranged a wedding banquet. When a man turned up who was not suitably dressed for the occasion, the king told his servants to throw him out. (See Matthew 22:11-13.) Jesus used this parable to tell us we will only be allowed in His kingdom if we are dressed in the "right clothes."

So what clothes are the right clothes? They are salvation clothes, washed clean by Jesus who died for us. Revelation 7:14 gives us a glimpse of heaven. We see a great many people in clean, white clothes, washed and made white in the blood of the Lamb. Yes, the Bible says the blood of Jesus washes us clean. When we ask the Lord to forgive our sins, then He gives us new, clean, white clothes – clothes of salvation.

Afterwards we can dress in more new clothes. The Bible calls these the clothes of living the right way. These clothes are the righteous acts of believers. (See Revelation 19:8.) Because we believe in Jesus, we are thankful, and that is why we do good deeds. These good deeds are like beautiful, bright new clothes.

The Bible says: "I have taken away your sin, and I will put rich garments on you" *(Zechariah 3:4).*

16 November

People of the Light

You are all sons of the light and sons of the day. We do not belong to the night or to the darkness (1 Thessalonians 5:5).

There are all kinds of people in your community. But the Bible says there are actually only two kinds of people in a community: people of the day and people of the night.

I would like to think that you are a person of the light. Then you needn't be ashamed of what you do and how you live. Then you want to be known as someone who loves the Lord Jesus and who follows Him. Then you don't want to be associated with the things of darkness or activities of the night, do you?

You don't have to be afraid of the people of the night or the darkness. They will always be around until the second coming of the Lord Jesus Christ. It would be very unwise to choose friends from their circles, though. There is a very real danger of their dragging you down to their level. Choose friends from the people who live in the light. Remember that your friends at school will know soon enough which crowd you hang out with. It's not always possible to avoid the company of people of the darkness. So never forget to be a good witness, and make sure your testimony is heard, loud and clear.

Live like a person of the light!

17 November

Good Works Aren't Always Big Works

And we pray ... that you may ... please [the Lord] ... bearing fruit in every good work, growing in the knowledge of God (Colossians 1:10).

Did you think "good works" are only the big and important tasks that you perform? One is inclined to think a good work is something like when you do missionary work in a distant country. This is not necessarily true.

Good works are the things Christians do because they are thankful that they belong to the Lord. They don't need to do "big" things. Let's give a few examples. Serving your parents by bringing them coffee in the morning once in a while is a good work. When you wash your dad's car (without complaining), that is a good work. Picking up empty cold drink cans and papers from the football field after a game is a good work.

So you see, good works are those tasks you perform because of a positive attitude deep inside of you. One does not do good works to be saved. No, Christians do good works because they have already been saved. Good works are evidence that you already belong to the Lord.

Ask the Lord what good work you can do for Him today. Then go and do it!

18 November

New Records

Ahab son of Omri did more evil in the eyes of the LORD than any of those before him (1 Kings 16:30).

The Guinness Book of Records is known for its fascinating list of world records. There are endless sporting achievements: the most test tries in rugby, the longest jump, the fastest race, and so on. There are a few fun ones too, like the longest kiss, the fattest lady, the ugliest person. You name it, and it's there.

There was a king in Bible times who also set a record. Of a long line of kings who were terribly wicked, he was the worst by far. He had a staunch supporter in his wife, Jezebel. She was a Baal worshipper and lost no time "converting" her husband and the people. Ahab not only built Baal an altar, but he also had a holy totem-pole put up. He did more to provoke the God of Israel than all the kings of Israel before him. (See 1 Kings 16:33.)

He died a gruesome death. He was hit by an arrow during a battle, and the dogs licked up his blood in the streets as Elijah had prophesied.

Do the right thing. It is highly unlikely that you will make the record books, but you will die happy.

19 November

Pray for Our Leaders

I urge then, first of all, that ... prayers ... be made for ... kings and all those in authority (1 Timothy 2:1-2).

Paul has another important task for young Timothy. He tells him how important it is to pray for the leaders of their country. The Christians in Timothy's time didn't agree with the government.

Maybe you have heard your parents complain about our country and that they are not happy with things the government is doing. Even if you don't agree with the people who rule over you, you must remember the Lord appointed them over you.

So you not only need to obey the laws, but also pray for those who rule the country: for our President, Congress, and state governors. They need wisdom from the Lord himself every day if they want to do the important work they have to do properly. It might be a good idea to write down their names in your prayer book and pray for each of them by name. The only way there can ever be peace in our country is if people learn to accept one another and to pray for one another.

What does the Lord expect from believers regarding governing authorities? (See Romans 13:1.)

20 November

No Other Gods

"You shall have no other gods before me" (Exodus 20:3).

"I could never kneel before a monster like that!" Louise says in Sunday school. The teacher has shown them a picture of people worshiping a bronze figure.

"Yes, but we have other gods today," the teacher replies. "Who can name a few?"

"Money," is Peter's immediate response.

The teacher knows his parents are very rich but never come to church. "Could be," she says. "What else?"

"Sports," says Maureen.

"Yes," the teacher says. "Sports are a good thing, but they must never be more important than the Lord."

"My mom says pleasure is my god," Kim says. "She says I watch too much television, so I don't have my quiet times."

The teacher replies, "If this is true, then we'll have to talk about it!"

"You can worship yourself," is Hector's opinion.

"How can you do that?" Ryan wants to know.

"When you are so selfish that you never have time for others, then you worship yourself!" the teacher says.

"Let's close our eyes and confess those things that are more important to us than the Lord, and let's tell Him that He is the only God we want to worship."

The Lord must be number one in your life.

21 November

Grow!

But grow in the grace and knowledge of our Lord and Savior Jesus Christ (2 Peter 3:18).

If a baby is to grow, he needs four things: food and water, fresh air, warmth, and exercise. Without these the baby will die. There are also a few things we need if we don't want to stay spiritual babies forever, as far as our faith goes.

Reading the Bible is just as important for our spirit as food is for a baby. They say a tortoise can be without food for five hundred days, but don't you try going that long without spiritual food! Before you know it you will be of no use to the Lord!

Praying is like breathing. A man apparently once held his breath for more than thirteen minutes. If he had gone much longer, he definitely would not have made it. We need to talk to the Lord regularly; otherwise we will suffocate spiritually.

Being with other Christians helps us develop spiritually. A coal of fire lying off by itself cools down quickly. But together with other coals it glows a long time. When we are among other Christians, we stay warm and are enthusiastic for the Lord much longer than when we are on our own.

To be a witness for the Lord or do other work for Him is to exercise our faith. And so we become stronger children of the Lord.

Read the Bible, pray, get together with other Christians, and work for the Lord. These things make you spiritually strong.

22 November

Like a Dove

At that moment heaven was opened, and he saw the Spirit of God descending like a dove and lighting on him (Matthew 3:16).

A dove is a symbol of peace and hope. At huge gatherings where people of different countries get together, such as the Olympic Games, doves are often released. The doves all fly up together. The sound of a dove cooing brings peace to one's soul.

When Jesus was baptized and ready to start His earthly ministry, something wonderful happened. Above Jesus and John the Baptist, heaven opened up, and the next moment something like a dove descended on Jesus. It was the Holy Spirit who was sent down to Jesus by the Father to help Him with everything He had to do. Jesus did wonderful work on earth. He healed the sick, drove out demons, forgave people their sins, performed miracles, preached, and taught. To be able to do all this, He needed the Holy Spirit. That is why the Holy Spirit came down on Him like a dove.

You also need the Holy Spirit to do what the Lord wants you to. We receive the Holy Spirit when we are born again, that is, when we accept Christ as our Lord and Savior. The Spirit doesn't come to us in the form of a dove like with Jesus, but He does come live in us.

The Bible says: "Be filled with the Spirit" (Ephesians 5:18).

23 November

God Breathed His Words into the Bible

All Scripture is God-breathed (2 Timothy 3:16).

What is meant by the words of the verse above? It means that He breathed His words into the hearts of the writers of the Bible.

Just like one speaks into the mouthpiece of a telephone, God spoke into the hearts of the writers of the Bible through His Spirit.

This doesn't mean the Lord spoke into a microphone and that the writers wrote words down automatically. No, God laid words in their hearts, then the words went through the sieve of each one's personality, and only then did they write them down. This explains why one can tell from a specific book whether the writer was a learned man like Paul or if he was a farmer like Amos.

Isn't it wonderful that the Lord used the personalities of the authors of the Bible? In the same way He wants to use you with your unique personality. After all, you received your personality from the Lord. You don't need to become someone else or like someone else when you start witnessing for the Lord. Just be yourself. Through His Spirit, He will use you as an instrument in His hand. Give testimony of what the Lord did for you personally, because then people will realize that you are sincere.

Thank the Lord for His wonderful Word.

24 November

Be Thankful

Give thanks in all circumstances, for this is God's will for you in Christ Jesus (1 Thessalonians 5:18).

George was busy with his homework. He didn't feel like doing it at all because he was tired and thirsty. His mother came in carrying a big glass of chocolate milk for him. George saw her but said nothing. When his mother left the room, he gulped the cold drink down and went on with his essay, still moaning about it. How do you think his mom felt?

We often treat the Lord exactly the same. He sees we need something, and He gives it to us. Then we just take it and go about our business as usual, without even saying thank you. You can thank the Lord in four different ways. You can be thankful in your thoughts, in prayer, in song, or you can do nice things for others because you are thankful.

In a certain region in the Alps, the herdsmen have the lovely custom of singing to one another when it is time to take the cattle and goats back home. They sing, "Up till now the Lord has kept us safe. Praise Him!"

Shakespeare, one of the greatest writers of all time, said that unthankfulness is the ugliest of all kinds of sin. It's even worse than stealing or swearing or being drunk, he said. Do you agree with him?

What things are you thankful for? See how many you can name in one minute.

The Lord deserves to be thanked.

25 November

Watch What You Say!

No lie was found in their mouths (Revelation 14:5).

In Revelation 14, we read about the 144,000 people who remained faithful to the Lord and are now with Him in heaven. A formidable thing is said about these people: No lie was found in their mouths! I wonder if there is one of us who can say this! One recent study found that people lie up to two hundred times per day!

I'm sure this isn't true of you. But the fact is that it's very easy to tell a little white lie and not even notice that you've done something wrong. It is very important to the Lord that His children always tell the truth. The devil – who is also called the "father of lies" – is going to try his best to lure you into telling a lie as often as possible.

Starting today, pay special attention to what you say. Make sure that all the stories you pass on are the truth and that the things you say don't contradict your Christianity. If you do catch yourself telling a half-truth, confess your sin right away. God is gracious; He will forgive you every time.

With what does James compare the human tongue? (See James 3:6.)

26 November

More and More like Jesus

Whoever claims to live in him must walk as Jesus did (1 John 2:6).

What is written here is that our lives must be like Jesus' life. Jesus is not on earth anymore, so we must show people what He was like. Wow, that's quite a job, isn't it? How could we ever manage to be as loving and good as Jesus?

Have you ever tried standing with your back to the sun on a clear day, then holding a mirror in such a way that the glare of the sun reflects on your face? If you have, you would have seen your face shine with an unusual light. In the same way, if you spend a lot of time with Jesus through prayer, then your life will also reflect all the good characteristics He had. People who read the Bible regularly and meditate on it and who talk to the Lord a lot usually start acting the way Jesus did. Do you know someone whose face is always beaming because he knows Jesus?

I heard a story of an important businessman who met a little boy. A bully had knocked the boy's belongings out of his hands, and the businessman helped him pick the scattered things up. The little boy was so thankful and surprised that a stranger could be so kind and helpful that he asked, "Sir, are you perhaps Jesus?" People long for someone like Jesus. We can try to stand in for Him.

The Holy Spirit lives in us and helps us to be like Jesus.

27 November

The Wall around Us

"And I myself will be a wall of fire around it," declares the
LORD, "and I will be its glory within" (Zechariah 2:5).

People build walls around their houses because it makes them
feel safe. They hope it will keep thieves and crooks out. In the
olden days, people also built walls around towns or cities. This
was to keep out the enemy who wanted to attack the city and
capture it. So there was also a strong wall around Jericho. The
Lord gave the Israelites a plan to make this wall fall over: They
were to march around the city once a day for six days and seven
times on the seventh day, and when the priests sounded the
trumpets, the wall collapsed. It was a miracle. The wall could
no longer protect the people of Jericho, and the Israelites took
the city.

We also need to protect our lives. But we need more than a
wall around our house or a burglar alarm to make a noise. We
need the Lord himself. The Lord protects His children because
He loves us. Even if we get into trouble, He is there to help us.
He sends His angels to look after us. It's as if He builds a wall of
protection around us so that the enemy cannot destroy us.

The Bible says: "The Lord is my helper, I will not be afraid.
What can man do to me?" *(Hebrews 13:6).*

28 November

Every Family Member Must Work

Our people must learn to devote themselves to doing what is good, in order that they may provide for daily necessities (Titus 3:14).

You are lucky if you have parents that take care of you. It gives children peace of mind to know their parents make an honest living and that it is important to them to provide for their children.

But don't forget — it is not only parents who need to take care of children. Children also need to take the responsibility of doing an honest day's work. The most important work you have at the moment is your schoolwork. But there are other odd jobs at home that you should not pass onto someone else.

Some children are not prepared to do anything around the house or help with the yardwork. This is not the way it's meant to be at all. A family is like one big body. If one of the limbs does not function, the body cannot work, walk, and move around the way it is supposed to.

Every member of the family must see to the tasks he or she has to do, and do them well, without complaining.

Never dump your responsibilities onto someone else.

29 November

Sharper than Any Sword

For the word of God is living and active. Sharper than any double-edged sword, it penetrates even to dividing soul and spirit, joints and marrow (Hebrews 4:12).

In our kitchen we have quite a few knives. Most of them are fairly blunt, but there is a bread knife that is sharper than a sword. Paul says the Word of God is sharper than any sword that has been sharpened on both sides.

What does this mean? It means that the Bible can cut open a person's heart and soul to lay it bare before the Lord. There is nothing you can hide from the Lord. He knows everything about you. After all, He made you, didn't He? He knows how your body works, how your mind works, what you think, and what you are planning.

Fortunately the Word of the Lord is not set on cutting up your life so that you need to be unhappy about it. The Bible's purpose is to bring you closer to Christ and to help you know how to live. If you are in a bad mood, keep in mind that the Word says your friendliness must be known to all people. If you are sad, remember that the Lord would like to see joy in your life.

The Bible will help you discover the qualities the Lord put inside you.

30 November

Angry about God's Grace?

"You are a gracious and compassionate God, slow to anger and abounding in love, a God who relents from sending calamity" (Jonah 4:2).

Let's say your brother was very naughty, and your dad promises to punish him harshly. Your dad sends you to go and tell him what's waiting for him. Then your brother comes and apologizes to your dad and promises never to do this again, and your father forgives him. How would this make you feel?

Would you do what Jonah did? To start off with, Jonah was not at all excited about speaking to the people of Nineveh about their bad behavior. Then after three days in the fish's stomach, he eventually decided to go after all and tell them their city would be destroyed in forty days' time. And would you, like Jonah, become angry and go and sit under a tree, sulking, because they repented and God decided to forgive them?

Jonah is like all of us – very human. He was angry that God acted like a typical father. He says, "I know you are a merciful God, and I should have known you would let these people get away with everything. Why did I waste my time coming here?"

God would not punish one hundred and twenty thousand people who repented. Jonah couldn't take it that God could be so kindhearted and forgiving.

Thank God for His never-ending grace for all of us who have sinned and need His forgiveness.

1 December

God's Way

If the LORD delights in a man's way, he makes his steps firm; though he stumble, he will not fall, for the LORD upholds him with his hand (Psalm 37:23-24).

On the wall in my husband's study is a very old picture of the "broad road" and the "narrow road" (Matthew 7:13). The broad road is a smooth and easy road offering a variety of pleasures, and there are many people on this road. But at the end of this road is destruction. The narrow road, on the other hand, is an up-hill, dangerous road, and few people see their way clear to take this road. Yet this difficult road is the road that leads to heaven.

It's not always easy to stay on God's road when you are young. There are many things you want to do; some things that you know only too well are wrong. If the road the Lord marks out for you in His Word seems difficult, just remember that He walks by your side, and He is always there to help and support you. And if your foot should slip, He will be there to help you up.

Even if it isn't the road with the most attractions or easiest route, it is the Lord's road and is the best one for you!

What does God do for people who are on His road? (See Job 31:4)

2 December

Love for Everyone

"I now realize how true it is that God does not show favoritism but accepts men from every nation who fear him and do what is right" (Acts 10:34-35).

One day there was a school principal who had a strange dream. He dreamed he was told to get all the pupils in his school together because Jesus was coming to visit them. He made them sit in neat rows on the football field. He liked order and method, so he put all the black children in front, the brown ones in the middle, and the white children at the back. But this didn't look right to him. So he decided to place them differently, with all the girls in front and the boys at the back. But again it looked all wrong.

While he was busy giving instructions for the seniors to sit at the back and the little ones in front, Jesus arrived! Everything now looked disorganized and the man was very disappointed that he wasn't able to organize everything well before Jesus came. So he just let the children sit as they were. He went up onto the stage, and when he was standing next to Jesus and looked down on them, he saw how nice this medley of children looked. Suddenly he realized that to Jesus we are all the same, regardless of skin color, gender, or age.

We must also not be prejudiced.

All people are equally important to Jesus, and He loves us all.

3 December

Be Humble

"The one who rules [should be] like the one who serves"
(Luke 22:26).

This must be one of the most difficult instructions the Lord gave His friends. It is not easy to be humble when you have an important job. And on top of that, all of us have this built-in wish to be important.

But always remember how Jesus, the most important man who ever lived, was prepared to wash the dirty feet of His disciples. Also remember that Jesus said humility is one of the fruits that will grow on the tree of our lives if the Holy Spirit lives in us.

What is humility? When you wash the pan, black with burnt cereal, at the youth camp because no one else wants to do it; when people forget to thank you for your contribution to the school newsletter and you let it pass; when you get the worst room in the school and you don't make a scene; when they forget to announce at assembly that you won the chess championships and you don't make an issue of it ... then you are a humble person, and our Lord is very proud of you!

And if you have done something well and people praise you, give credit to your Creator. Say like John the Baptist, "He must become more and I must become less!"

Because you are a Christian, you must be willing to be the least.

4 December

The Angel with Me

"He will command his angels ... to guard you carefully"
(Luke 4:10).

Angels are God's messengers and God's helpers. The Lord sends them especially to come and help His children on earth when they are in trouble. Angels are heavenly beings that we cannot see with our eyes. They are faster than a lightning flash, and the Bible also calls them flames of fire. Angels have been described as having wheels and sparkling with jewels (Ezekiel 10:9), and they are big and strong. They fight against the fallen angels who followed Satan (demons and authorities and powers). The fallen angels are afraid of God's angels, because they are stronger than the demons.

You and I are often helped by angels who are with us, even if we don't see them. One day in heaven we will be surprised to see how often the angels helped us when we didn't even know it.

We don't worship angels, because they were created like us, like humans. We worship the Lord who loves us so much that He sends His angels to help us.

The Bible says: "Praise be to the God of Shadrach, Meshach, and Abednego, who has sent his angel and rescued his servants!" *(Daniel 3:28)*

5 December

The Bible and this Book of Daily Devotions

How can a young man keep his way pure? By living according to your word! (Psalm 119:9)

Of course I'm pleased that you read from this book every day. You must remember, however, that a daily devotional cannot take the place of the Bible. A good thing to do is to look up the verse from Scripture given for each day in your Bible. The thoughts that we, the writers of this book, have written down are given just to help you understand the Bible better. Don't allow any book to take the place of the Bible in your life.

Read our verse for today again. Young people can keep their lives pure by living the way the Bible says. So it follows that the Bible is the most important book that any Christian can read and study. Perhaps it would be a good idea to read from this book, say, in the morning, and then at night, the whole chapter in the Bible from which the text was taken.

Remember: the Lord's Word is a light for you on the path of life.

6 December

God Is Everywhere

"Can anyone hide in secret places so that I cannot see him?" declares the LORD. "Do not I fill heaven and earth?" declares the LORD (Jeremiah 23:24).

When I was in elementary school, we loved playing hide-and-seek. We all had our own favorite hiding places, and sometimes it took our friends a long time to find us.

It's not difficult to hide from your friends or your parents. Sometimes you pretend not to hear when your mom calls you, don't you? But we can never hide from the Lord. Neither can we do or say or think things He doesn't know about. God is everywhere. He not only made you, but He also knows you through and through. He always knows where you are. He even knows what you think! You can hide absolutely nothing from Him.

If you're not really happy with this thought, then just remember that it also means you are never alone. You always have the Lord with you. He lives in you through His Holy Spirit so that you are never without Him, ever. And the next time you feel lonely, just close your eyes and talk to the Lord. He loves you and will never leave you.

What must you do to belong to the Lord? (See 1 Corinthians 6:19-20.)

7 December

Sing in the Dark

"Do not grieve, for the joy of the LORD is your strength"
(Nehemiah 8:10).

In Acts 16, one of the most amazing stories about the life of Paul is told. We read there how Paul and Silas were beaten with sticks and thrown into prison because they were preaching the gospel. And what did they do then? Moan and groan about their bruised and bleeding bodies? No! They prayed and sang and praised the Lord!

John Bunyan, the well-known writer of the book *Pilgrim's Progress*, was also thrown in prison because of his religious beliefs. In his dark cell was a chair, and its back was made of wooden bars. He hollowed out one of these wooden bars, made himself a flute, and on this instrument played the most beautiful music to the glory of God. The prison wardens could never find out where this heavenly music was coming from, because by the time they got to his cell, the wooden bar was neatly in place. Only after he was released from prison did they discover the flute. To this day, it is on display in a museum in England.

Satan always tries his best to take a Christian's joy away, but if you can manage a smile or sing a song or whistle a tune when you're having a hard time, the devil sees that you and Jesus are too strong for him. Then he leaves you alone and looks for other prey.

Jesus will always help us to be joyful, even when we are suffering.

8 December

Come Closer

Come near to God and he will come near to you (James 4:8).

Some people are afraid of coming too close to the Lord. God is so great and mighty, is it possible that He really wants to be close to me? This is what some people ask. Remember that Jesus' name is also Immanuel, which means, "God is with us." He wants to be near us. We needn't worry that we will get hurt or become too different if we are close to God. No, He loves us as we are, and when He is near us, then we can only be better people. Actually we should see how close we can get to God – the closer, the better.

When we accept Jesus, He lives inside of us through the Holy Spirit. Then our bodies are His home, and He shares everything with us.

But sometimes, even though the Lord lives in us, we can still carry on as if He is not there at all. We make our own plans and our own decisions without talking to the Lord first. We can also do the wrong thing even if He is inside us. We must try to live so close to Him that we do everything with Him and for Him.

Let's talk to Him every day. Let's learn to recognize His voice when He speaks to us through His Word. Let's decide to do what He expects us to.

The Bible says: "[The Holy Spirit] lives with you and will be in you" *(John 14:17).*

9 December

Treat Your Pets Well

A righteous man cares for the need of his animal, but the kindest acts of the wicked are cruel (Proverbs 12:10).

Do you find it a drag to look after your pets? It's nice to have a pet, I know. But in the long run, children often get bored with caring for them. Caring for a pet is not all you need to do. You can spend some of your time playing with your dog or teaching your parrot to talk. It's just not good enough to only give a few spare moments to your pet every once in a while.

Would you be satisfied if your mother cooked you some food only now and then, sometimes checked if you have clean clothes to wear, and very seldom made you sandwiches for school? No, she looks after you properly, and you can rely on her – every day. This is the way you should care for your animals too – not just sometimes, but all the time.

Look at the verse above again. If you look after your animals well, you start enjoying them, and they become a pleasure. But it must be done on a regular basis. Have you noticed how a dog wags its tail when its food is ready and you call it? This also makes you happy.

So concentrate on things you can do to make your pets happy. Just think how your dog will wag his tail if you surprise him with an extra bone. Then he will know you want to take good care of him.

God also created animals. Take care of them.

10 December

Friends Can Make or Break You

A man of many companions may come to ruin, but there is a friend who sticks closer than a brother (Proverbs 18:24).

I once had to visit a young man who was in prison. After passing through all the security gates and walking down the long corridors after the warden, the young man and I finally sat down in a small room, facing each other. He was so ashamed that I had to see him in these circumstances.

We had only half an hour to talk, so there was no time to waste. When I asked him, "Tell me, why are you here?" he swallowed hard and took a few deep breaths. Then he told me that he had a few friends years before who were a bad influence on him, and eventually he started shoplifting with them. Later, more friends crossed his path, and things went from bad to worse. The end of the story? He was brought to ruin by his friends, and he ended up in prison!

I really hope you don't have friends like these. Fortunately the opposite is also true: If you have a friend who warns you when you are about to do something wrong, you should be very thankful. The Bible says he is actually closer to you than a brother. Don't get angry with him when he warns you against something.

Think about your best friends. Do they know the Lord? Then they are closer to you than brothers. Why not thank the Lord for them right now?

11 December

Christmas – A Time of Joy

"I bring you good news of great joy. … Today in the town of David, a Savior has been born to you; he is Christ the Lord" (Luke 2:10-11).

Why is Christmas the most wonderful day of the year for you? The day you look forward to all year, the day your heart sings with joy? On that first Christmas, the angels who came to tell the shepherds that Jesus was born sang a beautiful song of praise. It is a message of joy that they brought. We are also joyful at Christmas because it is the day that God's promise of the Messiah came true.

God sent His Son to be born as an ordinary human baby, to live a sinless life, and to die on a cross, so that the sin that came into the world through Adam and Eve's disobedience could be washed clean by Jesus' blood.

You and I are sinners; we all sin. But at Christmas we celebrate with joy, because Jesus' birth and death on the cross erased that sin. If you tell God about your sin and try not to sin any more, He will forgive you, because Jesus paid for it on the cross. Now isn't that more than enough reason to be joyful at Christmas?

What did the shepherds do to show their joy? (See Luke 2: 20.) What can you do?

12 December

Be a Peacemaker

"Blessed are the peacemakers, for they will be called sons of God" (Matthew 5:9).

You probably know that bullfighters in Spain use a red cloth to anger and alarm the bull they are fighting. And I suppose you also know that soldiers hold up a white flag when they don't want to fight any more but want to make peace. But do you know that you are also given the opportunity to use a white or red flag everyday?

If you are someone who likes arguments, you are a red-flag person. But if you are peace-loving, you are a white-flag person. Think about the way you normally react. What do you do when someone squeezes in front of you when you're standing in a line? Or when someone teases you? Or when someone steps on your toe by mistake?

Remember, the Lord wants us to be peacemakers. He even wants us to try and make peace between other people. A little boy was once asked whose side he takes when his mom and dad fight, and his answer was, "I don't take sides. I go and stand between them and stop them from hurting each other!" This is what a peacemaker does. If he knows about two people who are upset with each other, he will try to help them make up. He doesn't tell stories that will hurt people, and he never stirs up trouble.

If you belong to the Lord, you will be a peacemaker.

13 December

Don't Be Afraid!

The LORD is the stronghold of my life – of whom shall I be afraid? (Psalm 27:1).

We all have something we are afraid of. Some people are scared of the dark, and others are afraid of dogs or burglars. What scares you most? Exams? Being alone? The Lord knew that we would all struggle with certain fears. That's why He says 366 times in the Bible, "Do not be afraid!" That's once for every day of the year and an extra one for leap year. We need not fear anything, because we have someone to protect us: the Lord himself.

The Golden Gate Bridge in San Francisco is one of the longest bridges ever built. It is said that while they were building the first half of the bridge, there were many accidents. Twenty-three people fell from the bridge during working hours and drowned in the ocean bay far down below! So they decided to put a safety net under the construction work. It cost them more than a hundred thousand dollars to put up, and it saved the lives of at least ten people. But then something else happened once the safety net had been put up. The work was done better, and the workmen worked much faster! Because they were not afraid anymore, they could give the job at hand their undivided attention and energy.

The Lord's children should do more than other people and never lose heart, because they have a heavenly Father to protect them.

We need never be afraid! God is with us.

14 December

The Lamb of God

You were redeemed ... with the precious blood of Christ,
a lamb without blemish or defect (1 Peter 1:18-19).

The Lord is as strong and mighty as a lion, but He is also as meek as a lamb. The Bible calls Jesus the "Lamb of God." In the Old Testament we read how people sacrificed lambs to pay for the sin in their lives.

Jesus died on the cross to pay for the sins of all people. That is why John the Baptist said Jesus is the Lamb of God who will take away the sins of the world (John 1:29). Isaiah lived a very long time ago, and he said the people in Jerusalem would lead Jesus to Golgotha like a lamb to the slaughter (Isaiah 53:7). Jesus didn't even try to free Himself. He didn't put up a fight. He didn't try running away. He knew He had to die, just like a lamb being slaughtered, because this was the way He would pay for our sins. How much he loves us! Have you thanked Him that He was prepared to die on the cross for your sins?

The Bible says: "He was led like a sheep to the slaughter,
and as a lamb before the shearer is silent, so he did not
open his mouth" (Acts 8:32).

15 December

The Lord Will Judge Fairly

"I will judge between one sheep and another, and between rams and goats" (Ezekiel 34:17).

When the Lord looks at all the people in the world, He also knows everyone's heart. He sees other things than you and I see. It's almost like a farmer watching his sheep. He can tell right away which sheep have the best wool and which do not. It's like our verse says – the Lord judges between the sheep.

The Bible also says the Lord distinguishes between sheep and goats. Once again, this is like the farmer who keeps his sheep separate from his goats. So according to the Bible, a day will come when the Lord will also separate people. In the Bible sheep are usually an image for people who belong to the Lord, who listen to His voice and who do what He says. Then there are those who do not do these things. The image of a goat is used to describe them.

So it's no good pretending you are a sheep in the Lord's fold while your heart is all wrong. Remember, He is also going to separate sheep from sheep. And in the end He will then also separate those who are not interested in belonging to Him at all (the goats) from His sheep. The Lord has chosen you to be a sheep, not a goat.

Be a good sheep and listen to God's voice.

16 December

Christmas Is a Time to Spread the Word

When they had seen him, they spread the word concerning what had been told them about this child (Luke 2:17).

At the time Jesus was born, some shepherds were looking after their sheep just outside Bethlehem. While they were sitting around the fire, a bright light shone all around them, and an angel told them that the Savior had been born. At first they were terrified, but the angel told them not to be afraid because the news was good news – the best ever!

The shepherds were so happy about the good news. "Come, let's not waste time, let's go to Bethlehem and see the Child who has been born," they said to each other. There they found Mary and Joseph and baby Jesus in the manger, just as the angels had told them. The shepherds told Joseph and Mary about the angel's message, and they also told everybody else they came across.

You cannot keep the message to yourself that Jesus was born for sinners and died so that we can live forever. Like the shepherds, you must also spread the news. Every Christmas you get the chance all over again to tell your friends that Jesus was born. Have you started yet?

Do you find it difficult to speak to your friends about Jesus? If you have a problem with this, find out in Acts 1:8 who can help you.

17 December

One Lie Leads to Another

"Is this the time to take money, or to accept clothes … ?"
(2 Kings 5:26).

Being sneaky is not a sin any more – or that's what many people think. If you can get something for nothing, why not? And if you have to lie to get it, so what?

This is not how God feels about it.

Elisha the prophet had a servant named Gehazi. He was a faithful servant, but he couldn't stand it that his master performed miracles for people without charging them anything. He got especially upset when Elisha healed Naaman, an important soldier from a foreign country, of leprosy. Gehazi did not keep in mind that Elisha's miracles were from God.

Gehazi secretly followed the man and told him a terrible lie. He said two young preachers had just arrived, and they had nothing. Would Naaman please give them money and clothes? And to top it all, he said Elisha had sent him. When he got back, Elisha gave him one look and asked, "Where have you been, Gehazi?"

"Nowhere, sir," he lied again.

He not only cast doubt on God's integrity to serve his own purposes, but he also lied without batting an eyelid. As punishment he and his descendants were struck with leprosy. Read the story in 2 Kings 5.

Greed and lies are brothers.

18 December

Against the Enemy

Submit yourselves, then, to God. Resist the devil, and he will flee from you (James 4:7).

The greatest enemy of every human being, and also of the Lord, is the devil. He talked the first humans into sinning in the Garden, and he is still at work trying to tempt us into doing things we shouldn't. He is the one who makes people hate and hurt one another, and he is the cause of wars.

The Bible says we should make a choice against the devil. Sometimes this is difficult, because he is very sly. He is so wily that we can't always tell he is the one behind all the bad things we feel like doing. He works through people, and he runs the show behind the scenes while he pretends to be an angel of the light!

That's why we need the Lord to show us how the devil works. The closer we are to God, the easier it becomes to know when the devil is trying to trick us.

We also know the devil has already been overcome by Jesus. The Bible says we must resist the devil. How do we do that? Tell him "No!" in the Name of Jesus. If he tries to hurt us, or to get us to believe his lies, then we tell him we would rather believe what the Lord says. That's why we need to know the Bible well. Let's choose to be against the devil. Let's rather choose Jesus.

The Bible says: "Be self-controlled and alert. Your enemy the devil prowls around like a roaring lion looking for someone to devour" (1 Peter 5:8).

19 December

Admit Your Mistakes

Then Saul said, "I have sinned" (1 Samuel 26:21).

There was a time when Saul wanted to kill David. One day he even tried to pin David to the wall with his spear! David was very upset that Saul was out to get him and he said, "The king of Israel has come out to look for a flea – as one hunts a partridge in the mountains" (1 Samuel 26:20).

Fortunately Saul was man enough to admit to his foolishness.

It's not easy to admit your mistakes, especially not to the person who was on the receiving end of your foolishness. We learn a very important lesson from Saul's life. But if you say you believe in God and belong to Him, it's not enough only to learn a lesson from someone's life; you must put it to use in your own life as well. Think about it. Is there someone you need to tell that you made a mistake? Do it as soon as possible. Sometimes the opportunity passes to confess mistakes and make up for them. So don't put it off. It is important to admit to the mistake you made. And if you can in any way make up for the suffering you have caused, do it!

Are you honest enough to admit if you are wrong?

20 December

Teamwork Is Important

For we are God's fellow workers (1 Corinthians 3:9).

Don't you think it's great being part of a team? It's good to play a sport with teammates on your side. Can you imagine a baseball team with only two players? I think you will agree it would be stupid to send a team like this onto the field to play the opponents! If you want a decent team, you need all nine players.

Don't forget, your brothers and sisters are part of the team you take on to the field with you every day. Your family is a team of which you are a member. You need one another. You can't live without them, because then the team is not complete. Show your brothers and sisters and other relatives how much they mean to you by the way you treat them. How about starting today?

The most important team you belong to is God's team. It is a wonderful team, and in it you are a co-worker in God's service. Thank the Lord for the privilege of being part of this team.

21 December

First Sick, Then Well

By his wounds we are healed (Isaiah 53:5).

Nurses and doctors do a good job. They care for sick people. They give medicine and treatment so that people can get well. We must pray for everybody who nurses the sick, that the Lord will give them wisdom and help them heal those who are ill.

People's bodies get sick. Some have backaches, others get the flu, and others have heart problems and so on. But people also get sick in their minds. Then they must get help from a psychologist.

The best doctor is the Lord. He makes use of doctors, nurses, psychologists, and many others to help sick people, but He is the great Healer. He came to help, especially with the sickness of sin.

Jesus gave the "medicine" on the cross of Golgotha so that we could be freed from sin. He died for us and paid for our sins. If we believe this, we are healed from the sickness of sin, which kills people. And if our bodies become ill, we must first ask Jesus to heal us, and then, if it is necessary, see a doctor.

The Bible says: "It is not the healthy who need a doctor, but the sick. I have not come to call the righteous, but sinners" *(Mark 2:17).*

22 December

Jesus' Birthday

Our Savior ... wants all men to be saved and to come to a knowledge of the truth (1 Timothy 2:3-4).

Many families ask a person who has a birthday coming up to give them a wish list. You might write down ten things you would like to have. If you are lucky, you will get one of these things for your birthday.

Christmas, as you know, is Jesus' birthday. Have you ever wondered what He would like for His birthday? In the Bible a few things are mentioned that are likely to appear on Jesus' wish list. In the Old Testament, for example, it says that He would rather have a heart filled with love than burnt offerings. And in the text above we see something else the Lord would like to have: He wants all people to know about Him so that they will get to know Him as their Redeemer.

What can we do to please Jesus this Christmas? We can be nice to other people, because He said if we do something for others, it's just like doing it for Him. We could also go to church and show Him that we love Him with our songs and our prayers. But the best present would be to bring people to Him. How about a letter, or a dollar or two, or a prayer for a missionary who is far from home this Christmas, telling people in distant countries about Jesus?

We must make Jesus happy this Christmas because it is His birthday.

23 December

Gifts for Jesus

Then they opened their treasures and presented him with gifts of gold and of incense and of myrrh (Matthew 2:11).

Very far from Bethlehem, wise stargazers (Magi) saw the new, bright star in heaven. They recognized it as the sign that a great King had been born. They climbed onto their camels and went to look for the King. In Jerusalem, King Herod's wise men told them that the Messiah would be born in Bethlehem.

The wise men followed the star until it stood still over the place where baby Jesus and His parents were.

When the stargazers at last found Jesus, they knelt down before Him, opened their bags, and presented their gifts of gold, incense, and myrrh. These wise men knew Jesus was the greatest King of all time. They were so happy to have found him, and that's why they gave Him valuable gifts. Gold, incense, and myrrh were very valuable in Jesus' time.

At Christmas we worship Jesus as the great King, and we give each other presents. If you want, you can also give Jesus a present. The present He would like best is for you to invite Him into your life. Don't you want to make Him a gift of your heart this Christmas?

Why did the stargazers take a different route back to their country? (See Matthew 2:12.)

24 December

F.R.O.G. F.R.O.G. F.R.O.G.

Christmas – Jesus Is Born!

And she gave birth to her firstborn, a son. She wrapped him in cloths and placed him in a manger, because there was no room for them in the inn (Luke 2:7).

Christmas is a time for celebration because Jesus was born. Two thousand years ago an angel came to tell Mary she would have a son. She was told to call her son Jesus, because He would be the long-awaited Messiah who would free God's people from their sins forever.

Mary married Joseph, the man she was engaged to. When it was nearly time for the baby to be born, Mary and Joseph had to travel to Bethlehem, because the king wanted a census to be taken. Everyone had to register in their own towns.

When they arrived in Bethlehem, there was nowhere for them to sleep, so they had to spend the night in a stable. There in the stable, Jesus, our Redeemer, was born. Mary wrapped Him in cloths and laid Him down in the animals' manger of hay. This was the very first Christmas.

Every year the children of God celebrate Christmas, not because we get presents, but because we are so happy about the wonderful Present God sent to this world such a long time ago, so that we can believe in Him and become His children.

Do you know a verse by heart that tells you about God's love for you and the birth of His Son? If not, then memorize John 3:16.

25 December

Who Is Your Role Model?

Whoever claims to live in him must walk as he did (1 John 2:6).

If you could be like anyone in the world, who would you choose? We all have a hero or someone we look up to. It could be one of your parents, or you could choose to be like a sports star or a television star.

The best example to follow, however, is the one set by the Lord Jesus. We don't always realize that He wants us to live like He did. This is what the apostle John means in our verse for today. Why not read it again?

The important question here is this: What does it mean to live "in Him"? It means living close to Him. If you manage this, you won't do things Jesus doesn't like. You won't only follow Him, but you'll also go where He sends you. Sometimes it's visiting a sick friend. To put it in a nutshell, if you live close to the Lord and you are obedient, then you live in Him. There's nothing mysterious about this; it's simply a way of life.

Is Jesus your role model? Do you try to live the way He did?

26 December

How Do You Boast?

"Let him who boasts boast in the Lord" (2 Corinthians 10:17).

I always find it very interesting to see how children boast. I don't mean boast in an ugly way, but in a biblical way. Let me explain. The guy who's top of the class tells his friends, "I'm just more brainy than you are!" This is not the biblical way.

Others should sing his praises, not him. It would be much better if one of his friends would say, "You're really smart!"

How should he react to this? If he simply smiles or nods his head in agreement, he is not being a good witness for the Lord. The best way to respond is, "Yes, I'm very grateful that the Lord has made it possible for me to do well at school."

But just a minute, this story is not supposed to be about someone else. I want to know about you. How do you boast? What is your reaction when someone pays you a compliment? Do you bask in your own glory, or do you use it as an opportunity to praise the Lord? The way you boast shows what goes on in your heart.

Thank the Lord for your talents.

27 December

Creatures of Habit

I delight in your decrees; I will not neglect your word (Psalm 119:16).

Yvonne was a bit disappointed. A month ago after a service on the beach, she made up her mind to read the Bible every day. She realized she needed to do this to make her stronger spiritually. She got off to a good start. That first week she read a chapter a day. But later on it dwindled to a verse or two, and now it suddenly struck her that the past week she hadn't even opened her Bible once.

On Sunday, Yvonne stayed behind after Sunday school. Their teacher told them they were welcome to ask her to pray for them about anything. "Ma'am, please pray that I will read my Bible regularly!" she said, embarrassed.

The teacher smiled and started drawing something on her writing pad. Yvonne snuck an inquisitive look at it. "It's a spider web," the teacher said. "The Spaniards have a saying: A habit is like a spider web at first, and later on, like a strong cable."

At first Yvonne didn't understand what the teacher was trying to tell her. Then, with a flash of understanding, she said, "I know! It means at first a habit is easy to break, like a spider web. But a habit you keep working on becomes as strong as a cable and just as difficult to break!"

"I will pray that you read the Bible every day this coming month. After that it might just be more difficult to forget than to remember!" the teacher said.

Get into the habit of reading the Bible every day.

28 December

Why Must We Honor Our Parents?

"Honor your father and your mother" (Exodus 20:12).

The fifth commandment does not ask if your parents are good or bad. It simply says you must honor them – whether they are good or bad is not the issue. It's God's ruling that children have parents, and so you must also do what God tells you to as far as your parents are concerned.

"But what if my parents don't do God's will?" you may ask. "What if they swear or treat each other badly?" The answer is, you must still honor and respect them even if you don't agree with what they do, because the Lord expects you to. You don't have to approve of the things they do wrong. But, you never have to put up with any verbal or physical abuse from your parents.

Look what the Lord does – He hates sin, but He loves sinners anyway. So He doesn't love your parents less because they have done something wrong. They are still His children. The same is true for you. If you misbehave, it doesn't mean you are not your parents' child any more, does it? They still love you even if you have been naughty. So ask God to help you honor your parents.

What is your reaction when your parents don't do what you think they should? Would the Lord be pleased with you?

29 December

Obey Your Parents

Children, obey your parents in everything, for this pleases the Lord (Colossians 3:20).

Barry thought his parents were too strict. They wouldn't allow him to do everything his friends were allowed to do. (Or that's what he thought.) For example, he had to be back home from a night out at ten o'clock. Some of his friends didn't have a curfew like that. But parents have good reasons for their rules.

One night Barry's parents went out to dinner. A friend came to spend the night so Barry wouldn't be at home alone. The boys were told to keep the doors locked, not to let anybody in, and to stay home and not go anywhere.

The minute his parents left, Barry and his friend slipped out, took their bicycles, and headed straight for a shopping center. It was truly their intention to be back home by half past nine and hopefully fast asleep by the time Barry's parents got back. But their plans didn't work out that way, because when they went to get on their bicycles at about nine o'clock, one was missing – stolen! By the time their parents got back, they were both in tears and felt very bad about what they had done.

The Lord wants us to listen to our parents.

30 December

Praise Him!

You are my God, and I will give you thanks; you are my God, and I will exalt you (Psalm 118:28).

The Bible says we must praise the Lord with our whole being. (See Psalm 103.) To praise the Lord is to glorify His name. We glorify His name when we say or sing that there is no one as wonderful as He is. We praise Him because He sent Jesus to us as the Redeemer. We praise Him because He is the great Creator of everything good. We praise Him because He forgives our sins.

We praise Him for all the good things there are for us to enjoy. We praise Him for health. We praise Him because we are not going to be dead forever but will live forever. We praise Him because He gave us His Holy Spirit and will be with us until He comes to get us one day.

We have very good reason to praise the Lord. We praise the Lord with our mouths and with our hearts. We say it, and play it on musical instruments, and sing it so that everybody can hear. Everything that breathes must praise the Lord. Will you praise the Lord today?

The Bible says: "I will praise the LORD all my life; I will sing praise to my God as long as I live" *(Psalm 146:2).*

31 December